Willem Vissering

**On Chinese Currency**

Coin And Paper Money

Willem Vissering

**On Chinese Currency**
*Coin And Paper Money*

ISBN/EAN: 9783744724487

Printed in Europe, USA, Canada, Australia, Japan

Cover: Foto ©Suzi / pixelio.de

More available books at **www.hansebooks.com**

# ON CHINESE CURRENCY.

## COIN AND PAPER MONEY.

~~~~~~~~~~~~~~~~~~~~~~~~~

ACADEMISCH PROEFSCHRIFT

TER VERKRIJGING VAN DEN GRAAD VAN

DOCTOR IN HET ROMEINSCH EN HEDENDAAGSCH RECHT,

AAN DE HOOGESCHOOL TE LEIDEN,

OP GEZAG VAN DEN RECTOR MAGNIFICUS

## Dʀ. P. VAN GEER

HOOGLEERAAR IN DE FACULTEIT DER WIS- EN NATUURKUNDE,

VOOR DE FACULTEIT TE VERDEDIGEN

op Woensdag den 27sten Juni 1877, des namiddags te 4 uren,

DOOR

## WILLEM VISSERING,

GEBOREN TE LEIDEN.

LEIDEN, E. J. BRILL.

1877.

# SIMONI VISSERING

VIRO CLARISSIMO

PATRI OPTIMO CARISSIMO

ET

# IOHANNI IOSEPHO HOFFMANN

VIRO CLARISSIMO

VENERABILI MAGISTRO.

HAS PRIMITIAS

TAM IN STUDIIS ECONOMICIS

QUAM IN STUDIIS ORIENTALIBUS

D. D. D.

## GRATUS DISCIPULUS

## AUCTOR.

# CONTENTS.

~~~

### FIRST NOTIONS OF MONEY.

Barter. — Origin of money and primitive species. — Denominations to express the idea of money, currency, medium of exchange. — Information of Kwan-tsze, the earliest writer on money. — Views on the character of money and the use of it in ancient times, by two Chinese scholars of the eleventh century. — Something on the use of money in the beginning of the Tseu dynasty. — Two passages quoted from "the book of rites of the Tseu". — Ma-twan-lin's critic. — Introduction of new coins by King-wang and advice given by Tan, duke of Mu.

### HISTORY OF MONEY UNDER THE GREAT HAN-DYNASTY.

The Ts'in-dynasty. — The golden yi. — The Han-dynasty. — The leave-coins. — Wen-ti grants the people to cast their own coins. — Speech of Kia-i against free-coining. — Practical view of the same question by Kia-san. — King-ti makes false coins. — Reign of Wu-ti. — His financial measures. — Representative money of skin-parcels and white metal. — Yik tseu coins. — Institution of one general state-mint. — Excess of false coining under Yuen-ti, and advice given by his Minister to abolish money. — Information on the relative value of money under the Han-dynasty. — History of Wang-mang. — His regency and re-establisment

# ADDENDA.

# PREFACE.

It is now two years since the first thought occurred to me to write a historical and critical inquiry into the metallic and paper currency of the Chinese, followed from original sources.

The source chiefly drawn upon and consulted by me has been "the Examination on Currency[1])" by the Chinese scholar *Ma-twan-lin*[2]), treated of in the VIII and IX Volumes of his great Encyclopedia.

*Ma-twan-lin*'s life and works have been described by ABEL REMUSAT in the "Biographie Universelle." He was born in *Po-yang*[3]), province of *Kiang-si*, probably about the year 1245, when the end of the *Sung*-dynasty was near, and the social condition of China was most miserable in consequence of an over-issue of paper money. Under the last emperor of this dynasty he held an important public office, but when the Mongols had conquered the Chinese empire, he resigned his post and devoted himself entirely to scientific studies. During twenty years he was engaged upon the composition of his great work from which the materials of this volume have been gathered.

1) 錢幣考.     2) 馬端臨.     3) 鄱陽.

In 1321 the first edition of his work was published under the title of *Wen hien t'ung k'ao* [1]).

According to *Ma-twan-lin's* own preface to his work 文 *wen*, signifies the historical chronicle, the purely historical facts as he found them in the Annals of the different Dynasties; 獻 *hien* are properly oral or written addresses and reports which are mostly the elucidation of the historical facts. I, therefore, prefer the Rev. Dr. LEGGE's translation of that title into "General Examination of Records and Scholars" to that of ABEL REMUSAT who tried to express its signification by the rendering "Recherche approfondie des anciens monuments".

Great is the praise lavished by European authors on Ma-twan-lin, and together with Confucius and Mencius he is of all Chinese authors the best known in Europe.

In the above mentioned biography ABEL REMUSAT says of him:

"On est certain de trouver sous chaque matière les faits qui y sont relatifs disposés chronologiquement suivant l'ordre des dynasties et des règnes, année par année, jour par jour. On ne peut se lasser d'admirer l'immensité des recherches qu'il a fallu à l'auteur pour recueillir tous ces matériaux, la sagacité qu'il a mise à les classer, la clarté et la précision avec lesquelles il a su présenter cette multitude d'objets dans tout leur jour. On peut dire que cet excellent ouvrage vaut à lui seul toute une bibliothèque et que quand la littérature Chinoise n'en offrirait pas d'autre il faudrait la peine qu'on apprît le Chinois pour le lire. On n'a que choisir le sujet qu'on veut étudier, et traduire ce qu'en dit Ma-twan-lin. Tous les faits sont rapportés et classés, toutes les sources indiquées, toutes les autorités citées et discutées. Il est à regretter qu'on ne se soit pas encore occupé d'exploiter cette mine précieuse, où toutes les questions qui peuvent concerner l'Asie orientale, trouveraient des réponses les plus satisfaisantes. Il y a même beaucoup de parties de Ma-twan-lin, qui mériteraient d'être traduites en entier....."

1) 文獻通考.

After a careful study of Ma-twau-liu I readily agree to this encomium passed on our learned Chinese; only in one respect I must differ from it. Ma-twau-lin is not always equally clear and distinct. Compressed constructions which often cloak his exact meaning are of too frequent occurrence; moreover, he is peculiarly fond of using words in a strange secondary signification, not explained in any Chinese Dictionary. A comparison of many passages, and a profound study of the difficult parts will at last enable the student to solve these riddles.

This explains perhaps the reason, why except the MARQUIS D'HERVEY DE ST. DENYS [1]) nobody as yet has listened to the call of ABEL REMUSAT, and edited part of *Ma-twan-lin's* Works.

———

As far as I am aware the important fragments in the two volumes of Ma-twan-lin's work are all quoted; those not interesting either with respect to language or history are paraphrased or entirely omitted. The explanation or interpretation of passages obscure either from the difficulties of the language, or because they were distinctive of the authors style, and showed a peculiar Chinese construction, I have given to the best of my ability, even when the economical part had no need of the information given in those fragments. In a few instances the difficulties were beyond my strength; these passages I recommend to the special care and attention of sinologues.

It having been my aim throughout to preserve the sense and spirit of the original, many pages will be found disfigured by

1) In his meritorious work "Ethnographie des peuples étrangers" traduit du Chinois, | de Ma-twan-lin, edited in the *Atsume Gusa*.

inelegánt phraseology, but though this may offend the ear of the ordinary reader, sinologues will undoubtedly appreciate a faithful rendering of the peculiar construction and choice óf words in the Chinese text.

To two remarkable phenomena in the Chinese language I have called attention as often as they occurred in the expounded passages.

1. The peculiar force of the final particle 矣 which, according to my conviction, is commonly used when the author or speaker expresses his subjective opinion, and which characterizes the thoughts and perceptions founded only on the individual nature of the thinking and speaking person; while, on the contrary, the final particle 也 gives to the words the character of an objective certainty proceeding from the nature of the subject itself.

In reading the classic authors my attention was directed to this fact by my much esteemed 老先生 Prof. HOFFMANN, and the more I advanced in my study of Chinese texts, the more settled my conviction became regarding the truth of his observation. The following examples taken from Classical authors may serve as illustration; to give here more I have thought unnecessary, as the passages of MA-TWAN-LIN, in which that peculiar force of 矣 is obvious, are all marked at the foot of the page.

CONFUCIUS says:

士 而 懷 居 不 足 以 爲 士 矣。

"To be a scholar and love one's ease is, I believe, not sufficient to be considered a scholar."

The distinction between the two particles is clear from the next example in whith both occur.

君 源 也。臣 流 也。
濁 其 源。而 求 其 流 之 清。不 可 得 矣。

"The King is the source, the subjects are the stream.

To make that source muddy, and yet to wish to have that stream limpid is, in my opinion, not possible."

MENCIUS too gives many instances.

是 心 足 以 王 矣·

"The heart seen in this is sufficient (to my conviction) to carry you to the Imperial sway."

The distinction of the two particles shows itself again in the next phrase.

寡 人 之 於 國 也。盡 心 焉 耳 矣。

(*The king says.*) "Small as my virtue is, in the government of my kingdom I do indeed exert my mind to the utmost."

Dictionaries commonly state that the character 矣 emphasizes the phrase. This is, however, no argument against my observation, as subjective views are mostly expressed with more emphasis than objective statements.

2. The great signification of the rhetorical inversion or ante-position in the Chinese language, in consequence of which that word and that part of the phrase on which falls the stress is transposed and emphatically begins the sentence. This is especially the case in the 獻 parts containing the speeches and reports, the style of which the author or speaker intended to be elaborate.

This same transposition is found in most European languages and some authors make frequent use of it.

"Ein frommer Knecht war Fridolin"

says SCHILLER, and begins his sentence with the predicate.

"A giant's strength we admire in him," writes CARLYLE under

the impression of the tidings of GOETHE's death. From every page of our modern literature examples might be gleaned, and in the writings of the ancients the same rhetoric peculiarity is found.

In the Chinese language and grammar that transposition has, however, greater significance than in any other language, as here all grammar depends on the position of the words, and when for the sake of rhetorical turns we are deprived of this guidance, and the Chinese author instead of 未有之 dares to write 未之有, the difficulties already besetting us greatly increase.

Ma-twan-lin's Book has in consequence of that inversion many a complicated construction which for a long time I was at a loss how to translate. The most important of these passages I have marked in a note.

---

And now I am at the end of my long labor, and see the book ready before me, I wish to express my grateful thanks to all who have assisted me by help or encouragement. To them whose names are found on the first page of this volume, I can give no better token of my deep acknowledgments than the dedication of the work they have shown to much sympathy with.

For much information I am also indebted to Prof. GUSTAVE SCHLEGEL, whose profound knowledge of the Chinese language was of invaluable assistance so me.

A copy of Ma-twan-lin's book I received from Prof. A. CARRIÈRE, Sécrétaire de l'Ecole Spéciale des Langues Orientales vivantes; at the request of Dr. R. ROST of the library of India Office, the Rev. Dr. JAMES LEGGE had the kindness to send me the copy of Wan ki's Continuation of Ma-twan-lin; through the kind intercession of his Excellence the Minister of Foreign affairs P. J. A. M. VAN DER DOES DE WILLEBOIS, I received from the Imperial Academy of Sciences at St. Petersburg the original bill of the *Tai-ming* dynasty with permission to make a drawing or photograph of it. Prof. A. SCHIEFNER, member and secretary of the Imperial Academy of Sciences at St. Petersburg was so kind as to offer me some Chinese bank-notes and bills of exchange of later times; and from Paris I received from the Ecole Orientale the scrip of a note, issued by a Chinese joint-stock bank at *Šang-hai*.

The photograph which is an exact reproduction of the original much worn bill, is obtained after a new process, invented by Dr. E. J. ASSER of Amsterdam, who had the kindness to supervise the execution of this work of art.

To these gentlemen and to many others, residing in my country, I openly tender my deep obligations for their ready and kindly aid.

Within a few days this volume will be launched from E. J. BRILL polyglottic printing-office into the world; very probably to be critizised and contested; but also, I am sure, to be appreciated by those who, taught by their own experience, know the amount of labor required to understand and explain a Chinese author.

The best wishes the author can give to his book on its way are those contained in the following passage of GOETHE's treasure of wisdom, "the West-Östlicher Divan"

> Vor den Wissenden sich stellen,
> Sicher ist's in allen Fällen!
> Wenn du lange dich gequälet,
> Weisz er gleich wo dir es fehlet; .
> Auch auf Beifall darst du hoffen,
> Denn er weisz wo du's getroffen.

LEIDEN. June, 1877.        W. V.

# INTRODUCTORY CHAPTER.

An important chapter of the economical history of China was the subject on which I purposed writing my Academical Dissertation for the acquisition of the degree of Doctor of Laws; and as the mysteries of the monetary history always have had great attractions for me, my predilection has led me to attempt an investigation of Chinese Currency and Banking.

How far this investigation may claim to be a Political Economical Study is a question which has already often been put to me, while I was collecting the materials from Chinese and Japanese sources. And when the economist, judging by the title, opens the book and sees so many Chinese characters, I fear he will feel some doubt if the work can be of any interest to him and if the economical value has not been put too much in the background because of the desire to explain difficult passages in the Chinese text. It is therefore that in this introductory part I have imposed upon myself the task of giving an answer to the above question.

Perhaps the same answer that I have often given to the same question might suffice here, that the history of a commercial people which is the greatest as well as the most ancient nation in the world, of whose literature vast and valuable stores are still extant, who had come to the solution of many a question, social and political, long before it agitated the Western world, and whose theories, and institutions are all found back in Europe years and years afterwards, that such a history is worthy of being closely studied and carefully searched. But I feel here called upon to waive an answer in such general terms and to speak more in particular about the economical value of the matter treated of in this study, the more so, as I wish to acquaint my readers beforehand with what they are to expect on a perusal of this volume.

However, before treating of the economical value of the subject, I may be allowed to state what on this head has already been communicated by European authors of different times.

There are many stories of medieval merchants and monks, which with more or less praise mention the use of paper money in the empire of the Great Khan, and at present hardly any work on Currency or Banking is published but gives some information as to the money and paper currency of the Chinese. Mr. MACLEOD [1]) and Mr. JEVONS [2]) tell us many particulars of Chinese paper money; DR. OTTO HÜBNER in his work "Die Banken" [3]) says that at present the system of Free Banks is in active operation in China and that it fully answers the purpose. M. COURCELLE SENEUIL *in voce* "Papier Monnaie" in the Dictionnaire de l'Economie politique, and M. BENADAKIS in his essay in the Journal des Economistes, entitled "Le Papier monnaie dans l'Antiquité [4]) and even the author of the Notizie interno all' ordinamento bancario e al corso forzato negli Stati Uniti di America, e in Russia has appended to his Allegati a little chapter entitled "La Carta Moneta presso le nazioni Asiatiche" [5]) All those authors show great interest in the same subject, and give a concise view of the history of paper currency in the Chinese empire. These communications lead us naturally to the sources drawn upon by them, and as the fountain-head of all we find:

1° A little information given by J. KLAPROTH in the first volume of the Journal Asiatique (1822) entitled "Sur l'origine du papier monnaie" [6]).

2° An essay of the late sinologue ED. BIOT, followed from Chinese

1) THEORY AND PRACTICE OF BANKING Vol. I, p, 179. DICTIONARY of POLITICAL ECONOMY *in voce* Banking p. 215 and *in voce* Currency p. 667—671. Mr. MACLEOD says at the end of his information on Chinese paper money: "We have given this account of Chinese paper money because we are not aware that any account of it has ever been published in English, and it may probably be new to our readers to learn that all the phenomena which have been displayed in Europe and America by the issue of paper money were exhibited in China many centuries ago".

2) Money and the Mechanism of exchange p. 198.
3) Leipzig 1854 Vol. II p. 421
4) Vol. 33. March 1874. p. 353 sqq.
5) Page 161. This book of which only the first part is printed as yet, is one of the many valuable economical and statistical works which are gradually edited by the Ministerio d'agricoltura, industria e commercio in Italy.
6) Cf. Mémoires relatifs à l'Asie par J. KLAPROTH 1826. Tome I p. 375.

sources, and entitled "Mémoire sur le Système monétaire des Chinois". This study has been published in 4 numbers of the Journal Asiatique, Anno 1837.

These then were the sources from which all further information on the subject was drawn, information which did not escape the rejuvenating influence of a distillation through so many brains.

What I myself read in these monografies made me the more desirous to consult authentic documents in which probably many things, which were vague and without connection would be explained when I could read the exact and chronologically arranged details which the Chinese with laudable zeal are wont to collect together on any subject they treat of.

I had the good fortune of having a copy of MA-TWAN-LIN's Examination on Currency lent to me, and moreover I had access to the treasures of the collections in the Royal Ethnographical Museum, to the Japanese Museum of the Zoological Society: NATURA ARTIS MAGISTRA at Amsterdam, and to the libraries of Prof. J. HOFFMANN and Prof. G. SCHLEGEL of Leiden, and so I set to work, still uncertain whether I should be able to produce anything not yet published by my predecessors. But the more I advanced in my study of the Chronicles, the stronger became my conviction that I was doing no superfluous work. The oldest piece, that of KLAPROTH, proved to be nothing else but a quotation from one of those numerous Encyclopedias in which all possible and impossible subjects are separately treated of, works always highly interesting to a Chinese scholar, being compiled from the great authors, and faithfully referring to the sources from which they are borrowed.

The second source, the essay of ED. BIOT has great merits but it has the fragmentary character of a magazine article. MA-TWAN-LIN, the principal Chinese author consulted by BIOT has divided his work into two parts, 1º the historical chronicle, 2º the economical theories and opinions contained in the reports and memorials presented to the imperial government by prime ministers, governors of provinces, and other high dignitaries, or in the speeches delivered in the meetings of the privy council and the ministers of state by the sages and learned of their time. MA-TWAN-LIN, a learned statesman and author of the 13th century of our era, has collected all these chronicles and state papers, and arranged them in chronological order so that from the most ancient date down to the author's own time we have a faithful record of all that relates to the province of learning, science, policy, etc. Of this extensive collection, however, the reports and speeches form the principal and most important part; everywhere they impart the elucidation of historical events which precede and follow; but infinitely more important they are as they give us an idea of the men who have had the greatest influence on their time. These fragments, however, require a careful study, shall they be rightly understood. Full of historical allusions comprehensible to the Chinese literati but to us, not having the necessary materials at our disposal, often unintelligible; moreover not simple and clear as the chronicle which communicates only facts, but full of distorted sentences, full of pedantic words taken in a signification which rarely occurs and which are borrowed from some classic author who perhaps in some exceptional case made use of them and lastly treating of notions which they felt to be true and tried to express, but which as yet had never been subjected to a rigorous scientific investigation.

In writing his Mémoire sur le Système monétaire des Chinois the French author has exclusively confined himself to the historical Chronicle; only once or twice he wanders from his subject to give a few lines of MA-TWAN-LIN himself, in which that Chinese scholar communicates his individual opinions after having treated of a whole period of Chinese history; but even then those fragments are so abridged that the speculative matter could merely be touched upon. The consequence is that many passages of the Chronicle are not sufficiently understood, and that owing to the omission of what would have given variety and relief to dreary dates and facts, the part on the history of metallic money is uncommonly dull and monotonous.

Of invaluable service, however, this worthy pioneer of Chinese science has been to me. I had but to follow the way mapped by him when he, like a second Marco Polo, for the first time undertook a journey through the immense Chinese empire and it was possible for me to cruise and wander about in every direction, where he, seeking for the way in the unknown and unexplored country was obliged to go straight forward. By the indefatigable labors of many European sinologues, HOFFMANN, JULIEN, LEGGE, and others, I had not those obstacles to overcome, which BIOT had to struggle with; in many cases the way was prepared, the direction indicated, and so I could reach the wished for end or at any rate come nearer it than was possible for the solitary traveller in 1837.

Now it will easily be seen why I have preferred this to any other form of composition for my work. A magazine article being extant, a study collected from original sources was wanted, if it were only to enable some one or other to compose a new article for a Periodical in which the history of Chinese currency is fully discussed.

I have continually connected the history of currency with the economical opinions of the different times, such as they have come down to us in the words and writings of the great thinkers who in China have occupied themselves with this subject.

But I have pointed out not only the good and the true principles, but also the follies and mad-cap theories which promulgated by influential Chinese were of equally great importance to the history of their time. Originally it was my intention to compare the opinions and theories of Eastern Asia with those of Western Europe and America; but gradually I have been obliged to confine myself to a few remarkable points of comparison, for fear of giving to this book the very encyclopedian character peculiar to all original Chinese science. In most cases I have given a concise view of the political history which directly bears upon the passages taken from Ma-twan-lin, and which were indispensable to understand our author, at the same time availing myself of these little introductions to devote a few lines to the economical part of the social conditions.

It was likewise part of my plan to incorporate into this book a view of the Japanese metallic and paper currency. Apparently this was a wide field for observations. Among the collection of Dr. VON SIEBOLD, brought from Japan and preserved in the Royal Ethnographical Museum at Leiden, there were a great number of so called mint-books, containing diagrams and descriptions of all varieties of Chinese and Japanese coins; the collection of Japanese coins in that cabinet is nearly complete, and, last not least, there are seven Japanese bank-notes, the oldest dating from the year 1688 and the latest from 1868. But what was my disappointment when, on examination, I found that the Japanese authors seem not to have had the least idea of the signification of money, their books on the subject containing, only besides other worthless trash, a dull account of the dimensions and weights of their coins.

After they had adopted the institution of money from the Chinese, the round square-holed copper pieces were but seldom used, the general measure of value remained, what it originally had been, r i c e.  The Japanese gold and silver money had by no means an intrinsic value corresponding to the nominal, which has been proved from a report of an essayist of the Dutch Bank at Amsterdam, who at the request of Prof. HOFFMANN has estimated the value of some hundreds of gold *Kobangs*.  The relative value of the different metals, as given in the Japanese Encyclopedia *San-tsai-dzu-i* [1]) is very primitive.  "A gold coin has the value of 10 silver coins, 1 silver coin is worth 10 copper coins, and 1 copper coin has the value of a measure of rice."

Behold the childlike simplicity of a people who isolated from the rest of the world, were not interested in having an exact ratio of value of the different materials which for centuries together have circulated as medium of exchange.  After the Japanese ports were opened to Europe and America, this state of things very materially altered, but not until the country was plundered by cunning speculators who imported the silver coins in wholesale to exchange them for the underrated gold.  A paper money too have they had, but their notions of this representative currency seem to have been as crude as those of metallic money, and having gold and silver coins, the want of a lighter medium of exchange than copper was so little felt that this institution never reached any high degree of development. Little pieces  of paste-board representing a very small value, circulated in some feudal territories, and were issued because the feudal lords or *daimios* who, not having the privilege to cast their own coins, wished to bring a currency in circulation which was a sign of their power in their own territory, and at the same time met the want of a sufficient quantity of metallic money.  Of these notes there is one in the above mentioned Museum, issued in 1731 by the feudal lord of *Awa* and *Awatsi* [2]); another current in the province of *Simabara* [3]) issued in 1776; a third of the year 1688 without mentioning the territory where it was in circulation, of a value of 5 silver *pu*, etc.  In all

1) 和漢三才圖會。
Vol. 59. p. 16 *a*.

2) 阿波淡路銀杞.  The bill has a value of *itsi-monme* 一爿𠁁モ / ン / メ

(about ¹⁄₃₀ tael or three pence).

3) 嶋原, The bill has a value of *Yin-ni-pu* 銀貳分 (about 2 s. 6 d.).

the mint-books at my disposal I have looked for a description and account of this paper money, but nowhere have I found any further information. Only the great Encyclopedia *San-tsai-dzu-i* [1]) has an article on the paper currency of the Chinese, which is characteristic enough to be inserted here.

宋元用鈔・尤極不便

雨泡鼠齧則成烏有

懷中纏衣皆致磨滅也

Under the reign of the *Sung* and *Yuen* dynasties paper money was made use of. It was uncommonly impractical. When in the rain it got soaked and the mice gnawed at it, it became unfit for use (lit. as if one possessed a raven). When carried in the breast-pocket, or the money-belt the consequence was that it was destroyed by abrasion."

This quotation will suffice to show that though the Japanese have known paper money, they have not had the least idea of its important signification.

The Japanese is by nature either a husbandman or a soldier; merchants belong to the lowest cast; they act only as intermediaries in the inland trade of the country.

When Japan was opened to the world commerce, the credulity of the government as well as of the people was the cause that designing merchants cheated them in all possible ways, till at length roused by heavy losses they were urged to study causes and effects and take measures in order to prevent further mischief.

Quite different is the character of the people in China. There nearly everyone is a merchant and trader above all things. And the reverse of what commonly happened in Japan is seen in China. A Chinese merchant will not easily let pass an opportunity to make a bargain; in his intercourse with Europeans he generally proves to be too sharp for them; in all commercial transactions he knows to get a little profit out of the *fan-kwei* (foreign devil), and to drive out the European merchant wherever he makes his appearance.

1) Vol 59. p. 15*b*.

With such a strong contrast of character it is not surprising that the monetary history of the Japanese has no importance whatever when compared with that of the Chinese.

In many branches of Chinese wisdom traces of economical principles are obvious, They have written on taxes and population as well as on money matters. The practical philosophy of CONFUCIUS teaches the most judicious way in which a state should be governed, and that the first duty of a prince is to make his people rich.

Once, when CONFUCIUS was passing through *Wei* in company with one of his disciples he was struck with the populousness of the State. The disciple said "Since the people are thus numerous, what more shall be done for them?" CONFUCIUS answered: "Enrich them." And when they have been enriched, what more shall be done for them?" The reply was — "Teach them." [1])

We read in MENCIUS "Let it be seen to that their fields of grain and hemp are well cultivated and make the taxes on them light: — so the people may be made rich."

"The people cannot live without water and fire, yet if you knock at a man's door in the dusk of the evening, and ask for water and fire, there is no man who will not give them, such is the abundance of these things. A sage governs the empire so as to cause pulse and grain to be as abundant as water and fire. When pulse and grain are as abundant as water and fire, how shall the people be other than virtuous." [2])

In MENCIUS we find another remarkable passage in which he, answering some sophists who wished to return to the primitive state of man when everyone provided] for his own wants, sets forth the advantages of an equal division of labor [3]). It reads as follows.

MENCIUS said: "I suppose that *Heu-king* sows grain and eats the produce. Is it not so?" "It is so," was the answer. "I suppose also he weaves cloth, and wears his own manufacture. Is it not so?" "No. *Heu* wears clothes of haircloth." "Does he wear a cap?" "He wears a cap." "What kind of cap?" "A plain cap." "Is it woven by himself?" "No. He gets it in exchange for grain." "Why does *Heu* not weave it himself?" "That would injure his husbandry." "Does *Heu* cook his food in boilers and earthen-ware pans, and does he plough with an iron share?" "Yes." "Does he

---

1) LEGGE Chinese Classics Vol. I p. 130. | 3) Vol. II p. 123—126.
2) Vol. II p. 338—339.

make those articles himself?" "No. He gets them in exchange for grain." Page

MENCIUS then said: "The getting those various articles in exchange for grain, is not oppressive to the potter and the founder, and the potter and the founder in their turn, in exchanging their various articles for grain, are not oppressive to the husbandman. How should such a thing be supposed? And moreover, why does not *Heu* act the potter and founder, supplying himself with the articles which he uses solely from his own establishment? Why does he go confusedly dealing and exchanging with the handicraftsmen? Why does he not spare himself so much trouble?" *Ch'ing-seang* replied, "The business of the handicraftsman can by no means be carried on along with the business of husbandry."

MENCIUS resumed: "Then, is it the government of the empire which alone can be carried on along with the practice of husbandry? Great men have their proper business, and little men have their proper business. Moreover, in the case of any single individual, whatever articles he can require are ready to his hand, being produced by the various handicraftsmen: — if he must first make them for his own use, this way of doing would keep the whole empire running about upon the roads. Hence, there is the saying, 'Some labour with their minds, and some labour with their strength. Those who labour with their minds govern others; those who labour with their strength are governed by others. Those who are governed by others support them; those who govern others are supported by them.' This is a principle universally recognized."

Taking a general view of the economical part of our subject we find in the history both of the metallic and paper money principles, which are perfectly true and correct. An evidence of this is the name "current merchandise", by which the Chinese already in early times expressed their notions of money. The theories of money and its signification contain many good elements, and in many cases it is clear that the Chinese were thoroughly aware that money, as a measure of value of all commodities, should have an intrinsic metallic worth corresponding to the nominal indicated by the legend, at which the coin is brought in circulation by the government.

Often do we hear the warning voice of the councilors of the crown, when they show the prince who in the most reckless manner issues bad money to meet the growing demands of his army, the dangers

*b*

Page which must result from these unlimited adulterations not only for the subjects who will have to pay more for all commodities, but also for the prince himself and the government, as the money issued at a higher value than the nominal will return to the prince 141 in a depreciated state and vast sums will be required to withdraw the bad medium of exchange from circulation. "If you consider the money without heeding its character, as an instrument 80 in daily use to further exchange, if you are too sparing of the copper and grudge the cost of the mechanical process" you will soon experience the fatal consequences of it, for the false coiners will spring up in swarms, desirous as they are of enjoying for themselves the profits now accruing to the state.

"And what is that little profit gained in coining bad money," exclaims another author, "compared to that so much greater profit that the money returns in its full value to the government, and 156 that his imperial Majesty having received back the money as taxes from the hands of the people can re-issue the same pieces at the original worth which they had when they were circulated for the first time."

"For then," says another minister again, "the money makes reprisal on the bad policy of the prince when you are obliged to 141 withdraw the debased money, because the money coined by the state and the bad currency coined by private persons cannot be distinguished from each other any more."

Let us listen to the sensible words of the venerable councilor at the court of *Wei*, where he says:

"The flourishing state of a reign is not the result of the money being large or small of size, if only that which is generally received as money has a real value, the government can change the out- 90 & 91 ward form without causing any trouble."

A learned author on money matters says among others: "If we penetrate to the foundation in arguing on the value and meaning of 158 money, we arrive at the conclusion that money is an object that in a time of famine cannot feed us, in a time of cold cannot clothe us, but coming to the service of all occupations, all sorts of precious things may be procured by it. Hence it may not be bad!"

Notwithstanding these traces of the existence of sound economical notions it will be seen from this work that on the whole the social condition in general, and the condition of the money especially has

been most miserable. Never have those budding ideas been able to [Page]
ripen into an organic whole that could form the basis of a good
system of coinage.

In the history of the metallic money we observe two important
factors which continually have impeded a fuller development. 1⁰.
the want of a sufficient quantity of precious metals.
2⁰. the influence of false coiners which was the consequence of the
rude technical execution and the deficiency in the art of coining
of the state money.

The first point needs not be further demonstrated. Our whole history furnishes evidences that gold and silver, found only in a small
quantity, could not circulate as a general medium of exchange in China.
Only during the reign of the Mongol dynasty (1260—1368) silver
bullion circulating as money was frequently made use of [1]), and
generally the larger credit notes of that time were estimated
in some ounces of silver. Occasionally our history mentions the use [20] [23] [51] [94] etc.
of precious metals as a medium of exchange of unlimited value, but
these cases are insignificant compared to the general use made of
copper and iron.

But owing to this use of substances which had a slight intrinsic
value, the art of coining must necessarily be simple and inexpen-
sive, as in the opposite case the cost of production of each coin
would soon have exceeded the intrinsic metallic worth. which likewise would have resulted in a depreciation in the market-value of
the coin.

The art of coining being so bad through all ages, it was natural
that especially when the government began to adulterate the money,
false coiners sprung up in great numbers and cast money in
wholesale by the same simple process as the State. The Chinese
have never understood the art of striking money, but every
little piece was cast in a mould made in fine sand, so that every
person was able to cast as much money as he wanted. Matters
were worst under the reign of the *T'ang*-dynasty; then everywhere
the money was counterfeited; no longer in secret places, but before
the very eyes of the state officials, on rafts and in vessels in the [104] [sqq.]
middle of the river, this illegal but profitable occupation was exer-

1) 銀錠一兩當錢一
貫. "One tael of silver bullion is equal | in value to a string of a thousand *cash*," we read in *Wang-k'i*'s Continuation of *Ma-twan-lin*.

Page
30—56
127
106-114 cised. Countless measures were taken to prevent the evil, twice even we read in history that the emperor granted the people the privilege to cast money for themselves. This measure was strenuously opposed and defended in several speeches which contain a wealth of remarkable economical opinions. But the results were even more fatal in the end than the wisest stateman could have foreseen and the government was soon obliged to retract the privilege.

The only effectual means of checking false coining, the Chinese, with all their fine speeches and beautiful theories, have never been able to find, viz. to render the mechanical execution of the coin so perfect as to make forgery impossible, a result they could have obtained, if they had understood the art of striking money instead of casting it.

And now involuntarily arises the question: How is it possible that the Chinese have not gradually improved in their art of coining, and that necessity has not taught them to devise that mode arrived at by all other peoples who have attained a certain degree of civilization. That question too I will attempt to answer, but before doing so, I wish briefly to consider the economical significance and importance of the history of the paper money, as this will lead us to the very same conclusions as are to be drawn from the history of the metallic currency.

I will not treat of the ephemeral apparition of the deer-skin parcels, the representative medium of exchange introduced by *Han-Wu-ti*. Though mentioned by European authors as the first appearance of paper money in 38—40 the world, it was nothing but a cunning trick of a sly prince, purposing to tax the well-lined purses of his state-dignitaries, nothing but a shamelers extortion, corroborated by the fact that a minister, looking through his Majesty's shrewd designs, was put to death because he was bold enough to speak his mind and object to such measures.

No more will I speak of the short apparition of a real paper currency under the *T'ang*-dynasty. It is indeed a remarkable event in the monetary history, but it makes no more impression than a 120-121 dissolving view; we do not know whence it came or where it went, it is like a dream which after horrible phantoms appears as a pleasing calm, but which likewise disappears without leaving any trace of its existence, and of which afterwards the dim outlines are hardly to be recalled.

100 But I will treat of the system as it shows itself under the *Sung*-dynasty, how it has developed itself without leading principle and

without any system, and how after an existence of about 300 years, Page it has at last been made away with, having entailed nameless misery on prince and people.

A few words I may however be allowed to advance as to the reason why the history of the paper money has been treated in a way somewhat different from the other parts of this book.

The reader will observe that the Chinese text in the last chapter is more bulky than in the chapters which treat of metallic money, and that, besides the general introduction with which the chapter begins, the passages, printed in large type, principally serve to give some explanations of the contents of the fragment which follows. My reasons for this deviation are these that the quoted passages all dating from one time, and the measures recorded, generally taking their origin in the same causes, these fragments of Ma-twan-lin's chronicle are better connected than those of an earlier date which contain incoherent information often of distant periods and different times.

But on the other hand I have given in this part all that could be given; the history of the institution itself was remarkable everywhere and the records comparatively so few that after having tried to explain them all, I could not help giving the whole without the least deduction. Only the order in which the fragments follow have I changed to establish a better connection between the different parts of the subject than is found in Ma-twan-lin's work.

As everywhere else in the world, the paper money had its origin in the want felt by the people to have a medium of exchange 167 in which payment could be made without the trouble of transferring specie from hand to hand. Especially in the west of China where in those times the heavy iron money circulated, such a substitute for the common medium of exchange was of inestimable convenience to trade. Soon the system developed itself, as seen from the little but striking passage, where the invention is told. That institution invented by one *Tšʻang-yung* [1]) was during the first period of its existence, however, entirely in the hands of private persons. The use of the money bills probably originated in the receipts for government products issued by the state to pay the purchases made for the army. 170-171

---

1) 張詠 As we read in *Wang-kʻi's* Continuation of Ma-twan-lin. Vol. XVIII p. 9*b*.

Page
107
It is of little importance how far the insolvency of those private banks necessitated the state to interfere. No doubt, the government had immediately seen what large profits were to be gained, if it obtained the monopoly of the issue of notes, and so we soon see all private banks abolished, and on the very spot where the institution had taken its origin, the government continued to issue "the convenient money."

Soon afterwards the new money became legal tender throughout the realm; it so readily accepted by the people who had so much confidence in it, that when the 22nd triennal term of redemption of the notes of the first series, issued for the time of 65 years, and
172, 173 convertible at the government bank every three years, had come, only a small number was presented for payment.

Now we already meet with a conversion of the old bills by new obligations. At the 23rd term, when the whole series fell due, notes for more than 1.250.000 string of copper money were still in circulation. To redeem these old obligations new bills were issued to that same amount, for a period of 25 terms of redemption, and since that time there circulated notes of two different echeances. Once struck into that dangerous path they continued their way, more bills were issued, and at last, we are told that in 1107, when the
174 war with the Tartars called for great sacrifices, the necessity of the state was met by a vast supply of paper money so that there circulated an amount of twenty times as much as 100 years ago when the first bills were issued.

Eager as they had been before to keep the notes in their possession, they were now anxious to redeem them, but though presenting them at the fixed interval no specie payment was obtained. The holders of these already considerably depreciated bills of exchange received instead of money a new sort of notes called credit notes. These bills were emitted for a period of 43 years, convertible every year, and were exchanged at the ratio of 1 new bill for 4 of the old. In order to keep the depreciated paper money in circulation
175 the same measures were adopted as in France when the paper money of JOHN LAW was only to be maintained in circulation by force. All payments must be made for a part in paper. In that case it was thought that it would be difficult to ascertain the decrease of value, for "when it was ordered by law that what in the future would be stipulated for in iron and copper money,

should be paid partly in bills, these would have a <sup>Page</sup> 175
value corresponding to that of metallic money".

The result of this absurd measure was not doubtful. The bills were soon reduced to $1/_{10}$ of their legal value. Influential officials warned the government not to destroy public credit by over-issuing the paper currency any more; they adviced that the government should set the example to accept the bills at their legal value at 176 the government offices, in that case all payments might be made in bills exclusively, or on payments in money a premium of from 10 to 20 per cent might be levied.

But this measure proved as ineffectual as others, and notes of a nominal worth of 1000 *cash* were at last reduced to a real value of no more than 10 *cash*.

Such is the history of the paper money current in the capital and the whole eastern part of the empire, except in some of the provinces of the south east, where the use of paper money was to be 177 introduced some time afterwards. But even worse was the condition to become in the western and north-western parts, where the armies were encamped and the fortifications were built to secure China against their warlike neighbors, the Tartars. Our author takes us back again to the district of *Šo* in the province of *Sse-tš'uen*, 181 where the paper money had taken its origin. He tells us how gradually the metallic deposit had been seized upon to meet the increasing expenses, and how all payments in behalf of the army were made in paper.

Some fragments give us information as to the enormous quantities which were emitted in a short time.

The first issue of paper money in those parts (in 970) was to an amount of one million string, in the year 1204 the number of 183 credit notes of *Sse-tš'uen* alone exceeded the sum of 53 million string. Many schemes for paying off part of the debt, conversions of debt by issuing new notes estimated in silver, were devised, but they were all leavened with fraud; repayment was promised and when 184 the credulity of the people had caused the notes to rise, other supplies were issued, payment was deferred and the people proved to be cheated, when they came to present the notes which according to the proclamations should be paid back. And the end of the history of the bills in *Sse-tš'uen* is described as follows: "In the year 1210 180

Page
186    when the old bills had been twice withdrawn from circulation, the
value of the new notes was at last equal to the old ones.

Another chapter treats of the history of the government
bonds or frontier bills with which the purchases made for the
army, encamped in those western parts, were paid and the outlay
on the border fortifications was covered. A curious circumstance it
is, that, when it was ordered that in the same place there should
be established a bank for the issue of another sort of notes, to suit
the convenience of the daily expenses of the soldiers and the retail
187    trade in the camps, a protest was made by the ministry because
the metallic deposit was wanting. In consequence of this protest
the bank was immediatatly abolished again.

Here too the ever increasing want led to an overissue of
paper money; those notes gradually made their way into the eastern
provinces where it was first ordered that they ought to circulate as
legal tender, and afterwards they were even printed and emitted there,
when in consequence of the hopeless war with the Tartars the Chi-
178-179    nese court was obliged to retreat to the south. How little confi-
189    dence the government itself put in the paper money is told where
we read that "in order not to have to look up entirely to the paper bonds to meet the wants of the empire, there were issued again
receipts for government productions which represented a value of
10.000.000 string annually. Moreover the government itself begins
to disown the notes by ordering that all taxes should be paid in
190-191    ready money; continually conversions are effected and redemptions
200    deferred, with the promise that at ensuing terms of echeance the
loss will be regained, but the consequence was that the notes continued to fall, an ruin and misery spread throughout the country.

Ma-twan-lin gives a separate chapter regarding the history of
paper money in the eastern provinces, which was instituted to circulate in certain districts exclusively. Its history is the same, and
here too in consequence of over-issue "the character of the paper money,
the balancing an actual possession of money, lost its effect." The
ultimate result was that thousands were inproverished and totally
ruined and such a cry of despair rose in the country as never afterwards was heard either in France after the failure of the Mississippi
207-209    scheme or in Austria in 1810. "After having tried during years and
months to support and maintain these notes, the people had no

longer any confidence in them, but were positively afraid of them.  Page 207
For the payment for government purchases was made in paper, the
fund of the salt manufactories consisted of paper, the salaries of all
the officials were paid in paper, .the soldiers received their pay in
paper.  Of the provinces and districts, already in arrear, there was
not one that did not discharge its debts in paper.  The copper money
which was seldom seen was considered a treasure.  The capital collected together in former days to supply the border fortifications was 208
quite exhausted, and was a thing not even spoken of any more. So
it was natural that the prices of commodities rose while the value
of the paper money fell more and more.  Among the people this
caused them. already disheartened, to lose all energy, the soldiers
were continually anxious that they did not get enough to eat, and
the inferior officials in all parts of the empire raised complaints that
they had not even enough to procure the common necessaries.  All
this was a result of the depreciation of the paper money."

The paper money had ruined the state and caused the decline of a
dynasty that for more than three centuries had occupied the throne, and
never after that time the bills issued by the state have been able
to recover from their deep fall.


In following out the history of the paper currency we find, as in
that of the metallic money, a great many good principles and notions
which, if they had been extracted from that chaos of injustice,
united into a system, and accepted as *norma agendi*, might have
had the most beneficial results.

In the beginning the payment of the notes was guaranteed by a 176
metallic deposit to an amount of about three-sevenths of the out-
standing notes; intervals of redemption were fixed, and a limit
was set to the issue.  Constantly the ministers and the councilors
warn the government that paper money which is worthless of itself.
must be backed by a fund for which it may be exchanged, shall
the people keep confidence in it, and circulate it as money from
hand to hand.  *Tung-lai* and *Ma-twan-lin* have both very plainly said 214
that paper is not money; they have pointed to its representative
character, and maintained that it is nothing but a means of trans-
mitting specie.

Ma-twan-lin writes:

"With the very first intention to institute paper-bonds, it was not 214-215 originally so that they were looked upon as money but they were then considered to be of the nature of the receipts for tea, salt and other government productions, balancing money only temporarely." . . . . . . . . . . . . . . . . . . . . . . . . . . . . . . . . . .

. . . . "And so much the more now that by means of a bit of paper of the size of one foot, a quantity of many pounds of copper could be substituted, now that by circulating the lighter the heavier was actually employed, and the strength of one man was sufficient to make that a quantity of tens of thousands of strings at a fixed time arrived at places some thousands of miles distant, what necessity was there that every part of the empire should have a paper money of its own, in consequence of which the people at last did not know anymore which to trust."

But not only in the time of its greatest decay do we find such correct notions of the paper money. Already in the definitions and names by which they tried to express their first apprehensions of the representative character of paper money, we see the right principle at the bottom of their thoughts on the subject. "The stretching of money" and "a bill balancing an actual possession of money or merchandise" were the long but well chosen names which contained their first notions and soon became the current expressions for paper money.

Scattered here and there we find various principles which, if — as in later time in Western Europe — a law of banking had been made, would have been introduced into the system. So we find regulations as to the convertibility of old, damaged, or torn bills into new ones, and as to what part of the old bills must be presented and be still legible in order to be exchanged for a new one at the payment of a little premium. Then follows some information about the way in which the bills were coined, the designs and the marks impressed on them, the paper of which they were made, the details of the art of execution; all these particulars showing the gradual development of the institution, but at the same time the total absence of anything that might be called a system. Furthermore there are the penalties remarkable for their resemblance to those which were instituted at the first appearance of forged paper money in Europe and America. On the bill of the Great *Ming*-dynasty we read: "Whoever fabricates or uses forged bills shall be beheaded, and he who informs against the forger or arrests him shall receive a reward of 250 ounces of silver."

On the *assignats de la République française* we read something similar: *"La loi punit de mort le contrefacteur, la nation récompense-le dénonciateur,"* and the American notes issued during the War of Independence bear the short phrase "To counterfeit is death."

Perusing the fragments quoted, more regulations and decrees will be found, which might have completed the system if the Chinese had been able to compose it.

But all these good elements and these right economical principles remained disjointed, and were only so many luminous points in the pitchy dark through which they groped their way to hit upon the exact mean, as Chinese philosophers love to call it. By their own stupidity as well as by irresistable causes from without they deviated more and more from those principles which should have led to a solution of the difficulties, and got involved in greater misery and wretchedness than the Western world has even experienced.

And now the question arises again: what has been the cause that the Chinese civilization, so much older than that of any other people in the world, containing so many good elements, has never attained to a higher stage of development, but has remained stationary in all respects in the same way as we have observed it in the history of their currency.

The question is a very debatable one, and it is almost impossible to point out a general cause of the fact. Some have tried to explain it by asserting that the inhabitants of North-eastern Asia, belonging to an inferior race of men, never can attain to the highest stage of mental development. This assertion is in some degree corroborated by the history of the east Asiatic nations, their exertions in science and art, which all show a remarkable inertness of thought.

It has, however, also been contested, among others by my worthy friend Mr. L. SERRURIER [1]) who in his studies of Japanese language, political and social history, has met with the same phenomenon, and who holds that the explanation must be found in the circumstance that the soil and climate have not necessitated these nations continually to devise means of defending their lives, of making their country inhabitable, and of protecting themselves against all the dangers which those tribes have had to overcome, who coming from the Western and Southern parts of Asia have peopled Europe. Such

1) The author of a very interesting little work "Something on Japan." (Een en an- | der over Japan) and editor of a part of the *Kasira-gaki*.

Page a struggle for existence sharpens the intellect, and is the parent of
that Science which never resting at last makes Nature her servant.
There is some degree of truth in this opinion, especially when we
consider the splended conquests of Science in the European society
in every branch of human knowledge, results which lead us to believe that the human intellect is boundless in its range.

But I have two serious objections to that assertion. Firstly that
in ancient times countries which were even more blessed than
Eastern Asia, viz. Greece and Italy, even in consequence of the
benefits of soil and climate have attained to a development which
in many respects is unequaled by the modern development born from
struggle and privation. What an admirably developed system of
laws did the Romans possess; a system which served for ages as
*norma agendi* and for the greater part continues to serve as such
even in the present times. So the ancient Greek are still the un-
matched statuaries, and of both peoples writings have come down
to us which show the high degree of development of their languages
and conceptions; and wherever in modern times in science or art
the highest point of perfection is aimed at, those relics of ancient
Greece and Rome are still the models generally looked up to.

If we draw a comparison between the progress made in art, law
and language by these peoples and that in China, we are inclined to
grant that a lack of natural capacity must have been the obstacle
which has prevented them from reaching the same height under nearly
similar circumstances.

My second objection may seem to be weightier yet. The Chinese
were by no means exempt from such labor and hardships as were
overcome by other peoples by energy and strength of intellect, but
Nature seems not to have bestowed upon them an equal share of
mental endowments. Some striking instances may be quoted to
prove this. The Chinese author *Kwan tsze* who lived 625 years be-
9 fore Christ writes: "When from east, west, north and south, all
over a surface of from 7 to 8000 miles all intercourse with these
parts was cut off by the flood, and in consequence of the difficulties to reach those regions neither ship nor cart could penetrate
thither, the people relied on the following sorts of currancy." To
this passage may be subjoined the following paragraph from the North
China Herald, Shang-hai, January 4th 1877.

"In Central China the provinces have been suffering famine following upon a drought, which caused the failure of the crops and consequent impoverishment and scarcity. Some measures of relief are being taken, but the want of good roads makes the carriage of rice to the distressed districts difficult, and it is to be regretted the Chinese government does not require the people to earn food by developing the means of communication."

So during a period of more than 25 centuries we see no progress in the art of constructing roads and of protecting the fields from inundation.

What a strong contrast China in this prospect presents to Holland. To render their country habitable the Dutch had to put out all their strength and engage for generations in stubborn conflict with the angry elements. Untiring industry and energy chained the Ocean and made the country, disinherited by nature, not only fit to dwell in, but rich and powerful. The comparison affords another striking instance of the difference between an all conquering power of the ever progressing development of the human mind in the one country, and a perfect inertness of intellect and submission to the power of nature in the other.

We have had occasion to show what misery was produced in China by a bad currency, and how they have never been able to find the right means to baffle false coiners. And this must be said of a people of merchants, while the Romans who felt much less inclined to trade have directly invented the art of striking money, as may be seen from the excellent fragment of the writings of the civilian PAULUS, lex 1 pr. *De Contrahenda emptione* (Dig. Lib. XVIII, 1) [1]) while we read in the *Lex Cornelia de falsis* (Dig. Lib. XLVIII, 10, lex 9 pr.) [2]) that the false coiners at Rome cast their money, so, that the better mechanical process of the government money made it easy there to distinguish between true and false coin.

That lack of natural capacity of the Chinese people we observe in all their intellectual proceedings, in the way in which they cultivated science, in their art and in their political institutions.

1) Origo emendi vendendique a permutationibus coepit; olim non ita erat nummus, neque aliud merx, aliud pretium vocabatur, sed unusquisque secundum necessitatem rerum utilibus inutilia permutabat; sed quia non semper nec facile concurrebat, ut, quum tu haberes, quod ego desiderarem, invicem haberem, quod tu accipere velles, electa materia est cuius publica ac perpetua aestimatio difficultatibus permutationum aequalitate quantitatis subveniret; eaque materia FORMA PUBLICA PERCUSSA usum dominiumque non tam ex substantia praebet, quam ex quantitate.

2) Lege Cornelia cavetur, eum qui argenteos numos adulterinos FLAVERIT falsi crimine teneri.

With some few exceptions, that which has originated in the minds of the Chinese can hardly be called science. Nowhere we find a system, but everywhere a mixture of elements, good and bad, an enormous encyclopedia, but without any logical succession of ideas, no basis laid by one generation to build on for the next, not even the capacity to connect and unite the scattered materials and work them to a whole. On the contrary every attempt to strive forward in science shows little or no progress and generally is confined to endless collations, compilations and commentaries, generally devoid of anything that may be called system.

A favorable exception to this form the writings of the ancient philosophers which are founded on a true and practical basis, containing the principles on which men will live happy on earth, and how to attain this end, how the prince must govern his people and the people must serve their prince, how the social relations both in the family and in the state must be arranged in order to come as near this object as possible. Here we find a logically developed system which has been a true gospel at its origin and has continued to exist as such but likewise without having been developed fuller notwithstanding it chiefly deals with the material interests of life.

As to the department of speculative philosophy, what has been produced after that time is so obscure and vague that one feels almost inclined to ask whether the learned philosophers themselves were able to account for the speculative theories they wrote down as genuine wisdom.

In art as in science we find the general and characteristic fault of attending too much to the details but too little to the whole, and besides, that stubborn adherence to customs, traditions, fixed rules and processes which developed Chinese art to a true talent only as to the details. Let us take, for instance, the Chinese art of painting; the outlines of a picture are boldly drawn but perspective is wanting; the details are executed to perfection but a leading thought is not to be found, and this is again the consequence of the following the old beaten track; every part being done according to certain rules. To improve upon these rules, to catch the spirit and not to cling to the letter is a thing a Chinese painter never thinks of.

A remarkable instance of this I have seen in a number of portraits of Chinese nobles who were evidently taken after life. The

painter had produced a striking resemblance of the head and attitude of his model, and in this part of his work he had unconsciously
followed the laws of perspective, while the state robes interwoven
with gold and flowers and the variegated carpet are executed as
minutely in the background as in the part of the picture which lies
nearest to the painters eye. And the reason why he in one part had
unconsciously obeyed the laws which the plane surface imposes on
him, and he neglected them in the other, is simply because there is no unity
of thought; in floor and carpet he neglects the laws of perspective only
because he knows the receipt to draw a floor or a carpet. He does
not observe this want of unity in the whole, and very problable it
would not be possible to convince him of his unprincipledness, for
he has worked according to rule, and rule in his principle.

Finally we find the same absence of unity in the political administration of the Chinese. The ancient constitution of the *Tseu*-
dynasty was founded upon the principle of centralization. Whole legions
of civil functionaries were spread over the empire and were respon-
sable for their actions to the central government established in the
capital; a thing of itself already impracticable. Such a system,
however, may have answered well in the beginning when the empire
was not extensive, but already under the *Han*-dynasty a centralization of the power of the government must needs cause a total
disorganization and the greatest frittering of power.

The Chinese empire was too extensive to become powerful when
governed in such a way. Petty princes and influential officials representing the central government in remote districts could with im-
punity commit the greatest extortions and injustice. Their despotism
generally made it necessary for them to assume a hostile attitude
against the central government and to be on friendly terms with
their homogeneous neighbors in case the emperor minding to punish
them, made war upon them. Hence no prince, however prosperous his
reign may have been, but has had to fight rebels. And was that system
of centralization a source of continuous confusion and warfare at times
when the reins of the government were in the hand of a well-meaning
powerful prince, worse evils arose when a tyrant was seated on the
throne, and abused the imperial dignity to satisfy his passions and desires.
Every feudal prince, every magistrate becomes lord and master of his
own terrntory, calls himself prince, king, emperor, or whatever
sublime title his imagination suggests, and whole periods occur

in Chinese history in which several dynasties, several emperors simultaneously sway the scepter in the most distant parts of the empire.

This state of affairs generally lasts till some warrior or statesman has spirit and energy enough to consolidate the lacerated empire, then he is proclaimed Emperor and becomes the founder of a new dynasty. The internal broils are quelled, and the external enemies driven back to their dominions.

A new period of prosperity has dawned owing; to the peace which now prevails and the incomparable fertility of the land situated between the *Kiang* and the *Ho*, there is abundance of food: "the teeth grow and the population increases" [1]).

At the accession of such a new dynasty we always read of reforms also in the monetary system, but hardly have some generations passed by when it is the old history again. A despot or tyrant either disregarding the warnings of wellmeaning ministers or urged by evil councilors sets the example of making bad money. Confusion, want and distress are the fatal consequences.

Provisions rise in price, trade is paralyzed, weeds cover the fertile fields, false coiners spring up like clouds, the officials appointed by such a government, commonly rascals themselves, extort the people; the posterity of those who were born in affluence die miserably from want and the bodies of tens of thousands, not killed by the sword of the enemy but starved with hunger, cover all the roads of the empire.

Four times in consequence of this absence of unity the Chinese empire has fallen a prey to its savage enemies the Huns, Tartars and Mongols, who in large numbers and with irresistable fury came in from the Western and Northern plains of Asia. Their chiefs ascended the sublime throne of the "Son of heaven," did all they could to ruin the people and after a short career shared the same fate as their Chinese predecessors.

In this way occurs everywhere the same phenomenon so clearly seen in the monetary history; the want of a progressive development and of an organizing talent which were to unite into a whole, into a system the good elements scattered here and there, and this notwithstanding the Chinese people lived in circumstances which made it necessary

---

1) 重 熙 累 盛 生 齒 繁 庶 is the phrase by which the Chinese author expresses that Malthusian theory.

for them to exert all their strength of intellect to accomplish radical inprovements. Involuntarily we are induced to ascribe such a leading characteristic to a lack of natural capacity which allows no development beyond certain limits. I may be allowed to communicate a remarkable concordance of this supposition derived from the state of social development, with the results of another branch of science, viz. the examination of the formation of the Chinese skull.

The Chinese skull frequently shows, firstly a particular deviation in the formation of the tempeial bone, called by Prof. VIRCHOW [1]) *Processus frontalis* (Stirnfortsatz der Schläfenschuppe), and secondly a noticeable narrowness of the temporal region (*Stenokrotaphie*); two phenomena which are generally observed in the skulls of inferior races.

In the Anatomical Museum of the Leiden University is a collection of 67 Chinese skulls, 5 of which have the deviation (*Processus frontalis*) and 20 of which show more or less the other phenomenon, the narrowness of the temporal region (*Stenokrotaphie*).

Professor VIRCHOW, p. 59 of the work quoted, writes "Ich komme somit zu dem Schlussergebniss, dass der Stirnfortsatz der Schlafenschuppe allerdings eine Theromorphie (Thierähnlichkeit) und zwar vorzugsweise eine Pithekoide (Affenartige) ist. Die noch nicht nachgewiesene aber sicher zu vermuthende defecte Bildung der temporalen Hirntheilen lässt es gerechtfertigt erscheinen, *in dem Stirnfortsatz und in der Stenokrotaphie überhaupt ein Merkmal niederer, jedoch keineswegs niederster Rasse zu sehen.*"

---

The reports of mediaeval travellers in Tartary and China, which first made known in Europe the wondrous use of pieces of paper as money, all date from the time when the paper money in China had already had its flourishing time.

1) Se RUDOLF VIRCHOW, Ueber einige Merkmale Niederer Menschenrassen am Schädel. Berlin 1875.

2) I got this information from my friend and fellow student Mr. P. DE KONING who having examined the aforesaid collection of Chinese Skulls, is about to publish a dissertation on the subject entitled "Description of Chinese Skulls" (Beschrijving van Chineesche schedels. Leiden v. d. Hoek 1877.) The number of 67 Skulls which were at his disposal is perhaps too small to draw a general conclusion regarding the Chinese. race, but remarkable it is that both phenomena are found in such a high degree (*Processus frontalis* at 8°/₀ and *Stenokrotaphie* at 30°/₀ of the whole number, whereas other examinations of skulls f. i. of Russians and other European races made on large scale showed only a proportion of about $^{15}/_{1000}$. GRUBER found the *Processus frontalis* on 60 of 4000 Russian Skulls. CALORI on 12 of 1074 Italian Skulls. Cf. VIRCHOW *cit.* p. 10.

The earliest communication is of a monk, GUILLAUME DE RUBROUCK (*Rubruquis*) who in the year 1252 was sent by Saint Louis, king of of France, to the court of the Mongol prince MANGU-KHAN. His report on the paper money is very insignificant: "*La monnaie de Cathay est faite de coton grande comme la main et sur laquelle ils impriment certains lignes et marques faites comme le sceau du Cham* ').

Much more interesting is the information given by MARCO POLO, the Venetian, who about 1275—84 resided at the court of KUBLAI-KHAN²). Inhabitant of the greatest commercial town in the world, an institution like that of paper money struck him with admiration which is evident from this glowing account ³).

It is found in the second book of his travels:

## CHAPTER XXIV.

### HOW THE GREAT KAAN CAUSETH THE BARK OF TREES MADE INTO SOMETHING LIKE PAPER, TO PASS FOR MONEY OVER ALL HIS COUNTRY.

Now that I have told you in detail of the splendour of this City of the Emperor's, I shall proceed to tell you of the Mint which he hath in the same city, in the which he hath his money coined and struck, as I shall relate to you. And in doing so I shall make manifest to you how it is that the Great Lord may well be able to accomplish even much more than I have told you, or am going to tell you, in this Book. For, tell it how I might, you never would be satisfied that I was keeping within truth and reason!

The Emperor's Mint then is in this same City of Cambaluc, and the way it is wrought is such that you might say he hath the Secret of Alchemy in perfection, and you would be right! For he makes his money after this fashion.

He makes them take of the bark of a certain tree, in fact of the Mulberry Tree, the leaves of which are the food of the silkworms, — these trees being so numerous that whole districts are full of them. What they take is a certain fine white bast or skin which lies between the wood of the tree and the thick outer bark, and this they make into something resembling sheets of paper, but black⁴). When these sheets have been prepared they are cut up into pieces of different sizes. The smallest of these

---

1) Cf. Recueil de divers voyages curieux par P. BERGERON. Voyage de RUBRUQUIS en Tartarie p. 91. Leide 1729.

2) He is known as the emperor 世宗 *Si-tsung* in the Chinese history.

3) The text is quoted from the splendid Edition of MARCO POLO's Book by Col. HENRY YULE, Vol. I p. 378—380. The account is so interresting when compared with the Chinese sources, which have been translated is the sixth Chapter that I have given it in full. In different other passages of M. P.'s Journal the use of paper money with the tribes he visited and who were governed by the great Khan is mentionned.

4) See the photograph to the Addenda.

sizes is worth a half tornesel; the next, a little larger, one tornesel; one, a little larger still, is worth half a silver groat of Venice; another a whole groat; others yet two groats, five groats, and ten groats. There is also a kind worth one Bezant of gold, and others of three Bezants, and so up to ten. All these pieces of paper are [issued with as much solemnity and authority as if they were of pure gold or silver; and on every piece a variety of officials, whose duty it is, have to write their names, and to put their seals. And when all is prepared duly, the chief officer deputed by the Kaan smears the Seal entrusted to him with vermilion, and impresses it on the paper, so that the form of the Seal remains stamped upon it in red; the Money is then authentic. Any one forging it would be punished with death]. And the Kaan causes every year to be made such a vast quantity of this money, which costs him nothing, that it must equal in amount all the treasure in the world.

With these pieces of paper, made as I have described, he causes all payments on his own account to be made; and he makes them to pass current universally over all his kingdoms and provinces and territories, and whithersoever his power and sovereignty extends. And nobody, however important he may think himself, dares to refuse them on pain of death. And indeed everybody takes them readily, for wheresoever a person may go throughout the Great Kaan's dominions he shall find these pieces of paper current, and shall be able to transact all sales and purchases of goods by means of them just as well as if they were coins of pure gold. And all the while they are so light that ten bezants' worth does not weigh one golden bezant.

Furthermore all merchants arriving from India or other countries, and bringing with them gold or silver or gems and pearls, are prohibited from selling to any one but the Emperor. He has twelve experts chosen for this business, men of shrewdness and experience in such affairs; these appraise the articles, and the Emperor then pays a liberal price for them in those pieces of paper. The merchants accept his price readily, for in the first place they would not get so good an one from anybody else, and secondly they are paid without any delay. And with this papermoney they can buy what they like anywhere over the Empire, whilst it is also vastly lighter to carry about on their journeys. And it is a truth that the merchants will several times in the year bring wares to the amount of 400,000 bezants, and the Grand Sire pays for all in that paper. So he buys such a quantity of those precious things every year that his treasure is endless, whilst all the time the money he pays away costs him nothing at all. Moreover several times in the year proclamation is made through the city that any one who may have gold or silver or gems or pearls, by taking them to the Mint shall get a handsome price for them. And the owners are glad to do this, because they would find no other purchaser give so large a price. Thus the quantity they bring in is marvellous, though those who do not choose to do so may let it alone. Still, in this way, nearly all the valuables in the country come into the Kaan's possession.

When any of those pieces of paper are spoilt — not that they are so very flimsy neither — the owner carries them to the Mint, and by paying 3 per cent. on the value he gets new pieces in exchange. And if any Baron, or any one else soever, hath need of gold or silver or gems or pearls, in order to make plate, or girdles or the like, he goes to the Mint and buys as much as he list, paying in this papermoney.

Now you have heard the ways and means whereby the Great Kaan may have, and in fact *has*, more treasure than all the Kings in the World; and you know all about it and the reason why.

*Marco Polo*'s information has already frequently been mentioned in connection with the Chinese historians of the Mongol dynasty, and after the detailed account of the issue of paper money under the reign of *Kublai-khan* given by PAUTHIER in his edition of *Marco Polo*, the Chinese text may justly be looked upon as a superfluous appendix. Yet was it not useless to compare these reports with that part of the history of paper money in *Wang-k'i*'s Continuation of *Ma-twan-lin* which bears upon the time of *Marco Polo*'s residence at the Chinese Court. The perusal of this passage has lent greater force to my conviction that the important history of the paper money after the great bankruptcy caused by it under the *Sung*-dynasty was already past and gone by in China. Our Venetian was too much in admiration of this remarkable institution to see the dark side of the picture. The Khan actually "made such a vast quantity of this money which cost him nothing that it equaled in amount all the treasures of the world". Moreover we read in the Chinese Chronicle that it was made to the smallest amount and that there circulated bills for 1 and 2 *cash* [1]). An imperial decree issued in the 3rd month of the period *Tsung-t'ung* (1281) ordered that the premium on the conversion of old *Hoei-tsze* into new ones should be raised from $2^0/_0$ to $3^0/_0$ to indemnify the state for the cost of printing and ink [2]). Here too were depreciation and conversions of all kinds the natural consequences of over-issue which terminated in a great state-bankruptcy at the close of the Mongol dynasty.

Subsequent travellers in Tartary and China have also made mention of paper money. *Frater* ODERIC DE FRIOUL (1318) seems to allude to paper money when he relates the way in which taxes are paid to the great Khan.

1) We read of bills called 厘鈔 worth $^1/_{1000}$ of an ounce of silver = 1 copper cash.

2) Marco Polo's statement perfectly accords with this decree. *Wang-k'i* XVIII 3a—b (工墨費).

The people of this country say, that they have one duetie inioyned unto them by their lord, for every fire payeth ono *Balis* in regârd of tribute and a *Balis* is five papers or pieces of silke, which are worth one floren and an halfe of our coine, Tenne or twelve housholds are accompted for one fire" [1]).

In 1322 Sir JOHN MANDEVILLE, the physician was in Tartary and his story which is inserted in all books treating of the history of Banking, reads as follows [2]).

"This Emperour may dispenden als moche as he wile, withouten estyma-"cioun. For he despendethe not, ne makethe no money, but of Lether em-"prented, or of Papyre. And of that money, is som of gretter prys, and "som of lasse prys, aftre the dyversitee of his Statutes. And whan that "Money hathe ronne so longe that it begynnethe to waste, than men beren "it to the Emperoure's Tresorye; and than thei taken newe money for the "olde. And that Money gothe thorghe out alle the contree, and thorghe "out alle his Provynces. For there and beyonde hem, thei make no Money "nouther of Gold nor of Sylver. And therefore he may despende ynow, and "outrageously."

The last information is of JEAN DE CORE, bishop of SULTANYEH [3]).

Le grant Kaan fait monnoie de pappier là où il a une enseigne rouge droit ou millieu, et tout environ sont lettres noires. Et est celle monnoie

1) The passage is quoted from the Second Volume of the Principal Navigations, Voyages, etc., by RICHARD HACKLUYT. London 1599. page 60.

2, Remarkable it is indeed that neither from the account of any medieval author nor from the informations of the modern economists anything is known of the use of paper money in a great commercial town of Europe, at the same time that in China under the reign of the *Sung*-dynasty paperpmoney was invented. MACLEOD writes in his Dictionnairy of Political Economy in voce *Currency*. "The first paper money that we are aware of in Europe was that issued by the city of Milan in the 13th century."

But in an Arabian manuscript recently found in Spain, and treating of the Sclavonic race we read that about the year 960 of our era, shred money circulated in the city of Prague. This manuscript is preparing for publication at St. Petersburg under the title of AL-BEKRI's "*Nachrichten uber die Slaven und deren Nachbarn*". Prof. M. J. DE GOEJE who is possessed of a proofprint of this work, has kindly allowed me to borrow the following fragment from it (p. 29), which is interesting to our subject. The Arabian author got his information from a Iew who stayed for some time at the court of Otto I.

"Ibrahîm ben Iakûb der Israelite sagt: " . . . . Die Stadt Frâga ist aus Steinen "und Kalk gebaut. Sie ist die reichste der "Städte an Handel . . . Ihr Land ist das "beste der Länder des Nordens, und das "reichste an Lebensmitteln: der Weizen wird "bei ihnen verkauft um einen Knschâr, so "viel als ein Mann braucht für einen "Monat; Gerste wird verkauft um einen "Knschâr Futter eines Pferdes für 40 Tage, "und 10 Hühner werden bei ihnen verkauft "um einen Knschâr. Und es werden im "Land Bwj'ma (Bohemen) leichte kleine "Tücher gemacht von sehr feinem netzför-"migen Gewebe, welche zu nichts gut sind. "Der Preis derselben ist bei ihnen jederzeit "10 Tücher für einen Knschâr. Mit ihnen "handeln und verkehren sie untereinander. "Sie besitzen davon (ganze) Gefässe und sie "(die Tücher) gelten bei ihnen für Reich-"thum und für die werthvollsten Gegen-"stände. Mit ihnen wird eingehandelt Hirse, "Mehl, Pferde, Gold, Silber und alle Dinge.'

3) l'Extreme Orient au Moyen-age par LOUIS DE BACKER. Paris 1877. p. 341—42.

de greigneur ou mendre pris selonc la enseigne qui y est. L'une vault une
maille, l'autre un denier, et ainsi plus ou mains. Et ilz avaluent leur
monnoie d'or et d'argent à leur monnoie de pappier.

Ly emperères dessusdis a tresors si trèsgrans que c'est merveilles et est
pour celle monnoie de pappier. Et quant celle monnoie de pappier est trop
vielle et dégastée, sy que on ne la puet bonnement manier, on l'apporte
as monnoiers du roy, à la chambre du roy, deputez à ce, et se la enseigne
de la monnoie où ly noms du roy y appert aucunement, ly monnoier du
Roy rendent nouvelle pour la vielle trois moins sur chascun cent pour la
rénovation. Ilz font aussy tous leurs previlèges en pappier.

A Chinese author whose work is quoted by *Wang-k'i* [1]) writing
about the history of the money bills of the Mongol-dyn-
asty says: "Already were the bills in consequence of the overissue
no more fit to measure the value of all merchandise, and when in
consequence of the confusions of war there was for the government
expenditure no sufficient quantity of money to meet the want, continually new bills were printed, the result was that the bills had
no value while commodities fetched high prices, and when at last
they were not accepted any more, that law by which they had
been instituted, was repealed. At the time that they had their full
value, the bills were generally used as balancing money but in the
times of their decay when the deposit which should have backed
them was not sufficient, more paper money was constantly made,
till at last they (the bills) were not current any more."

"If the law of redemption shall be carried out an equal amount
of copper money should be deposited when bills are issued, as it
was when in *Sse-tš·uen* for the first time bills of exchange were
emitted. The private persons who managed this issue took care that
the bills came in when the money went out, whereas when the bills
were issued the money was deposited, and in this way money and
bills circulating side by side measured all merchandise of the empire,
and in those days there was not the least reason why they should
not circulate. But in the present time they do not know how
heavy they shall make the punishments, simply to compel the people
to circulate them, but in proportion as the punishments became
severer, the use made of the bills became less, and this resulted
at last in their not being current any longer and their circulation
being out all at once."

1) *Su wen hien t'ung k'ao* XVIII 9*a*— | tains the most important part of the account.
10*a*. The translation is free and only con- |

The paper currency which "the grand khan spended outrageously" was one of the reasons that the Mongols were expelled from the country, but a short time after the Chinese *Ming*-dynasty began by trying once more to palm paper money upon the people. In the year 1375 the bill was issued, a photograph of which has been appended to this work. The history of these bills is little more than a weak echo of what has already been said about the paper circulation which for a long time dragged forth its insignificant existence. · Occasionally history mentions a conversion or an order that the paper money should be accepted as legal tender, but no loud complaints, no state bankruptcy have resulted from it, very probably as the people having learned the value of a government-paper currency, made but little use of it.

About the middle of the 16th century when the Mandchu brought China under their sway, the paper currency was abolished, and ages passed away without any attempt being made to revive the old institution; its very existence seems to have been forgotten, so much so, that the Jesuit pater GABRIEL DE MAGAILLANS who many years preached the Gospel in the Western regions of China and also resided in *Peking* about 1668, in his "Nouvelle Relation de la Chine" can remark: "Il n'y a aucune mémoire dans la Chine et on ne trouve aucune marque dans les livres qu'on se soit jamais servy de monnayes de papier dans ce royaume comme MARC POLO le dit dans dans son second livre."

Not until two centuries later paper money was made use of again, in consequence of the want trade felt of a lighter and more convenient medium of exchange. Il reappeared in the same form as that in which it was first issued by "private persons" in 960 in the province of *Sse-tš'uen*. "Notwithstanding it is no legal tender", a French diplomate [1]) writes, "it is everywhere accepted and seldom it occurs that the bills issued by some bank or other circulate at a discount." Considering the history we have related this statement in my opinion might be reversed and run: Because it is not legal tender and because it is no concern of the State it is generally accepted as money.

The words of this French diplomate corroborate the statement

1) Lettre datée de Peking 12 Avril 1869 de M. le Comte DE ROCHECHOUART, chargé d'Affaires de la France en Chine. — Journal des Economistes 1869. Vol. XV , p. 103 sqq.

made by some authors, that the present system of free banking seems to work favourably in China. Truly a remarkable contrast! While in Europe free-banking gradually disappears as impracticable and monopoly of the State itself or at any rate under immediate control of the State is becoming the general theory, we see in China the very opposite take place.

And how to explain the fact that free-banking works its way so well? The information given by several diplomates answers that question. The circulation of paper money issued at a certain place moves within narrow limits, and within the immediate neighborhood of the town; in no wise without the province; hence the people generally know whether the bank which issues the notes be solvent or not. Furthermore, the several money shop keepers and bankers of a town or district enter into a kind of bond agreeing to honor one another's bills and only he who has sufficiently proved to be solvent is admitted into the bond. Hence the different banks control one another and if one happens to become insolvent the consortium is apprised of it before the public, and takes measures to prevent great losses.

Credit exists only to the extent of advances of money on sufficient security. Deposits and mortgage seldom occur. Bills circulate and are bought and sold at the Exchange of Peking, but as far as we can judge, Chinese banking confines itself to issuing and repaying bills.

At the end of this work an interpretation will be found of two bills, one emitted by the State, the other, a scrip issued by one of the numerous joint-stock banks in *Šang-hai*. It may seem contradictory to speak of a bill emitted by the State, after having just told that since the conquest of China by the MANDCHU, the government issued no paper money any more. The contradiction is, however, explained by the fact that the State acts in the quality of a private person in order to enjoy some of the profits accruing from Banking. Therefore it has also adopted the name of a commercial firm and subjected itself to the very same regulations which other private banks have to obey to, in order to retain the favour and confidence of the public.

# CHAPTER I.

BARTER. — ORIGIN OF MONEY AND PRIMITIVE SPECIES. — DENOMINATIONS TO EXPRESS THE IDEA OF MONEY, CURRENCY, MEDIUM OF EXCHANGE. — INFORMATION OF KWANTSZE, THE EARLIEST WRITER ON MONEY. — VIEWS ON THE CHARACTER OF MONEY AND THE USE OF IT IN ANCIENT TIMES, BY TWO CHINESE SCHOLARS OF THE ELEVENTH CENTURY. — SOMETHING ON THE USE OF MONEY IN THE BEGINNING OF THE TSEU DYNASTY. — TWO PASSAGES QUOTED FROM "THE BOOK OF RITES OF THE TSEU". — MA-TWAN-LIN'S CRITIC. — INTRODUCTION OF NEW COINS BY KING-WANG AND ADVICE GIVEN BY TAN, DUKE OF MU.

The primitive mode of commercial exchange in China, as in all other countries, was barter, the interchange of certain products of the earth, such as wheat and rice, or of men's manual labor, as silk, arms, etc., by means of which the necessary and much desired articles were obtained. It is, however, remarkable that while all other nations, in Europe as well as in Asia, have had a primitive currency recalling the lowest state of civilisation, the hunting and pastoral state, — when by means of furs and cattle exchange was effected — no trace of the same phenomenon is to be found either in Chinese history or language. The earliest record of money shows that the "blackhaired people" in the remotest times stood already on the third step of the ladder of civilisation, and that a subject of "the Son of Heaven" was either a husbandman or a merchant. For it is related that

1

神 於 貨 爲 有
農 國 帛 市 無
列 以 日 市 以
廊 聚 中 日 交

*Šin-nung* (the second known emperor of China, who reigned about the year 2737 B. C.) instituted a market-place in his Empire in order to gather merchandise and silks. By day-time market was held to exchange the articles which people had for others which they had not.

But at the same time that among the common people, who earned their livelihood by cultivating the soil and feeding silkworms, barter was prevalent, there seems also to have existed a kind of coined metallic money, current among the travelling merchants, the circulation of which was however very limited, as it was not used by the people who lived by the produce of agriculture.

Ma-twan-lin alludes to that ancient money in the beginning of his "Examination", and the same subject is treated of historically and rather economically by two Chinese scholars, who lived in the middle of the 11th century of the christian era. From both treatises we intend giving a passage. Besides, many old Chinese and Japanese mint-books show us drawings of those ancient coins, most of which, however, are covered with characters, in an old

and nearly illegible writing-manner. One of them I have copied as I found it in a Japanese book in possession of the zoological Society Natura Artis Magistra at Amsterdam [1]).

According to my Japanese informant the characters, read from the right-hand side to the left, are 安邑貨二金 which means current merchandise of the second metal (circulating in) the peaceful capital. With

1) To the kindness of the Director of this Society Mr. G. F. Westerman and of the conservator of the Japanese Museum and library Mr. G. Janse, I am indebted for the free disposal of several useful materials.

second metal silver is meant. It was cast by King-*Yü* of the *Hia*-dyuasty 夏ノ 禹王鑄 ル, who reigned twenty-two centuries ago in China.

What Ma-twan-lin gives in reference to the money of ancient times is very little. As it is most likely a piece of a very remote date, and at the same time furnishes us with some ancient denominations of currency, we will first quote it, and then proceed to the explanation of the various names by which, in ancient and in modern times, money and its different qualities are designated.

或 或 三 夏 莒 人 謂 謂 有 高 有 自
刀 赤。品。商 人 謂 之 之 熊 陽 錢 太
或 或 或 之 謂 之 泉。氏。氏。矣。昊
龜 錢 黃 幣。之 布。商 陶 高 謂 以
貝。或 或 金 刀。齊 人 唐 辛 之 來
布 白 爲 虞 人 齊 氏 氏 金。氏。則

Since the reign, of *T'ai-Hao* (B. C. 2852) money is supposed to have been extant [1]. In the reign of *T'ai-Hao* it was called *Kin*, metal, in that of *Yeu-nai-ši* (B. C. 2697) and of *Kao-sin-ši* (B. C. 2435) it was called *Ho*, merchandise. *T'ao-t'ang-ši* called it *Ts'uen*, (a character now signifying a fountain) the people of *Šang* and *Ts'i* called it *Pu*, a hempen or silk piece of cloth, and the people of *Ts'i* and *Keu* called it *tao*, knives. The money of the first three dynasties of *Yü*, *Hia* and *Šang* (2255—1766 B. C.) was made of three different sorts of metal, yellow, white and red, and consisted further of cloth, knives and tortoise shells.

There is some evidence that in the remotest times, in which history is a blank, there was in China a currency of shells, much resembling the Wampumpeag cowries, found among the American natives, when the first New-England settlers arrived there in 1630. Firstly, because all the words denoting buying 買, selling 賣, riches 財。貲, goods 貨, store 積, property 資,

---

1) Note the final particle 矣 by which | no objective certainty but the subjective meaning of the author is expressed.

prices 買, cheap 賤, dear 貴, and many others referring to money and wealth are composed of the ideographical sign which denotes the word shell 貝 [1]). Secondly, because *Wang-mang* the usurper, who took possession of the Imperial throne 14 A. D., wishing to return to the ancient state of things, introduced again the old forms and sorts of money, and among them 5 different varieties of shells of an arbitrary value. Further there is a passage in the *Šu-king*, the historical chronicles, informing us that anciently shells were considered as precious articles. For we read that king *Pwan-kang* (1400 B. C.) laments the greediness of his ministers: "Here are those ministers of my government, who share with me the offices of the State, and yet only think of hoarding up cowries and gems," 具乃貝玉 [2]). Two songs in the ancient "Book of Poetry" make mention of shells as "an ornament embroidered in silk [3]), and strung together by vermillion threads, fastened as an ornament on a warriors helmet [4])."

The different denominations of money are:

1°. 布。幣。刀。 *Pu, pi* and *tao.* Hempen and silk cloth and knives were the earliest articles of trade generally used for money, and as the first weighed metallic money was an imitation of the shape and a representation of those articles, the same denominations remained to designate those coins. The *pu*-coins represent a piece of cloth, a dress, and the *tao*-coins are in their outward form an imitation of a sword or knife. Even between the character 布 *pu* and the form of the coin

---

1) J. Klaproth was the first that in the Journal Asiatique directed the attention to that fact.

2) *Šu-king* IV. VII. 2. 14. Legge p. 240.
3) *Ši-king* II. V. 61. Legge p. 346.
4) *Ši-king* IV. II. 4. 5. Legge p. 626.

*pu*, of which we give here an illustration, there is a resemblance which still more distinctly may be seen from the form 帗,

the same character in the old seal-writing. The conclusion is easily arrived at that 布 or 巾 is the original ideographical form representing .cloth, dress [1]).

The illustration of the knife-shaped coin is of one used under the usurper *Wang-mang* (14 A. D.) and found in the valuable work of the Russian diplomate BARON DE CHAUDOIR, Recueil de Monnaies de la Chine, St. Pétersbourg. 1842. (Planche II.) The character engraved on the coin is 代 to exchange, which here is used for 貨 article of barter, merchandise. It is the same as the third monogram 貨 on the coin of the Emperor *Yü* (page 2). Together with the knife-shaped coin the character 刀 as a denomination of currency is lost. 布 and 幣 (hempen and silk cloth), however, are still extant, as we will see in the passages quoted from Matwanlin, and the second word, used by itself or as part of a compound, has become the standard term for currency [2]).

2°. 貨 *ho*, MERCHANDISE, ARTICLE OF TRADE (*merx*), composed of property and the verb

---

1) I have copied the coin from a Japanese mintbook. A description of it will be given in Chapter II, Currency instituted by Wang-mang.

2) See, for instance, the title of Ma-twan-lin's Examination 錢幣考。

to change is likewise one of the oldest names of currency, and may already be seen on the coin of the emperor *Yü*, and up to the present time, taken by itself or as part of a compound, it is used in the same sense, as for instance in the frequently occurring 通貨 general or current merchandise 貨布 lit. cloth-merchandise, or the cloth-representing coin, the name of a coin in use under *Wang-mang* (14 A. D.) 錢貨 money-merchandise, etc. [1]). The economical truth, that money is a merchandise which should have its own intrinsic value, a truth so frequently lost sight of in our modern history of money, has become with the Chinese a rooted truth by the constant use of the denomination 貨; and frequently we see in Chinese history, that whenever the sovereign has arbitrarily altered the weight or standard of the coins, his prime minister remonstrates with the argument. "Money as a MERCHANDISE should have an intrinsic value."

3°. 錢 *tsien*, COIN, COPPER CASH, is the general name for the round and square holed Chinese coins in common use. In combination with other characters already treated of, as for instance 錢貨 . 錢布, it is used for the general signification of Medium of exchange.

Another quality of money, is expressed by Chinese economists by the character 權 *Kiuen*, properly meaning to weigh or balance on the steelyards, equivalent; for instance, 先有所謂穀粟泉布之權. Formerly, they had what is called the equivalent of a currency consisting of grain and rice. — And a little further on the passage is found: 以

1) Mat. VIII: 21 *b* 其輕重可得貨之宜 Its weight may be the reason that it is fit for currency 古者 以龜貝爲貨 The ancients made currency of tortoise shells.

泉布爲權。常不使權勝本. Money was made the equivalent, but they did not always take care that that equi-valent was adequate to its origin (was what it was intended to be when it first was instituted). [Mat. IX: 36 *b*].

4°. 圜法 *yuen-fat*, properly ROUND or CURRENT RULE is a denomination found in the "Rites of the *Tšeu*-dynasty" [1], in which we read that the administration of the State-finances was divided among nine different principal offices or boards 九府圜法. The signification of 圜 is, according to a definition of Ma-twan-lin's, similar and current 圜謂均而通也.

5° There are several other terms, as 寶 *pao*, precious object, treasure. For instance the expression 通寶 "current money" in addition to the year-name of the fabrication of the coin, is the constant design of the coins of the *T'ang* and subsequent dynasties (800—1877). Further, 貫。緡 and 鏹 which all three have the signification of a string of 1000 *cash*.

6°. Finally, there is the remarkable word 泉 *ts'uen* which at present means, fountain, spring. We see it in a seal-writing on the ancient coins as a denomination of money, and now it is still used in daily occurring expressions to denote money, as 泉貨。泉布. An attempt has been made to explain its signification by saying that money streams and, so to say, spreads over the community as water coming forth from a fountain, but on authority of a scholar under the *Sung*-dynasty, this is a misinterpretation, and the monogram 泉 of the old coin is not even related to the modern character 泉 fountain.

1) This book was written more than eleven centuries B. C. and is still extant. When treating of the money under the *Tšeu*-dyn. we will quote two passages from that "Book of Rites" having reference to the budget and the management of state finances.

But let us hear *Ts'ing-ts'iao*, who according to Mayers [1]) was a scholar distinguished by almost universal knowledge.

夾祭鄭氏曰。古文錢字作泉者。言其形。如泉文。錢字變而作刀。言其形。再變而為圓法。圓法郎太公所作。自圓法流通於世。民便之。故泉與刀廢。後人不曉其文也。觀古錢之篆文。後世借為錢字。故泉之篆文。其實泉之篆文。下體之泉。本末不從水也。先儒不知。謂流於泉。布於布寶。利於刀。此皆沿鑿之[2])義也。

*Kia-tsi* of the family-name *Tsing* says — "In classical style the word money is expressed by the character 泉 and has reference to the form of the coin; synonymous with this character but different in form is the character sword, which has reference to the instrument (anciently used as money). Another synonym is *Yuen-fat*, which was instituted by *Tai-kung* (the duke of *Tseu*). Since that time *Yeun-fat* has passed through different ages, and as the people thought it convenient, *ts'uen* and *tao* were discontinued, and posterity does not more understand the meaning of that character. If we look at the shape of ancient coins, (we observe) in seal-writing the character 泉 (⊡) which later generations have substituted by the monogram 錢. If they, therefore make the derivation of the (ancient) mark *Ts'uen*, they make of it the character 泉 which has the meaning of water-fountain. But the seal-character of the real 泉 (of ancient coins) is in its lower strokes not composed of the radical 水 water. The most eminent scholars do not know either its origin or end (whence it arose or what has become of it) and when they say that it streams faster than a fountain, that it spreads more (widely) than cloth-parcels, that it is more precious than gold and more advantageous than knives, these (various opinions) are nothing more than sailing along the coast and boring in the direction of truth.

---

1) Chinese Reader's Manual. I. 61. *Kia-tsi* is the pseudonym of the author.

2) 之 = 往 going to.

From the form of the primitive species of which we gave the illustrations, it will easily be seen that money took its origin in barter. The Romans derived their pecunia from pecus and on their first coins engraved the figure of an ox or a sheep, the Chinese did very much the same thing when, instead of their knives and articles of clothing, they gave to a weighed quantity of different kinds of metal the shape of articles of clothing and of knives, which henceforth served for money. ·

There exists a fragment of one of the most ancient Chinese authors on the origin of money, which relates in a rather ingenuous way how circumstances led the ancient sovereigns to make money as a means to relieve the wants of their people.

遠。能 絶 周 困。鑄 禹 之 金 者。之 旱。管
其 通。壞 七 東 幣 以 無 鑄 湯 無 禹 子
至 爲 斷。八 西 以 歷 糧 幣 以 糧 五 曰。
之 其 舟 千 南 救 山 賣 而 莊 有 年 湯
難。途 車 里。北 人 之 子 贖 山 賣 水。七
故 之 不 水 去 之 金 者。人 之 子 人 年

Kwan-tsze says[1]): "In the seventh year of the reign of king T'ang (B. C. 1766 the founder of the Šang·dyn.), there was a drought and in the fifth year of the reign of king Yü, (B. C. 2205 the founder of the Hia-dyn.) there was a flood. Among the people who were in want of rice-gruel (food), there were who had sold their children (for slaves); king-T'ang then took the metal of the Tšoang-mountains, and cast money that he might ransom the sold children of the people who were in want of food. King-Yü took the metal which was found in de Lei-mountains, and made money of it to relieve the distress of his subjects. When from east, west, north and south, all over a surface of 7 or 8000 li (miles) all intercourse with these parts was cut off by the flood, and in consequence of the length of the way and the diffi-

---

1) Kwan-tsze was one of the most renowned statesmen of antiquity. In 685 B. C. prime Minister of the feudel State of Tsi he greatly contributed by a prudent government to the rise of his native country among the rival principalities of that time. He has written a work on government and legislation of which the piece quoted is probably a fragment. See Mayers Chin. Read. Man. I. 203.

託用於其重。以珠玉為上幣，以黃金為中幣，以刀布為下幣。三幣握之，則非有補於暖也；食之，則非有補於飽也。先王以守財物，以御人事，而平天下也，是以命之曰衡。衡者，使物一高一下，不得有調也。

culties to reach them neither ship nor cart could penetrate thither, (the people) therefore relied on and employed according to their weight (the following sorts of currency). Pearls and gems were used as the first, the yellow metal as the second, and swords and cloth as the lowest sort of money. As to the effects of these three different sorts of money, if you took a handful of them, they could not supply (you) with clothing (lit. to warm the body) and as to eating them, there was no possibility of getting satiated. In order to protect the precious goods, to promote the welfare of their subjects, and to bring the kingdom to a perfect state of order, the ancient sovereigns gave the instruction, saying: by weighing in a balance, the result will be that articles, one of which is high and the other low, will not obtain the quality of being equal".

A note, given by Ma-twan-lin to elucidate the last sentence, where mention is made of the invention of the steelyards in order to measure the value of objects of different size, runs as follows:

若五穀與萬物平，則人無其利；故設上中下幣，而行輕重之術，使一高一下，乃可權制利門，悉歸於上。

"When the relation between the five species of grain and all living beings is proportional, people have no occasion to adopt those several sorts of money (high, middle and low); but by applying the expedient of weighing, one may obtain that one object is high and the other low. And by weighing the goods, one will get an advantageous issue which will wholly agree with the above-mentioned (expedient of making use of several different objects for money).

But those old forms of the medium of exchange soon proved to be very inconvenient, and the right principle, that money,

1) 萬物 the universe, all creation.

whose destination it is to roll about the world, should· be round of form, soon became a firm conviction with the Chinese; hence it is recorded that in the reign of the *Tseu*-dynasty (1022 B. C.) money was made, which was round of shape and had a square hole in its centre. This convenient form once adopted, is, as it were, petrified in Chinese society. If, at different times, weight and quality vary, with a few exceptions which shall be duly mentioned, the form has remained unaltered during nearly 30 centuries. In this case also the spirit of invention had reached its climax, and the Chinese rested satisfied faithfully to follow the example of their venerable ancestors without any important deviation from the beaten track.

The metal of which money was made, was in ancient times of three different kinds — gold, silver and copper; the last however, rather a species of bronze composed of copper, tin and lead. As the country itself was not rich in precious metals, gold and silver, as we shall see, were in use only in the earliest times, when currency was little needed; moreover, these metals were totally unfit for Chinese society on account of their high. valuation. Gold had ten times the value of silver, silver ten times the value of copper, and when we learn, according to a fragment from the "Statistical returns of articles of commerce and food" in the days of de *Han*-dynasty (about the birth of Christ), that one individual of the lower class of people did not even spend one cash a day to supply his wants 日 用 有 不 滿 一 錢, it is evident, that a currency of great intrinsic value was of little use in those simple times. Generally, the gold and silver coins were used as presents to princes, and as rewards to the highest officers of state for meritorious actions performed by them. *Sui*, a scholar in the reign of the *Sung*-dynasty gives us the following information on the subject: "If by the government great outlays were made, or great rewards were given, they usually consisted of metal, and especially of yellow metal. In the time that the *Han*-dynasty ruled over the empire, gold and silver were still used as currency, but after the reign of the Emperors *Siuen-ti* and *Yuen-ti* (B. C. 73 and 48) gold as money began to be exhausted. After the reign of the Later or Eastern *Han*-dynasty gold was very seldom used, and by the great spread of the religious doctrines of *Buddha* and *Lao-tsze*, gold was employed to adorn the images (of those sages) made out of wood and clay. And as it then ceased to be used as money, it was made into vessels and used as ornaments of dress", [Mat. IX 41*b*].

Occasionally we read in history of iron money, which circulated besides copper, but which did not answer on account of its want of portability, little intrinsic value and the general unfitness of the material to supply the place of money.

What idea did the Chinese attach to money? what were its functions and character? and how is it that in olden times money was not made at all or in very small quantities, while in later times metallic money could not be made in sufficiently large quantities? These questions are treated of by two scholars, who lived in the reign of the *Sung*-dynasty (about A. D. 1000 — 1100), and as their views of the matter are not unworthy of being brought under the notice of Western economists, I have translated those parts of the two essays, which refer to the money among the ancients [1]). Further on, when treating of paper-

---

1) I have, moreover, added the Chinese text to the translation, as the fragments contain many curious Chinese phrases and constructions interesting to sinologues.

money, we shall once more quote these authors, who, on this subject are still much more important, living as they did at a time in which China was visited by one of the greatest of calamities that can befall a people, viz. "an over-issued and depreciated paper-currency."

ESSAY BY LIU-TSU-KIEN [1]).

量 者 公 而 有 之 作 之 古.所 貨 之 東
資 天 諫 作 凶 周 幣 幣 如 由 之 設.萊
幣 災 景 布.荒 官 救 皆 管 生 物.乃 呂
權 流 王 又 則 司 民 綠 子 者.權 是 氏
輕 行.之 考 市 市 之 凶 論 考.財 阜 曰.
重.於 設.單 無 凡 饑 年.禹 之 貨 通 泉
作 是 古 穆 征 國 考 故 湯 於 之 財.布

Tung-lai of the family-name Lui[2]) says: "The institution of money, that is to say, the collecting together of some current precious object or merchandise (lit. article of trade) took its origin in the weighing of some precious article. If we inquire into its origin in ancient times, we learn from Kwan-tsze about the money of the emperors Yü and T'ang, that in bad years they made money in order to relieve the distress of the people suffering from famine. And if we inquire into it (the state of money) at the time that the market-justices instituted by the Tšeu-li[3]) (managed the affairs), we see that whenever the country was visited by famine and failure of the crop, taxes were not levied on the market, but that currency was fabricated, and if we consult the account of the remonstrances made by Mù, duke of Tan, against the measures introduced by the ruler King-wang of the Tšeu-dynasty, (it appears to us) that the ancients, as soon as calamities from heaven floated and spread (over the earth), measured the riches according to their weight and made of them a currency by which they saved their people.

---

1) Mat. IX 35a sqq.
2) Tung-lai was the pseudonym of Liu-tsu-kien (1137—1181 A. D.) according to

Mayers I n°. 466. one of the most renowned scholars of that time.
3) Tšeu Kwan is the ancient name for Tšeu-li.

賦所布者數積權已流農藏論幣
甚以不皆所鏺方先通桑者九以
少九過以至有有不衣數年之救
所貢權三多所先過食萬之積民
謂九輕穀亦施有權財千初。
俸賦重粟何。若謂一貨緒未古
祿。取為補是穀時之何嘗人
亦用之本盈無粟之本哉。所論
是錢於。虛本泉宜。。論財
頒幣民所之。布而錢所財貨
為謂財雖布謂。。但

If however the ancients make mention of treasures 1), they only mean the produce of the soil, and it had not yet occurred that several millions of cash strung together, hoarded up in treasuries, were taken in this sense. And what was the reason? Because to clothing and food, produced by husbandry and the cultivation of mulberry trees, they used to attach the idea of 'wealth, whereas the circulating money (lit. the currency, which was continually streaming and going on) did not surpass the quantity required to meet the necessity of it at a fixed period.

Formerly, there was what is called the equivalent of a currency consisting of grain and rice. As these (articles) were generally given (when anything was bought), how should it (then) have been possible to supply the necessity of measure and quantity (lit. the number of superfluity and want), in the case they had heaped on an excessive quantity of cash, whilst they were in want of the special basis (of exchange of that time). And as in the reign of the three dynasties and before this time 2), people, when speaking of wealth and taxes, always considered grain and rice as the basis, the properly so called money did not surpass a fixed quantity necessary to measure the weight (of things).

Because the taxes levied on the people were taxes in kind and tributes, the use made of money in paying them, was very scarce, and as to the bestowal of salaries and emoluments, this was managed in the same way. Fields were distributed among princes, noblemen and great

1) 九年之積 properly the store of nine years. — In three prosperous years of agriculture, the crop of one year was not needed for food by the people, but stored up for bad years that might come. Here such a store of 27 years' labor is taken in the sense of treasuries.

三代以前 UNDER and BEFORE the three dyn. cf. 以上 frequently found in the history of *Wang-mang*'s money. — Chapter II.

錢石職自者而時作錢爲祿地田
布亦之有甚已作幣之末）所爲爲制
爲是高古少所先權作以多寡君祿
重以下意到此儒輕益三寡亦卿
穀所謂王得以謂惟緣代亦未大
粟謂意公漢通金錢凶之未嘗夫
制萬石佐初有金凶年人嘗以不
祿石至吏有無銅年饑多以過
尚千石以天以無荒用錢以
未石以班下均凶所少錢布采
以百泉尚多年以地布爲

dignitaries (according to their ranks), and the only difference was in the size of the piece of land owned, and so it did not occur that money was considered as official pay. For the reason that the people under the three dynasties possessed a great deal of land, there were no idlers and as the use of money was scarce, the consequence was that money was of little importance. Only when bad years brought on famine and distress, money was made, and the reason of it was, according to the statement of ancient scholars, that gold and copper had no bad years. According to the want of the times they made it, that by means of it, (the commodities) which the one had and the other had not might circulate, and thus effect a due proportion between abundance and want, and nothing more [2]). These now are the reasons, why formerly under the three dynasties, currency is seldom made mention of.

As we come to the time that the *Han*-dynasty occupied the throne, the old custom still existed. In order to distinguish the rank and offices they held, from the king and his nobles down to the assistant officers, the terms tens of thousands, thousands and hundreds of *stones* (picul of rice) were made use of, and because in the same way all salaries were reckoned by grain and rice, the currency was not considered very important yet.

1) 末作 an idler, (lit. a *nothing-doer*) = 游手. The author means by it false-coiner. The student of Ma-twan-lin's text will see that at the next page, which we omit in our translation, the expression

末作 is found twice again, firstly in combination with 浮游, secondly with 游手. [Mat. IX 36b]

2) *Nothing more* lit. *and there stop*, is a frequently occuring expression denoting that the phrase is at an end.

### ESSAY BY ŠUI-SIN OF THE FAMILY YE [1]).

水心葉氏曰。錢之利害有數
說。古者因物權之以錢。後世
因錢。權之以物。錢。所起
起於商買。通行錢幣之變起
近之制。物不可以四方。故至
金錢行之。然不可以自行用以
至少。自桑漢三代之世。至錢
今日非錢不行。以後浸多。於
以錢極少者。當時三代民有常前
一家之用。自穀米布帛蔬菜業
魚肉皆因其力。以自致計其
待錢而具者無幾。止是商買
之貿遷與朝廷所以權天下

*Šui-sin* of the family-name *Ye* says: "On the advantage and disadvantage of money there are several theories. The ancients used goods (commodities) which they weighed in order to serve for money, and the subsequent ages used money, which was weighed in order to serve for goods (riches) [2]). The origin of money is to be found with the merchants who travelled all through the four quarters, as they went to trade in regions far off and near, and because goods could not be dealt in by means of themselves, they were dealt in by metallic money.

But in the period when the three dynasties ruled over the Empire, the use of money was very limited. Since the *T'sin* and *Han* swayed the scepter, it gradually increased, and at the present day no business is transacted without the use of money. As formerly under the three dynasties money was very scarce, every one of the people was continually engaged in supplying by manual labor whatsoever was needed for the support of his own family, grain and rice, silks, vegetables, fish and meat. The available (lit. waiting) money when gathered, was computed to amount to a very small quantity, only so much as was required by the merchants to pay for the products of the government which they bought.

---

1) I have not found his name in Mayers or elsewhere. From his writings it appears that he lived nearly at the same time as the foregoing *Tung-lai*.

2). The meaning is this: Anciently goods were used as money, now money is considered as goods (riches). The pun in the Chinese text makes a literal translation difficult. The term 物 is used in a double sense. Firstly, it stands for goods, merchandises. Secondly, for goods, riches.

之物。然後賴錢幣之用。如李悝平糴法，計民一歲用錢，只一千以上，是時已為多矣。蓋三代之時，尚不及此。土地所宜，與夫民之所自食，非穀粟則布帛。而民之所用，金錢亦無待於金錢，故用之亦少。所用之數，以歲計之，亦不然。後世輕重之制則不然。物物由錢起，故因錢制物之多少。百物皆由錢起，布帛則有丈尺之數，穀粟有斛斗之具。其他凡世間飲食資生之具，皆從錢起，銖兩多少貴賤輕重。

But when afterwards the service of money was more and more adopted, and *Li-huei* [1] laid down a general regulation as to the purchase of provisions for governmental use, it was considered that every individual needed 1000 pieces of money or a little more, a year. And this was rather much for that time, for under the three dynasties it did not amount to this figure. What was offered to the spirits of the earth [2]), and what was consumed by the mass of the people, if not grain and rice, then certainly it was silks, and because every one of the people made them for himself, there was altogether no room for metallic money, and as the people quietly attended to their business, there was no want of metallic money either, and therefore the use made of it was very limited, and the quantity which was then used, was, if reckoned over a whole year, still below the generally accepted estimate of that time.

But the regulation of its quantity in subsequent ages was quite different. A hundred (different) things originated in money, in consequence of which all goods were measured by means of money. When (formerly) it was pieces of silk, they were measured by *tsangs* (10 feet) and *tsik* (feet), and when grain and rice, the measurement was ascertained by *hu* and *meu*. All other provisions that arose, and were hoarded up in subsequent ages, are, since money gradually got more important, meas-

---

1) *Liu-huei* was a minister of prince *Wen* of *Wei*. Mayers I n°. 345 does not state any particulars about him.

2) 宜 are sacrifices brought to the spirits of the earth. See *Su-king* V. 1. 1. 10. Legge p. 487.

皆由錢而制。上自朝廷之運用。
下自民間之輸貢。州縣委藏之商買用。
貿易。皆主於錢。故不得用錢。
倍不於前。而三代不得少。後百
世不得前。而三代各以斷其後
國以自治。一國之物。自足以供
一國之用。亦非是天下自可
關之物。亦不至貿心下通之。
上又明立禁戒不要力使天下心窮
力遠須故書曰。惟土物愛厥心
藏老子曰。致治之極。民甘其食
美其服。樂其俗。隣國相望雞犬
之聲相聞。民至老死不相往來。

ured by money as to weight, quantity, price and value. From the most important (articles) transported in behalf of the government, down to the smallest tribute paid by the people as taxes, what is gathered in provinces and districts, and what by travelling merchants is transacted, all this is governed by money; and that is the reason why later generations use 100 times 100 the money, which the earlier (generations) employed. But how is it that the three dynasties had not too little, and the later generations not too much money. The three dynasties had all isolated their kingdom (from all other countries), that they might manage their own affairs; and what was produced by one country, was also sufficient to supply the wants of that same country. And (those productions) did not circulate through the whole kingdom, nor was it allowed to export the goods, and so it had not come to that pass, that people were obliged to spend the strength of their minds to get a living. The ruler, moreover, in a judicious way, instituted inhibitions, and it was not yet necessary, that the exhausted forces of the empire where required in the remote regions[1]. Hence the book of Records says "When they love only the productions of the ground, their hearts will be good", and *Lao-tsze* says: "The highest state of perfection of good government is reached, when the people think their food sweet, and their clothes beautiful, when they rejoice in their uneducated simplicity; when the inhabitants of neighboring states, who are so near each other, that

1) As it was when the author wrote this treatise, and China was in constant war with the barbarous tribes on the North and West frontiers, and a great deal of North China was already invaded by Tartar princes.

小厚薄。皆隨時變易。
多。制度不一輕重大
錢之所由多用。錢既
後世錢多。此數者皆
金錢安得不多。所以
北互則又多於前世。
四方。安商買往來南
之民。嘗指不交通於
之患。無桑如一。天下
名。而國。雖越有州知異
爲一少。後世天下異既
得不錢如此。安
其無所用錢如此。安

they can see one another, and hear the crying and barking of their fowls and dogs, have grown old and die without having had mutual intercourse." In such a condition there is no need for money, and it is easy to obtain, that there be no want of it. (lit. that it was not scarce).

Afterwards when the empire was united into one kingdom, though the different names of provinces and districts were still existing, and the great assault of the T·sin(-dynasty) had not yet happened, and the people did not feel sorry that they did not know each other, and that arm and finger (i. e. high and low) were equal, it was still possible for the people not to' trade, and not to penetrate into the four quarters. In those early times, however, tradesmen were continually coming and going, and kept up a constant intercourse between South and North, and thus it was easily obtained, that metallic money was not plenty (for it was not generally needed).

The reason why the quantity of money was afterwards so large, was because it was so generally made use of, and as there was such a large quantity of money, calculation and measure were not always the same, so that in the course of time, weight, size and thickness were continually altered.

### THE TŠEU-DYNASTY.

In the year 1122 B. C. the Šang or Yin-dynasty, the second of the so frequently spoken of three dynasties, was overthrown, having ruled over the empire more than 600 years; the last tyrant being dethroned by the duke of Tšeu, eldest son of the Chief of the West, who mounted the Imperial throne under the title of *Wu-wang*. His younger brother *Tan*, who in history is generally known under the title of 周公 *Tseu-kung*, or duke of *Tseu*, composed a work, in which he lays down the rules, according to which the new dynasty was to govern the empire. This work is still extant, and its precepts continue to be looked upon as a guide to the government of the State.

Having given some information on the different sorts of medium of exchange, current in the beginning of the reign of this new dynasty, Ma-twan-lin quotes two fragments from the book on the state laws and regulations of the *Tseu*-dynasty, which refer to the administration of the state finances, and which undoubtedly are the oldest historical records, which so minutely bear witness to the high degree of development attained by the administrative government of those times.

I will first give the historical facts in their original form, and proceed with the most important parts of the quotations from the *Tseu-li*.

以 方。而 賈 周
斤 輕 重 易 制
爲 重 一 物。以
名。以 斤。黃 商
　 銖。錢 金 通
　 黃 圜 方 貨
　 金 函 寸 以

In behalf of the merchants, the *Tseu* made a current merchandise in order to serve as a price in the exchange of goods. The gold was of the size of one square *Tsün* and weighed a *Kin*, the copper coins were round and had a square hole in the centre, the weight was ascertained by *Tsus*. The gold currency (took its name from the weight and) was called *Kin* (pound).

Silks of a certain length and breadth, called a *p'i* 疋, were also a unit of value, but as copper-*cash* was by far more convenient, being easilier spread than cloth, better strung together than silks, and more profitable than the gold coins, it soon was preferred and generally used.

布．征　則　荒　市　周¹⁾
而　市　札　國　官
作　無　喪．凶　司

The justices of the market, instituted by the book of rites of the *Tšeu*-dynasty ¹) made money in bad years when the people were visited by a failure of crop, epidemics, or a great mortality; and taxes were not levied on the market.

According to the translation of *Tšeu-li* by M. E. Biot (I 315 n°. 3), a great deal of money was cast in bad years in order to enrich to people. — A slight economical error for that time, to be sure.

By the rites of the *Tšeu*, there were instituted nine different boards of administration for the revenues and expenses of the crown and the State 九府圜法. We omit the special denominations of each of them, they are to be found in *Tšeu-li* and *Ma-twan-lin*, but we will look more closely at the regulation of the budget and the general expenses of government, which will show us, that already in those remote ages, people were guided by principles which we find back in our modern politics.

之　之　旅．喪　凡　之　王　之　者．之　百　之　外
財．幣．共　紀　祭　衣　及　公　有　用．物．入　府
凡　齎³⁾其　會　祀　服　后　用　法　凡　而　出．掌
邦　賜　財　同　賓　之　世　也．百　有　待　以　邦
之　予　用　軍　客　用．子　共　官　法　邦　共²⁾布

The *Wai-fu* or administrator of the Exterior magazine, manages the revenues and expenses of the state finances, in order to provide for a hundred different things, and he is prepared for (lit. awaits) all the necessary outlays of the country, which are regulated by law. (The expenses of all the public functionaries are fixed by law). He supplies the necessary outlays for the *liste civile* (dress and wardrobe) of the king, the queen and the hereditary prince, and the general expenses of sacrifices, entertainments of princes and their nobles, coming as guests to the court, mourning arrangements, court receptions and assemblies of the troops; and further for

---

1) The *Tšeu-li.* 周禮 was formerly called *Tšeu-kwan* 周官, and is here called by that old name.

2) 共 is here continually used for 供.

3) 齎行道之財用也.

小用皆受焉。歲終則會。惟王及后之服不會。〇泉府掌以市之征布。飲[1]市之不售。貨之滯於民用者。以其賈買之。物揭而書者。以待不時[2]而買者。凡賒者。祭祀無過旬日。喪紀無過三月。凡民之貸者。與其有司辯。而援之以國服為之息。凡國事之財用取具焉。歲終則會其出入而納其餘。

travelling expenses, and the precious articles given away as presents.

In general he receives all the money used for small expenses in behalf of the state, and at the end of the year he makes his balance, only the expenses of the king's and the queen's wardrobe are not included in it.

The *ts'uen-fu* (which according to the *Tšeu-li* is the collector of taxes) manages the money which is paid as taxes on the market. He collects the goods which are not sold in the market, which are preserved for the use of the people. He publishes and puts down the commodities which he has bought, according to their market-price, and waits for the buyers who may at any time wish to buy them.

Whenever they want the goods for sacrifices, the buyers on credit may, as a rule, not delay their payment beyond ten days, (and if the purchased wares are destined) for mourning, they may not delay to settle their accounts beyond three months.

He consults the justices of the market about those persons who borrow money from him, and reckons the interest according to the wants of the State. He uses to receive and gather all the treasures in behalf of the state-service. At the end of the year he makes the balance of revenues and expenses, and delivers the surplus (to the 職幣 according to the *Tšeu-li*).

Now follows one of the few treatises of Ma-twan-lin himself, in which he expresses his opinion on the financial system of the *Tšeu*-dynasty. — We have abbreviated the piece a little, and given only that part which contains the author's own peculiar notions on the nature of money. It runs as follows:

---

[1] 飲 is here used for 斂. | [2] 不時 = always, incessantly.

古人創泉布之本意。實取其流
通。緣貨則或滯於民。用而錢則
無所不通。則泉府而一官。最為便
民。滯則買之。泉時而欲買者。多先
賣之。無力者則賒貸與之。盖多
王視民如子。則洞察其隱微。而初
方濟其缺乏。仁政設也。尚於不原此。
非專為謀利。取勤¹)其一語。以斷其
立官之本意。而買之於方滯之
天下大事。可乎。而買之際。此與
時。賣之於欲買之際。此與常平
賤糴貴糴之意同。泉府則以錢
易貨。常平則以錢易粟。其本意

When the princes of antiquity first formed the fundamental idea of currency, they really had directed their attention to its continual streaming and circulating. If that currency consisted of merchandise, some princes hoarded it up for the use of the people, but whenever it was really m o n e y, there was not a single piece which did not circulate.

The one official who collected the taxes, the *Ts'uen-fu*, was very convenient to the people. Whenever the market was heavy with provisions he bought them, and when there were people who at all times came and were desirous of buying, he sold them. And if they were in want of ready money, he sold the goods on credit, or (first) he lent them the money they wanted, and (afterwards) gave them the goods. In this way the ancient sovereigns considered the people as their children. They instituted a thorough inquiry into the distress of the people, which was concealed from their eyes, and everywhere they relieved distress and want, and what regards their benevolent government, there was indeed nothing superior to that. Originally it was not with an intention to take profit that they determined to take interest, and is it right not to inquire into the fundamental idea of the institution of that official, but always to harp upon ¹) that same saying, that it was in order to curtail the great public service of the kingdom? He bought the provisions at a time that they were plentiful everywhere, and he sold them at the time when the demand for them was great. Now, this was united with the intention to buy generally cheap and to sell dear (when prices had risen.)

---

1) 勤 = 譏 to repeat, to assume the language of another, used in a contemptible sense. In Dutch nabauwen.

皆以利民。非謀利也。然後世常平之法，轉而為所糶，且以其濟儲，宅用不其民，則惟恐利數之不多，是之不羡，於之亦之理財法。視之矣。

The collector of taxes used his money to exchange it for goods and generally for rice, and the original intention was altogether to benefit the people, and not to increase their own profit. But ensuing generations have subverted the good customs of antiquity; with united strength they effected the purchase of grains, but what they accumulated, they used for quite another purpose, and not in. behalf of the people. Then, they only feared that the number (of consumers) should not be great, and that their profits should not be excessive, and therefore they considered it (those purchases of grain with united strength) also as a reasonable way to manage the finances [1].

Now, the necessity that money should have the property of divisibility, begins to be felt, as appears from the next fragment in which Ma-twan-lin again pursues the thread of his history.

周景王二十一年，患錢輕，更鑄大錢，徑一寸二分，重十二銖，文曰大泉五十，肉好皆有周郭，以贍農不足。

*King-wang* of the *T'seu*-dynasty fearing that the money was too light, made in the 21th year of his reign (523 B.C.) great copper coins of a diameter of 1.2 *tsün* and of a weight of 12 *tšu*. The design was *Ta-ts'uen* or great currency 50 ($^{50}/_{100} = {}^{12}/_{24}$) [2]. The body of the coin and the hole were all round furnished with a raised edge (in order to prevent the filing off of copper dust) [3]. But to meet the requirements of husbandry, they did not answer the purpose.

---

1) The last sentence is antethical to the preceding "the ancient sovereigns considered the people as their children."

2) An ounce was 24 *Tšu*. Thus, 12 *Tšu* represent 50% of an ounce. As according to Amiot 1 *Tsün* = 0.0205 m. the diameter was on an average 0.0246. According to another statement nine of these pieces had a length of the foot of *Hoang-ti* = ± 0.25 m. in which case the diam. of one piece must have been 0.0275. It is utterly impossible to ascertain the exact size of ancient Chinese measures, because it was frequently altered, while the names remained the same.

3) A difficult passage — 肉 is the flesh or substantial part of the coin, Jap. ミミ *Mimi*, 好 is the square hole in the centre, Jap. アナ *Ana* = 孔, 郭 is pro-

王將鑄大錢。單穆公曰。不可。古
者天災降戾。於是乎量資幣權
輕重以賑救民。民患輕。則為作
重幣以行之。[幣2) 輕物貴也。於是
乎有母。則以權子而行。而行。若
不堪重。則母權以行。母而行。不
廢重。於是多作輕而行民皆得
小利之。今王廢輕而作重民大
其貲能無匱乎。若匱而王用失
所乏乏則將厚取為民民不給
將有遠志。是離民也。且夫有備
未至而設之。有至而後救之。是
不相入也。可先而不備。謂之急。

As the king was about to cast (those) "large coins", (his Minister) *Mu-kung*[1]) of *Tan* said: "You ought not to do this. Anciently they always tried to ward off the calamities of heaven, and therefore they measured their precious objects by weighing them in light and heavy ones, in order to relieve the people. And whenever the people feared that the money was too light, they made a heavier currency, and brought it in circulation. (For, says a note, when the coins are light the wares bought with them are dear). And thus they had the mother (i. e. the large coin as unit of value) and the child (the little coin) was weighed in circulation, so that the people got them both. If (on the contrary) the heavy money was unfit, they made light money in great quantities, and brought it in circulation; they did not, therefore, abolish the heavy coins, and thus they had the child (as a unit) and the mother weighed against it in circulation. So the big and the little money were a benefit to the people.

But now that the sovereign abolishes the light and institutes the heavy coins, the people lose their wealth in consequence of it; and can this be without their becoming exhausted? and if the people are exhausted and the sovereign wants them, he will have a people in sorrow and want,

---

perly a wall to defend a city, here the raised edge. In a Japanese book on Chinese coins, the following passage occurs —

新ニラス 錢ヲ鑄ル肉ニ好チニ 周ヲ郭チシテ。 Anew he cast coins, the outer edge and inner hole of which are furnished with a surrounding raised rim. Cf. 古今泉貨鑑 vol. I. p. 13a.

1) *Mu-kung*, is a name which frequently occurs under the *Tseu*-dynasty.

2) Occasionally, I have inserted in the Chinese text a note of Ma-twan-lin's in parenthesis [].

弗　日　竭　汗　而　塞　王　用　且　之　先　可
聽。　矣。　也。　也。　爲　川　府　以　絶　召　之　後
王　　無　其　漬　原　猶　寶　民　灾。　謂　而

and this being so, he will have to levy heavy taxes in behalf of the
people, and they, not being able to pay them, will have far-reaching
thoughts (will estrange their hearts from their sovereign), and the end
will be that the people leave the country.

But, moreover, to have taken measures for what is not necessary,
while they are still to be taken for what is impending; and then afterwards
to be obliged to repair the evil (caused by this injudicious way of proceeding), will never do (lit. cannot enter together.) To be able to take
measures beforehand and not to do so, is what I call to draw misery
on ourselves; and to arrange beforehand what we are able to do afterwards, that is what I call to summon up calamities.

Besides, you cut off the custom of the people to fill the treasury of
their king, and that is as if you were stopping up rivulets and sources
to make a dirty pool. The drying up of it will be the result in no
time. The king however did not listen.

----

# CHAPTER II.

Other papers referring to money matters under the *Tšeu*-dy-
nasty do not exist. In his next historical record Ma-twan-lin
passes a great many years when he brings us to the feudal
state of *Ts'in*, at the time that the last of the *Tšeu*-emperors is
about to be dethroned by his too mighty and independant vassal.

楚莊王以爲幣重，更以小爲大，百姓不便，皆去其業。孫叔敖爲相，市令言於相曰：市亂，人莫安其處，次行不定。……王定……故遂令復如故，而百姓乃安。

"*Tsu tsoang-wang* [1]) in order to make the money heavy, made the little coins equal in value to the great ones, but as this was not suitable to the people, they all left their business. *Sün-siok ngao* [2]) was (then) prime-minister. The market-master, speaking to the prime-minister, said: "The market is thrown into confusion, none of the people is quiet in its dwelling place, and trade is unstable". The prime-minister *Siok Ngao* reported it to the king, who gave order to return to the old state (of things), and the people were thereupon tranquillized."

In the year 221 B. C. the *Tseus* were at last dethroned by prince *Tsing*, pretended son and heir to *Tsoang-siang-wang* [1]), who now under the name of *Si-hoang-ti* (the first illustrious ruler [3]) 始皇帝 put an end to the division of China into many feudal states, and united the whole empire under his sway. Now, when the *Ts'ins* had united the empire, there were two different sorts of currency. The gold coin called *Yi* was the first sort and had a weight and value, as a note observes, of 20 ounces or taels.

（二十兩爲鎰以鎰爲金之名數也）[4]).

銅錢質如周錢，文曰半兩，重如其文。而珠玉龜貝銀錫之屬爲器飾寶藏[5]，不爲幣。

The copper coins were in substance equal to those of the *Tseu* dynasty; the design was "half an ounce" and their weight was according to that design. But pearls, gems, tortoise shells, silver, tin and what further is connected with these, were used as

1) 楚莊王 = 莊襄王 who 250 B. C. ascended the Throne of China. Mayers I. 228.

2) Mayers I. 129.   3) Mayers I. 597.

4) In Mencius' time (B. C. 372—289) the *Yi* also was a current unit of value, as appears from two passages of his works. See Mencius B. I. 2th part,

IX. 2. "There you have a gem which may be worth 10.000 *Yi*." And B. II. 2th part, III. I., where mention is made of presents of so and so many *Yi* offered to Mencius by several princes. The Rev. Dr. Legge reckons it at a value of 24 taels, but from Ma-twan-lin we learn it was only 20.

5) 臧 is here used for 藏.

implements, toys, and precious articles, hoarded up in treasuries, but they were no (more) money.

## THE HAN-DYNASTY.

The descendants of the first illustrious ruler who tried to secure the succession of his line during "a ten-thousand ages" by an atrocious and tyrannical policy, did not long enjoy the possession of "all territory under heaven." His son and grandson were murdered by intriguing eunuchs, and 14 years after the accession to the Throne, the *Ts'in* dynasty was extirpated, and "a soldat de fortune," *Liu-pang* 劉邦 1) who made himself renowned in the revolution and struggle against the existing power, took his place and founded the great *Han*-dynasty which, during four centuries, was Master of the Empire. (204 B. C. — 190 A. D.)

匹 萬 躍。市 之³⁾ 不 周 金 鑄 用。秦 漢
百 鑄。米 物 民。軌 之 一 莢 夾 錢 興
金。馬 至 痛 以 逐 制。斤。錢²。令 重 以
　 至 石 騰 稽⁴⁾ 利 而 復 黄 民 難 爲

As they judged the money of the *Ts'in* too heavy and inconvenient to be used,. the *Hans*, in the first time of their rise, made the people cast, the *leave-coins*, so called, because they were as thin as elm- leaves 2), the gold coins were again of the size of a pound as under the *Tšeu*. But those little copper coins were irregular (not of a size) and threw away all the benefit of the people. By the gathering and storing up of commodities, prices enhanced enormously. The price of rice increased to 10,000 *cash* a stone (picul) and a horse was sold for 100 gold-pieces.

1) Mayers I. 414.

2) 如 榆 莢 也·

3) 之 = 其 Cf. Julien. Syntaxe Nouvelle I. p. 159. The construction is: 利 v. trans. to benefit, and 之 民 its object. I have found a similar construction, Mat.

VIII. 7a. 逐 爭 其 民 in the speech of the minister *Kia-I*. Cf. p. 35 note 2. N. B. here 其 is used instead of 之 Julien, *in loco* gives a similar instance.

4) 稽 貯 滿 也·

Accordingly, queen *Kao-heu* (185 B. C.) brought again in circulation pieces of 8 *Tšu* equal in value to the half-ounce coins
of the preceding dynasty, but at the same time the profusion of
elm-leaves remained in circulation, because it was impossible to
draw them back.

Our chronicle is now fast approaching to the reign of the Emperor Wenti who during 22 years occupied the imperial seat,
and is considered as a pattern of humanity, a prince, who in
all he did, considered the weal of his people.

In the 5th year of his reign, Wenti caused again coins to be
cast of 4 *Tšu*, the design was "half an ounce."

放　錢.除
鑄　使　盜 　　With an intention to root out false coining,
民　鑄 　　he let the people free to cast their own money.

But this measure did not at all please his privy councilor and
minister *Kia-I* who expected from it nothing but calamities to the
government and the people; and his plea against free-coining which
was delivered to the emperor, has always been considered as a
masterpiece of sound reasoning. And whenever in later times the
question arises anew whether it be better that money is made by the
government or by the individual subjects, the opinion of *Kia-I* [1]),
is always brought forward as an irreversible proof that only the government is able to provide for good and valuable currency. And
indeed, it is a remarkable piece, not only for its economical
worth, but also as a specimen of Chinese eloquence, though we
may find it somewhat too lengthy. As it contains also some interesting and curious Chinese expressions and constructions, I will give
the fragment as I have found it in Ma-twan-lin. It runs as follows:

---

1) On *Kia-I*, see Mayers N°. 245, where | the institutions of the state, and that some
is said that he introduced many reforms in | of his writings still exist.

夫縣法以誘民。使入陷穽。
之所疑榜笞奔走者甚泉。
抵罪多者。一縣百數。及吏
罪日報。其勢不止。乃者民
因欲禁其厚利微姦。雖黥
造幣之勢。各隱屏而鑄作。
法有起姦。今令細民人操
爲利甚厚。夫事有召禍微。
則不可得贏。而殽之甚巧。
然鑄錢之情。非殽雜爲巧。
以鉛鐵爲它巧者其罪黥。
得顧租¹⁾鑄銅錫爲錢。敢雜
○買誼諫曰。法使天下公

Kia-I remonstrancing (against the proposed measure) said: ·The law causes that it is granted to everyone in the empire to melt and cast copper and tin together in order to make money, but whosoever dares make false (coins) by alloying this mixture with lead and iron, shall have his crime branded in his face. But what concerns the circumstances of casting money, we know that he who does not mix it, and does not make false coins, will not be able to get any profit out of it, whereas he, who mixes it only in a slight degree, will get a large profit. By this fact, therefore, evil is summoned up, and this law will be the cause of crimes and debauchery. Since it is your command that the common people shall entirely have the power of making money in their own hands, everyone will secretly cast and make it. And though the punishments to be branded will be the daily penalty of this crime, in consequence of the desire (of the government) to check the making of large profit and the adulteration of the coin in a slight degree, the influence produced (by these punishments) will not be great enough to put down this evil. At this time the number of those who atone for that crime, will be large, — several hundreds in every district — and besides, the number of those who, suspected by the public functionaries, run away for fear of the bastinado, will be also very great. This law of the country leads the people astray, and will be the cause of their falling into a snare.

1) 得顧租 lit. to hire and to rent, is here with the signification to be enga- ged in. Or, as Ma-twan-lin observes in a note 顧租謂雇傭.

孰積於此。疊禁鑄錢死罪
積下[1]。今公鑄錢縣罪積下
為法若此。上何賴焉。又積下
用錢若此。郡縣不同。或用重錢輕
百加若干。不用吏急錢平壹
不受法。則大為煩苛。則市力肆
之乎[2]。則大為煩苛則
能勝。縱而弗呵苛則
異用錢文大亂乎。苟非其術
何鄉而可哉。今農事棄捐術
而采銅者曰蓄釋其未耜
冶鎔吹炭姦錢曰多五穀
不為多善人怵而姦邪愿

And what will more accumulate the number of crimes than this regulation? In former times, when the casting of money was prohibited, the guilty of death among the lower classes of the people were more frequent. But now that every one may cast money, the number of those condemned to be branded will greatly increase among the lower classes. But what advantage does the government derive from a measure like this? For the (different sorts) of money which will be used by the people in (different) provinces and districts, will not be of the same value. Some people will make use of light coins, (and if so) how much must they add to a hundred pieces[3] (in order to pay other people who are measuring the value of a thing by heavy coins)? Other people (on the contrary) use heavy coins, and an adequate weight (quantity) of goods will not be obtained by them. Which of the different sorts of money (at the moment circulating), is legal tender is not evident[4].

If the public functionaries are zealous and honest, they are greatly troublesome and vexatious, and yet their exertions will not be able to conquer the evil; if on the contrary, they are indulgent and not ardent in the pursuit, the people at market will make difference in the use of coins, and the different designs of the coins will cause great confusion. And if they too (the functionaries) are false in their dealings, pray, to what pass

1) Mat. explains this sentence by 言死 罪多委積於下.

2) 乎 is here more exclamative than interrogatory.

3) The meaning of the last sentence, rather difficult to understand, owing to its peculiar construction, is elucidated by the following note of Ma-twan-lin's: "If a coin has the weight of 4 *Tsu*, 100 pieces of that legal money will weigh 1 pound 16 *Tsu*, and now is the question when the money in which the sum due is paid, is less in weight, how many pieces are to be added to a hundred in order to make the payment equivalent and complete." i. e. how many per cent is the difference?

4) Different sorts of coins of foregoing dynasties, e. g. the elm-leave-coins, the half ounce, 5 *Tsu* and 3 *Tsu* pieces were all still in circulation.

勿　致　今　布　數　禁　起。則　令　之　知　甚　民
令　也。博　瀆。矣。棄　其　禁　之　此。不　陷
布。何　禍　於　銅　市　利　不　不　鑄　詳　而
則　謂　可　天　姦　之　深。得　其　奈　之¹)
民　七　除　下。數　罪²。盜　錢。其　議　何　刑
不　福。而　使　不　盜　又　則　術。必　而　戮
鑄　上　七　其　勝　鑄　鑄　錢　其　日　忽　刑
錢　收　福　然　也。不　如　必　禁　國。戮
黥　銅　可　博　也。故　法　足　雲　重。必　之。如　將

may we not be brought. At present husbandry runs the risk of decaying, and the number of people who seek to obtain copper, daily increases. They leave their ploughshares, they melt and cast, and blow the charcoal. The bad coins are daily made in larger quantities, while the five species of grain are not made to increase. The virtuous are led astray, whereas the wicked are respected; the people are falling into a snare, and the number of executions will be enormous and without judicial inquiry. What expedient will put an end to such a desolate state in the empire. If the functionaries who now advice you, knew that, they surely would say: Forbid it, forbid it, that these evil practices may cease, for the wounds inflicted by it are sore indeed! If your Majesty commands that henceforth the coining of money shall not be free, the money, no doubt, will become heavy again, and the advantages accruing therefrom will be important. But even the penalty of being outlawed by all the market-folks²), will not be strong enough to check the false coiners, who have sprung up like clouds. The number of false coiners will not be conquered for, while the law prohibits their number to be large (lit. overflowing), the copper (which every one may easily obtain) is the cause that it will be so (i. e. that false coiners are still to be found³).) It would, therefore, be a great calamity, if copper was made to circulate all over the kingdom. That great calamity, however, may be warded off, and seven blessings will be the consequence of it.

1) In 之刑。之 = 其.

2) 棄市之罪 is the penalty of proscription by the votes of the people, according to the Tsu-li 秋官 fol. 6b. 記所謂刑人于市與眾棄之也. It is what the historical records call the punishment inflicted on a person at market, when he is driven out by the multitude. Traduction du Tscu-li de M. E. Biot. Tome II. p. 322. § 26. „Il écoute la voix du peuple demandant l'exécution ou la grace."

3) The meaning is that the circulation of copper will be the reason that the law is of no avail.

罪不積一矣
偽錢不蕃民不相疑二
矣采銅鑄作者反
於耕田三矣銅畢
歸於上上挾銅積
以御輕重錢輕則以
以術之之重則以
術散之貨物必平
四矣以作兵器以
假²⁾貴臣多少有制
用別貴賤矣矣以
臨萵貨以調盈虛
以收奇羨則官富

Which are then those seven blessings? If your Majesty draws back the copper, and prohibits its circulation, the people no more will cast money, and the sentences to be branded will not increase — this firstly — ¹). The bad money not increasing in quantity, the people will no more suspect one another — this secondly. — Those, who at present try to get copper to melt and cast money, will again turn back to their ploughs and fields — this thirdly. — The copper will at last come to the crown again, the collected copper is then stored up in order to regulate the circulation of money (lit. to regulate light and heavy). Now, if the money is too light, (i. e. that it is so abundant, that weighed against goods it has little value, or as there is more currency than is wanted) the government has recourse to the expedient of collecting it. Is it (on the contrary) too heavy (i. e. is the currency circulating too scarce in proportion to what is required, and therefore heavy when weighed against goods) it has recourse to the expedient of diffusing it, and a stability in the prices of merchandise will be the result. — This fourthly. — By making implements of war (of this superfluous copper), (provided) the prince have excellent and honest ministers, the quantity of copper in store will have certain limits, if one uses to consider the rate of its market price ³) — this fifthly. — In consequence of the reduc-

1) Here also the choice of 矣 as final particle is important. These blessings are no certain facts, but mere suppositions of the minister *Kia-I*.

2) 假 is used for 嘉, See Williams.

3) The meaning of this rather obscure sentence is, that the State may get some profit, when honest ministers will observe the course of the metal, and draw back the superfluous copper, when the copper currency is too abundant, and make of it implements of war, which are always highly valued. At the same time the effect of this will be that the government store of copper will have certain limits. Sinologues will be aware how exceedingly difficult it is to render into plain English those brief Chinese phrases, which by a literal translation would be altogether unintelligible. For instance, the single words 輕 and 重 meaning light and heavy, want the explication, which in the translation I have put in parenthesis, otherwise the meaning would not be understood — 貴賤 dear and cheap, are to be taken as a compound, signifying, rate, course or market-price, just as the compound 多少 means quantity.

資而末民困
六矣制吾棄¹⁾
財以與匈奴
逐爭其民²⁾則
敵必懷七矣
故善天下
者因禍爲爲
福轉敗而爲
功今久退七
福而行博禍
臣誠行博
不從傷之上

tion of the prices of all articles of commerce (as soon as the money has a fixed legal value), when the periods of abundance and scarcity are in due proportion, and the government will be rich and well-fed, in consequence of the obtaining of surplus and profits, the people will no more be exposed to want, — this sixthly — And if we destine our hoarded treasure, to be given to the *Hiung nu* (the *Huns*), we shall put an end to the quarrels with that people, and our enemies will be brought to peace, — this seventhly. — Therefore he who governs the empire in such a way as to turn the existing evils into so many blessings, will do a meritorious work. Since many years the seven blessings have been opposed, and the evils have generally been predominant. Your ministers honesty is injured by it. His Majesty however did not follow the advice.

Besides, another peril was impending, as Ma-twan-lin tells us, in his next fragment. In the neighboring feudal States of *Wu* and *Tang*, the vassals were rather independent and made their own money, which caused uneasiness for two reasons. 1°. "That this currency, being of a better quality, might easily get an extensive circulation in the empire." 2°. "The wealth of those vassals was rapidly increasing by it, and as soon as it equaled that of his Majesty, it was evident that they would rise in rebellion. The emperor was, therefore, not quite at his ease, as to the result of his free-coining system, and again asked the advice of another minister of the crown, called *Kia-Šan*, who very practically decides the question as follows.

---

1) 棄 lit. pushed aside (as not needed). | 2) As to the construction, compare page 29 note 3.

賈山上書諫，以為錢者無用器也，而可以易富貴。富貴者，人主之操柄也。令民為之，是與人主共操柄也，不可長也。其後復禁鑄錢。

*Kia-šan*, the superintendent of the issue of State papers [1]), pleading against (the adopted measure) said: He, who considers the currency as an implement of no avail (as a prerogative of the crown), may occasion the change of riches; now riches are the handle, which is held by the rulers of men. If you let the people free to make (the money), it is much the same, as if they share the holding of that handle with the princes. That cannot last a long time. — Thereupon the emperor again forbade the people to cast money.

*Wen-ti*'s successor, the emperor *King-ti*, is said to have made money of false yellow metal, and by doing so, he infringed the laws of the market. But the people then made use of the money introduced by the feudal prince of *Tang* 鄧, and false coiners appeared, who beyond all limits practised their profession. Only a great many sentences were able to put a stop to their unlawful proceedings.

A more interesting part in the economical history of China is the reign of the next Emperor *Wu-ti*, who during 54 years occupied the throne. His was a glorious reign. He was victorious in his wars in the North-West against the formidable Huns; the whole South Western part of China, — the modern province of Yün-nan — was brought under the scepter of the Son of Heaven, and his generals carried the Chinese arms into the heart of Asia. Literature flourished, and an imperial University was established,

---

1) 土書 *Sang-šu* is probably the same as the frequently occurring 尚書 *Sang-šu*, which was a title of the prime ministers under the *Han*-dynasty; (Morr. *in voce* 官 25—26). The compound in 上 is found only three or four times in Ma-twan-lin's records. Under *Han-wu-ti*, *Wen-ti*'s successor, 中書 is found as a title of a president of a central board of administration.

to disseminate the study of classical history and wisdom. The emperor himself made many a splendid progress with his gorgeous court, and gave magnificent feasts. The consequence of all those blessings was, that an enormous quantity of money was wanted, and as the base and worthless copper-*cash*, was not at all sufficient to pay for these sumptuous outlays, several sorts of representative currency were introduced.

This expedient had the same fatal result in China, as in so many other countries were it was afterwards employed. In the beginning, it seemed to be the cause of an inexhaustible source of wealth, but when the splendid times and the delusions had passed away, the State was almost on the verge of financial ruin.

*Wu-ti*, in the first year of his reign (140 B. C.) brought in circulation coins of a real value, bearing the design of three *tšu*, but five years later these coins were suppressed again, because they were counterfeited and clipped, and pieces of 5 *tšu*, the standard-money of the *Han*-dynasty, were introduced again.

Counterfeiting made the money abundant in quantity but of little value, whereas goods were not so superfluous and rather high in price (錢益多而輕物益少而貴); and in the distant parts of the empire, pieces of cloth were again used as a medium of exchange. Now the public officers proposed to abolish the existing pieces, which had a nominal value of half an ounce[1]), but which really contained only 4 *tšu*, and to make again pieces of a weight of 5 *tšu*, furnished all around with a raised edge of the same substance (metal) in order to prevent the coins from being filed out, with a view of taking the copper dust. (鑄五銖。周郭其質令不得磨錢取鋊).

1) Half an ounce is 12 *Tšu*.

元。年。金。幣。
狩。造。及
四。白。皮

In the fourth year of the period *Yuen-šeu* (119 B. C.) a currency of white metal and deer-skin was made.

Ma-twan-lin quotes two pieces having reference to the introduction of that earliest of token-money, and as they contain remarkable particulars of the origin, value, and use of the deerskin currency, I will give the whole text and its literal translation without any further comment. Only I wish to observe beforehand, that these skin-tallies were purely to k e n s, and have had nothing in common with the leather-money, which was, during a long time, current in Russia. This Russian skin-money had a truly representative character, as the parcels were used instead of the skins from which they were cut; the skins themselves being too bulky and heavy to be constantly carried backward and forward, only a little piece was cut off, to figure as a token of possession of the whole skin. The ownership of the skin was proved when the piece fitted in the hole.

Ma-twan-lin tells us: [VIII 8*a*].

大 商 財 穀 鑄²) 或 而 家 民 是 公 造
空。買 役 數 鬻 累 不 之 重 天 卿 錢
時 而 貧。百。鹽。萬 佐 急。困 子 議。幣
縣 轉 滯 富 冶 財 金 公 黎 於 與 更 以
官¹)

At that time the emperor's treasury was very empty, and among the rich merchants there were some who accumulated their wealth (riches) to succor the poor, they forwarded several hundreds of measures of grain, and converted (their riches) into food²); there were others who (for their own profit) heaped up tens of thousands (pieces) of money, and who did not relieve the pressing want of the multitude. The black-

1) 縣官。is the Emperor. See *K'ang-hi*'s Dictionnary in *voce* 縣。縣官 謂天子也。王者官天下。故日縣官.

2) lit. they melted to food.

行。薦享。侯直以鹿聘皮司府有瞻
璧。必宗四續皮享。幣。言多白用。
然以室。十爲方今諸曰。銀鹿時
後皮朝萬。皮尺以侯古錫。而禁
得幣觀王幣。緣白以者有少苑

haired people. were suffering great distress. It was then that the son of Heaven, together with all his ministers, deliberated to make again a currency in order to supply what was needed. Now it was. forbidden to rear white stags in the parks, and in the privy treasury there was a mass of silver and tin. One of the functionaries observed (lit. spoke, saying). As to the skin-currency of the ancient kings, the feudal princes used to offer them as presents when they were invited to court. At present, you take pieces of the skins of white stags, measuring a square foot and embroidered on the hems, to make of them a skin-currency, of a value of 400,000 (copper coins a piece), (and) whenever kings, feudal princes, and noblemen of imperial clans, are come up to court to have an audience with his Majesty and to offer presents, they ought to receive those skin-pieces as badges of honor. Thereupon they will be brought in circulation (as they will always be desired by persons who wish to have an audience).

For those gifts of the emperor, the nobles who went to court, had to pay the fixed sum of 400,000 coins, as appears from the second fragment bearing on the subject. It runs as follows:

死。奏稱。萬。皮璧侯異。問白事。○
異上本薦直朝對大鹿帝時
腹不末反數賀。曰。司皮與張
胇[1]悅。不四千。以今農幣。湯湯
坐湯相十而蒼王顏以造用

When Tšang-t'ang was holding the office (i. e. was prime minister) and the Emperor, together with him (T'ang), instituted the currency of the white deer-skin, he also asked the opinion of I-yen, the minister of agriculture. The answer was: "to-day all the kings and feudal princes who are coming to a general levee at court (make) use of the azure badges which have a value of (only) some thousands. (coins). Instead of those badges, now the skins are presented to them, for which they

1) 腹胇 To hide in the innermost part of his belly.

have to pay in return 400,000 (coins). The origin and the end are not counterbalanced (i. e. the two obligations are beyond all proportion)." The sovereign was not pleased, and as *T'ang*, the minister, reported that *I-(yen)* was hiding his real meaning in his inmost heart, the emperor ordered him (*Yen*) to be put instantly to death.

Another representative currency instituted by *Wu-ti* consisted of three coins of a different size and form, made of tin and silver melted together, and of a nominal value far beyond the intrinsic. The outward forms and the figures with which they are covered, are symbolical. In an old Japanese mint-book I have found an illustration of a worn copy of two of them, and the French Jesuit Père du Halde in his work entitled »Description de l'Empire de la Chine" Tome II p. 166, gives also a drawing and description of them. As an illustration to the communications of Ma-twan-lin I have appended wood-cuts of these remarkable coins.

日。莫 如 龍。天 白 又
金 如 馬。地 用 金。造
三 龜。人 用 莫 以 銀
品。故 用 莫 如 為 錫

Ma-twan-lin continues: (The emperor) made also a white metallic currency of a mixture of silver and tin, and considering that in Heaven there was nothing superior to the dragon, and on earth nothing superior to the horse, and among men nothing superior to the tortoise, he, therefore, said in reference to those three sorts of metallic coins. —

其 圜 日
一 之 撰
曰。其 直
重 文 三
八 龍。名 千
兩。

Of the first was said: It shall have a value of 8 ounces (taëls); make it round; its devise shall be a dragon; its name shall be *Tšuan*[1]), and its value 3000 (coins).

1) *Tšuan* has the signification of regulator, a pattern.

五百。　方之。其文馬。直　二曰。以重差小

Of the second was said: Make it different and smaller (in comparison to the first mentioned), and of a square form, its devise shall be a horse; its value 500 (coins).

直三百。　其文龜。　小橢¹)之。　三曰。復

Of the third was said: Make it still smaller and of an oblong form, its devise shall be a tortoise and its value 300 (coins).

兩。　三重四　重六兩　兩則二　一重八

While the weight of the first was eight ounces, that of the second was six, and that of the third 4 ounces.

From the drawing we see that the figure of the tortoise is not drawn on the third coin, but the surface of the coin reminds us of the back of a tortoise-shell with its sexangular figures. The character 王 *Wang*, meaning THE KING, is found on every sexagon, and seems a representation of the human being *par excellence*.

As to the symbolical part of these coins, Japanese and Chinese authors provide us with many explanations, of which we will give some without any comment. In a Japanese mint-book I have found the following passage "The round exterior form of coins is

1) *T'o* has, according to a note, the signification of oblong 下而長.

emblematical of heaven, whereas the square form of the inner hole is an imitation of the earth[1])." The Chinese represents to himself the earth as a great square, and so he speaks of the 四方, the four sides, in the signification of all territory under heaven, and of the 四海, the four seas, as the universe, because the seas, in their turn, surround the earth. The firmament is a round operculiform covering over the earth.

The dragon, the emblem of imperial dignity, is composed of parts of several animals just as the Egyptian sphynx; one part of the year he dwells in the clouds, and another part of the year his residence is the ocean. It may be — but we advance this as a mere suggestion — that the dragon is the symbol of fertility and creative power, as it is associated with the watery principle of the atmosphere, and composed of parts of several animals; perhaps the sphynx, turning its back to the Libyan desert where all fertility ceases, has an identical signification.

The horse is emblematical of the earth, as the earth moves round the sun in twelve months and the pregnancy of the horse equally lasts 12 months. MEDHURST in voce 馬 says "*The time of its gestation is 12 months, hence taken to indicate the earth with its 12 months to a year.*"

The tortoise was anciently used in divinations. Further indications concerning the symbolic of dragon and tortoise are to be found in Mayers I no. 299. 451. Legge III p. 335 sqq.

The end of those glittering and medal-like coins was sad. They were counterfeited on a great scale, not only by the people, but also by the state officials. Their value in exchange diminished rapidly, and the people ceased to use them as objects of value; and though the emperor tried to avert the evil by no more issuing them, his efforts were of no avail, and at the end of

[1] In a Chinese work the same is expressed by 內方象地外象天圓.

the year in which they were first coined, they did no more circulate.

Now, again a new kind of money was coined, which in the first time of its existence met with better fortune. The pieces were called *Yik-tseu* 赤仄 which literally means be nded round, or surrounded with red; or as Ma-twan-lin describes it. "The raised edge of the coin was made of red copper. 以赤銅爲其郭也。 One piece was worth 5 (probably 5 *tsu* pieces), 一當五. The functionaries who collected the taxes, used not to bring again the false *Yik-tseu*-coins in circulation. But only two years had passed, and the new coin was again very bad in consequence of counterfeiting, and as even the sensible people did not think it right to use the coins at the legal rate, they were also abolished.

廢。之民赤其
不巧仄後
便。法錢二
又用賤。歲。

Now *Wu-ti* having learned wisdom by adversity, found out the right principle, and money was made of a real value according to its design, and every province and district did not as formerly make its own money, but a state-mint was established in the capital of the Empire, and three high officials of the *Šang-lin*, (an Academy of science of that time) [1]), were appointed mint-masters. They had to do their utmost effort in order to provide the whole empire with a good and valuable currency. To all money, not issued by the *Šang-lin* officers, the character of legal tender was denied. And all the metallic currency formerly in use was drawn back, and brought to the *Šang-lin*-mint in order to be melted and recoined, and as they considered it too expensive to destroy the few false coiners who still remained, they made

---

1) 上林 *Šang-lin*, the forest of superior men, was an Academy of science founded by *Wu-ti* of the *Han*-dynasty. Mayers I 592.

盜 大 唯 the most formidable and skilled of them workmen
爲 姦 眞 in the service of the state [1]).
之。乃 工    With this account end the records of *Wu-ti*'s reign.

For about forty years nothing remarkable seems to have happened. The 5 *Tšu* pieces, issued by the *Šang-lin* mint-masters, will, no doubt, have been very good during the first years, but counterfeiting was soon again in full vigor, and under the reign of the emperor *Yuen-ti* it seems to have been so frequently practised that a learned statesman presented a memorial to the Throne, in which he earnestly proposes to abolish metallic money and to go back again to the use of grain and cloth as a medium of exchange. That memorial, Ma-twan-lin's next fragment, runs as follows: [VIII, 9*b*].

姦 者 本 心 無 錢 多 鑄 耕 十 探 禹 元
邪 不 逐 動 厭 滿 富 陷 民 萬 銅。言 帝
不 能 末。搖。足。室。人。刑 坐 人。一 鑄 時。
可 半。耕 棄 民 猶 藏 者。盜 不 歲 錢 貢

Under the reign of *Yuen-ti* (48—32 B. C.). *Kung-yü* says: "The number of persons who, in order to make money, are grasping at copper, amounts to 100.000 in the course of one year. The people cease to plough, and being engaged in false coining, they incur punishment. (Besides) many rich men accumulate money in treasuries, and are filling their dwellings with it, and yet they are not satisfied. The minds of the people are agitated [2]), they leave their present employment and throw away their prospects. (Husbandry) cannot afford to lose half of the hands that plough the field, and the false coiners are not to

---

1) However important many pieces of Ma-twan-lin may be with respect to the Chinese language, being necessarily confined to space, it is impossible for me to give the whole of the Chinese text. The remarkable expressions and curious constructions, however, will be carefully noted down at the foot of the page. In this fragment we have an expression which reminds us of a latin construction. 於 是 悉

禁 郡 國 毋 鑄 錢. Thereupon it was generally forbidden in provinces and single parts of the empire to cast money. Interdictum erat ne funderent monetam.

2) We have here 本 末 in another sense again. The origin is here the existing state, the present; the end means the future.

禁。宜罷貪珠玉金銀。鑄錢之官。毋復以爲幣。除其販賣租鉄¹)之律。租稅祿賜。皆以布帛及穀。使百姓一意農桑。議者以爲交易待²)錢。布帛不可尺寸分裂。禹議亦寢。

be checked, (in their unlawful doings). It would be reasonable, therefore, to put an end to that grasping at riches (lit. pearls, jewels, gold and silver). If the officials who cast money, are henceforth prohibited to make currency, we may break with the practice of reckoning in commercial dealings the equivalent by cash¹) (lit. in silverweight). If taxes, salaries and rewards, were all reckoned by means of silk, cloth and grain, the people would henceforth turn their thoughts on husbandry and the cultivation of mulberry trees."

Now, as for that advice to supersede²) in exchange the metallic money (by silk and grain, it is an inconvenience that) silk-pieces do not admit of being divided and torn to feet and inches (i. e. that sort of money had not the necessary quality of divisibility). The advice of (Kung) yü was also put aside).

古者以龜貝爲貨。今以錢易之。民以貧。故宜可改幣。上問丹。丹對言可改。章下有司³)議。皆以爲難卒變易。錢以來久。

Another councilor, called Tan-tšuen 丹傳, also speaking against that measure said: "The ancients used tortoise shells as a currency. Now, if it is because they changed it for money that the people are impoverished, it would be reasonable to make a change in the medium of exchange." And as the emperor asked Tan (tšuen) if it were possible to alter it, Tan replied that it was possible. But the advice of the officers of the privy council of State was also asked, and they judged that it was difficult to make a sudden change in the money which for a long time had been in circulation.

From the days of the Emperor Hiao-wu-ti (117 B. C.) when the Šang-lin officers began to make money, till the year

---

1) A note says, 租鉄 signifies: the reckoning of the price of an object sold; what one recieves in return for (the object sold) in Tsze and T'su (in silverweight) — A Tsze = 6 T'su.

2) 待 is most likely used instead of 代.

3) 章下有司 are the officers of the privy council of State.

成錢二百八十億萬餘。 1 A. D. under the Emperor *Ping-ti*'s reign, they had made copper coins to an amount of more than 280.000.000.000 pieces.

The next fragment contains an information on the relative value of money in the time of the *Han*-dynasty, collected from the historical records of that dynasty and communicated by an author who lived under the *Sung*-dynasty between A. D. 1000 and 1100, and who compares it with that of his own time. The author's pseudonym is 石林 *Ši-lin*, and of his family-name he is called 葉 *Ye*. He observes: "In the historical records of China, the chronicles of *Wang-kia*, it is related that in the time of the emperor *Yuen-ti* the treasury of the imperial palace amounted to 4.000.000.000, and the privy treasury contained 1.800.000.000 pieces of money; and he adds that that is

以今計之不足以當權貨務盛時一歲之入 much. If you consider it in relation to the present time, it is not yet so much as is paid in one year in duties at a custom house, where a considerable import and export of wares takes place. In the time of the *Han*-dynasty, the money was very heavy, whereas the goods were light [1]), and the prices of grain were very low, for they were only 5 *cash* a

故嘉言是時外戚貲千萬者少正便有千萬亦是今一萬貲中下戶皆有之 bushel. Therefore says *Kia* (*Wan-kia* the author of the chronicles), that a man possessing 10.000.000 *cash* enjoyed a life (lit. wealth) free from care, and few principal officers did possess it, but it is also true that at present the average of middle-class and lower families possess that sum of 10,000 strings of cash.

1) Heavy and light are here in the signification explained at page 32.

According to the regulations of the *Han*-dynasty a prime minister and the military commanders-in-chief of cavalry and infantry 大司馬。大將軍 had a monthly income of 60.000 *cash*. Imperial historiographers and governors of provinces received 40.000. A commander-in-chief got, moreover, 350 bushels of rice monthly, and so it went on in a progressive ratio downwards, so that a public functionary of inferior rank got 100 stone (picul). There were also some who got 8 bushels and a little more monthly". In this way the author proceeds, and, as under the reign oft he *Sung*-dynasty, when *Šĭk-lin* of the family *Ye* lived, there was much money, but all commodities and provisions were scarce and dear, and the governement sought to remedy the evil by introducing a new sort of money in large quantities, he ends with stating as his opinion that the value of goods does not depend on the quantity of money existing, but on several other circumstances. The high prices of provisions, therefore, will not fall by a sudden increase of the quantity of money. In plain words he says: 蓋錢之多寡，係幣之輕重，不在鼓鑄廣狹也。 "The quantity of money (necessary as an equivalent to buy goods, i. e. the prices of commodities) and the value of goods do not depend on the larger or smaller quantities of money, which are coined". From this sentence we see how deeply *Šĭk-lin* was already convinced of the economical truth that "INCREASING THE QUANTITY OF MONEY IS NOT AUGMENTING THE WEALTH OF THE PEOPLE."

1) It is remarkable that the character *p'i* 幣 in this fragment, several times is taken in a signification contrary to what it commonly expresses; here it stands for goods, wares, whereas it generally signifies money, currency. In the beginning of this fragment a sentence, a common antithesis in Chinese construction, shows that abnormality very plainly. 漢時錢極重而幣輕. In the *Han*-period the money was very heavy whereas wares were light (i. e. low) in value: See page 46, note 1. At the next page it occurs a third time.

Now the same author proceeds to inform us how much at that time the people used for their daily expenses.

又曰如魏文侯相李悝言一夫治田百畝畝收粟一石半爲百五十石一夫五口人月食五石半百畝之入以四十五稅九十石爲食餘其四十石錢三十計錢千三百五十社問嘗新春秋之祠只用錢三百而用其餘錢以爲五口之衣衣人率用錢三百五人終歲用十五百今只餘千五十不足四百則固不嫌錢之少也然王使幣[2]輕亦何至是蓋日用猶不滿一錢不知何以爲生

As *Li-huei* the prime minister of *Wen*, the vassal of *Wei*, relates: "One man manages a hundred *Meu* (acres) of land; the acre produces one picul and a half of rice, total 150 piculs; one family consists of 5 mouths [1]) and a man eats one picul and a half a month. On an income of 100 acres a tax of 15 piculs is levied, and as a man uses 90 piculs for food, there remain 45 piculs. The picul has a value of 30 coins, together (the 45 piculs) 1350 coins. For sacrifices to the tutelary gods in their hamlets, the autumnal offerings of first fruits and the offerings in the spring to their ancestors alone, they already use 300 coins, and the remaining money must find the 5 persons in clothes. For the clothing of one man 300 coins on an average are wanted, thus, at the end of the year, 5 men have used 1500 coins. But as there remained only a sum of 1050 coins, there were 450 short.

Hence you surely should not attribute it (this state of things) to the scarcity of money. For although the prince takes care that the prices of commodities [2]) are low (lit. light), how should he be able to make them thus low (i. e. how

1) Just the same what we reckon a family at in our statistical returns.

2) The sentence is not quite clear, owing to the signification of the word 幣, which in this passage has again a meaning opposite to that which it has commonly with other authors (See Note page 47) I shall be happy if any Sinologue will give another and better interpretation of the three objectionable sentences of *Wang-Kia's* chronicles. [Mat. VIII 10a—11b].

would he be able to make them so low that they should be in proportion to the small sum which the common people can lay out). If they cannot even spend one *cash* daily, I don't know on what they live.

### WANG-MANG THE USURPER.

*Wang-mang* was a nobleman of royal descent, living at the court of the Emperor *Tš'ing-ti* of the *Han*-dynasty (32—6. B. C.). He was generally esteemed by the court as well as by the people for his high accomplishments and noble conduct; but unfortunately an insatiable ambition was the main-spring of all his good actions. At the age of twenty-eight he was already Commander-in-chief of the army, and when the emperor came to die, he became regent during the minority of the hereditary prince.

Incited by his ruling passion, ambition, he thought of becoming emperor himself, and aided by the imperious dowager Empress, mother to the deceased emperor, he attained his object. The two children who successively occupied the throne for a short time, were destroyed by the intriguing court-party of which *Wang-mang* was the master-spirit; one was poisoned, and the other was relegated in a state of strict confinement.

Now *Wang-mang* himself mounted the imperial throne and brought distress and ruin down upon the country and the people by the mad way in which he governed the state. The changes and alterations he made in the currency, minutely recorded by Ma-twan-lin, are striking instances of his tyrannic government, and, as we shall see, the very money brought in circulation by him greatly contributed to accelerate his fall.

4

When *Wang-mang* acted as regent[1]), he annulled the decrees enacted by the *Han*-dynasty and reverted again to the money of the *Tseu*-dynasty, the mother and child weighed in proportion to each other (See page 25). He also made again the pieces of *King-wang* of the *Tseu* of exactly the same dimensions and design.

Besides he re-introduced the knife-shaped coins, and called them *Ki-tao* 契刀 and *Ts'o-tao* 錯刀. The former, properly meaning knives to make agreements or bonds, had an arbitrary value of 500 *cash*; the latter were called gilded knives, because the characters engraved on these coins, denoting the name and value, were washed with gold 以黄金錯其文; their value was 50 *cash*.

*Ma-twan-lin* after giving a minute account of the dimensions of the several parts of these coins, tells us a dispute between two scholars, one of whom asserts that those two knife-shaped coins of the same size did not answer the purpose, the gilded characters of the second sort being soon filed out and effaced by constant wear and tear, so that no difference whatever was to be seen between the two sorts. The other who writes about 800 years after the money was brought in circulation, maintains that this opinion is false, as still in his time there exist some of *Wang-mang's* knife-coins, which are uninjured both in design and form, consequently quite answering the purpose. — I suppose that this worthy scholar will have had a specimen carefully preserved in a cabinet of antiquities. There are some in the Musea at Leiden, London and St. Petersburg, but they show only the outer form of the coin [2]).

---

1) lit. was dwelling in the regency 居攝.

2) M. DE CHAUDOIR in his Recueil de Monnaies de la Chine, etc. gives two illustrations of *Ki-tao*, on which the cha-

The ancient 5 *tšu* pieces still remained in circulation as long as *Wang-mang* was regent.

貨　錢　而　刀。字　恭
小　布　更　契　有　即
錢。之　作　刀。金　眞。
品。金　及　刀。以
名　銀　五　乃　爲
日　龜　銖　罷　書
寶　貝　錢　錯　劉

But when (*Wang-*)*mang* actually took possession of the imperial throne, and looking at the word 劉 saw that it was composed of the character 金 metal and 刀 knife ¹) he abolished all *ts'o-tao, ki-tao* and 5 *tšu* coins, and made several new sorts (of currency) of gold, silver, tortoise shells, cowries and copper *pu* (pieces imitating the shape of a dress. See page 4.), and he called them precious merchandise and little money.

*Wang-mang's* new currency consisted of 6 different copper coins, one gold-piece which, in imitation of the ancient rule of the *Tšeu-*dynasty was called 斤 *Kin* (pound) and had a value of 10.000 copper coins, and two silver coins of different value, the unit of which was a 流 *lieu*; both had a weight of eight taels, but the coin made of the silver found in the districts 朱 *Tšu* and 提 *Š'i*²), being of a better quality, was worth 1580, while that made of an inferior quality of silver, found elsewhere in the empire, was worth 1000 *cash*. Of tortoise shells, there were four different sorts of

racters denoting the value 五百 are engraved. This is in striking contradiction to the information of *Tšang-yen*, a Chinese author who lived before the eighth century of our era. In a description of these coins, he positively says: 其文 左曰契右曰刀。無 五百字也. "Its mark on the left side is *Ki*, on the right side *Tao*, but they bear not the character 500 (denoting the value)". Now either M. DE CHAUDOIR's imagination has been too lively or the *Ki-tao*, he copied, were antiquities of recent origin. In the numismatical cabinet of the Leiden University I have recently found some specimens which are obviously false, as they are not in the least damaged. They also bear the denomination of value, which *Tšang-yen* denies to them.

1) 劉 *Liu*, is the family-name of the *Han-*dynasty, founded by *Liu-pang* B. C. 195 [Mayers I N°. 414] and is composed of 金 metal and || or 刀 knife and now the usurper feared that the metal-knives would keep the remembrance of the *Han-*dynasty alive in the hearts of the people. And as history informs us, he was not quite wrong in doing so, for a seditious little song the subject of which was the money of the *Han-*dynasty contributed ten years later to *Wang-mang's* fall.

2) *Tšu* and *Š'i* were parts of *Kien-wei* in *Sse-tšuen*. Ma-twan-lin gives this uncommon sound to 提 in one of his notes.

various size and denomiuations, which had au arbitrary valuation. Further 5 different sorts of shells or rather pairs of shells called 朋 *peng*, and finally 10 different sorts of 布 shaped coins, an illustration of which is to be found at the next page. In general the new currency consisted of 28 different sorts, made of 5 different substances and designated by 6 different denominations [1]).

But the people did not approve of this new currency, the metal not being pure and solid; they were all in a maze of doubt, 百姓憒亂, and after a short time they did not use the money any longer, but continued to employ again the 5 *tšu* pieces of the *Han*-dynasty.

恭患之下詔敢挾五銖錢者爲惑衆。投諸四裔。於是農商失業食貨俱廢。民沸泣於市。道坐賣買田宅奴婢鑄錢抵罪者。自公卿大夫至庶人不敢稱數。

(*Wang*)-*mang* being alarmed at this state of things, issued a proclamation, (in which was said): that whoever ventured to hide the 5 *tšu* pieces in order to lead astray the multitude, should be banished to the remotest parts of the empire. Thereupon husbandmen and merchants lost their occupation, food and merchandise ceased to be produced, and the people in the market wept bitterly and were heart-broken. It is said that in this time no one durst determine the number of those, — nobleinen, courtiers, and great officers as well as lower people — who as a punishment for their crimes of counterfeiting money, were condemned to be sold for slaves, to do house and fieldwork.

*Wang-mang* was aware that his people were suffering severe distress. He, therefore, again abolished all this new eccentric coinage, and only one "little copper piece" remained together with the suitable "great coins."

---

1) Only 5 substances because the 錢 and 布 were both made of copper.

In the year 14 A. D. he again brought in circulation some of the abolished copper coins, but made a slight alteration in the valuation. 頗增減其價直。

One of these coins was called 泉布 ts'uen-pu. Another of the same form is the piece called 貨布 ho-pu, a diagram of which is to be seen at page 4. It has been appended once more in order to enable the reader to follow Ma-twan-lin's description of the dimensions of the several parts of the coin, as he probably found them in the *Han-šu* (the Annals of the *Han*-dynasty). The copy has been taken from a Japanese work on the subject, which is generally very exact in its statements. I have only translated those informations on the proportionate dimensions leaving it to the amateurs to ascertain from it the measures in use under *Wang-mang*.

貨布長二寸二分廣一寸首長八分有奇其廣八分其圜好徑二分半足枝長八分間廣二分其文右曰貨左曰布重二十五銖直貨錢二十五。

"The *ho-pu* has a total length of 2,2 *tsün* (2 *tsün* and 2 *fun* [1])) and is 1 *tsün* broad. The head has a length of 8 *fun* or a little more, and a width of 8 *fun*; the round hole has a diameter of 2 *fun* and 1/2. The foot-branches are 8 *fun* long and the space (between the feet) is 2 *fun*; the design is at the right hand *ho*, merchandise, and at the left hand *pu*, cloth, the weight is 25 *tšu* and the value 25 copper coins."

But the recent innovations did not gain the approbation of the people, and with new force they took to the temporarily inter-

1) A *fun* = 0.1 *tsün*.

rupted business of private coining. At first *Wang-mang* put to
death all who violated the laws, but there were nevertheless
so many false coiners that he began to feel alarmed.

迺更輕其法。私鑄作泉布
者與妻子沒爲官奴婢吏
及比伍知而不舉告與同
罪非沮寶貨民作一歲
吏免官犯者愈衆又五人
相坐皆沒入郡國檻車鐵
鑢傳送長安鍾官愁苦死
者十六七時童謠曰
黃牛白[1]腹
五銖當復。
好事者竊言王恭稱黃述
欲繼之故稱白腹五銖漢
貨言漢當復并天下。

He commuted his punishment and ordered that every false coiner with
wife and children should be reduced to the condition of state-slaves,
and the functionaries who were aware of the existence of (false coining)
in the *Pi* and *Wu* sections (under their supervision)[2] and did not be-
tray them to the authority, incurred the same punishment, and those
who did not stop the interdicted species current with the people were
suspended in their offices, for the time of a year. The result was that
the officials left their employment, and the number of those who acted
against the laws was beyond all measure. As soon as 5 men were found
together they were arrested and put in prison, and the prisoner-vans[3]
and iron fetters of all parts of the empire delivered their prisoners to
the mint-master[4] of *Tsang-ngan* (*Sing-nan fu*, the capital in that
time). The number of those who daily suffered a painful death was very
large (lit. 16 or 17).

Now at that time there was a seditious popular song:

"The imperial ox has a white belly
The 5 *tsu* pieces ought to return."

1) 白 white is the color signifying
evil, also that of mourning. Biot trans-
lates in loco, page 461. Le boeuf sacré
est gras.

2) 比 *Pi* and 伍 *Wu* are denominations of municipal sections or wards, instituted by the *Tseu-li*. Cf. *Tseu-li* I 256
n° 28.

3) lit. carts with cages on them.

4) 鍾官主鑄錢者.

The champions of the right cause expressed thereby in a covert way that *Wang-mang* was designated by the yellow (ox), and the explanation was, that they wished to put an end to his tyranny. That is the cause why they alluded to the white belly. The 5 *tšu* pieces were the currency of the *Han*-dynasty, and they meant by them that the *Han* ought to return, in order to unite the kingdom again.

In 23 A. D. the usurper *Wang-mang* was murdered and the descendents of the *Han*-dynasty again took possession of the ancestral throne under the name of the "Later or Eastern *Han*-dynasty."

### THE EASTERN HAN-DYNASTY.

天 六 從 解 難 從 許 三 五 土 武 雜 初
下 年 之 釋¹ 十 公 事 府 銖 書 初 用 王
賴 始 世 更 餘 府 遂 奏 錢 言 馬 布 莽
其 行 祖²⁾ 具 府 求 寢 以 言 援 帛 亂
便 五 建 表 乃 得 及 爲 事 宜 在 金 後
銖 武 言 隨 前 援 未 下 如 隴 粟 貨
錢 十 帝 牒 奏 還 可 三 舊 西 建 幣

Shortly after the troubles occasioned by the bad government of *Wang-mang*, silk, cloth, metals, and rice, were used as currency. In the year 25 A. D. *Ma-yuen* who at that time was *Šang-šu* in *Lung-si* ³), advanced his opinion that it would be reasonable to cast again as formerly the 5 *tšu* coins; the question was brought (lit. went down) ⁴) before the *San-fu* (the mint-college) which, in a memorial to the throne, was of the opinion that it could not be granted, whereupon the affair

---

1) 釋 signifies to explain, to open out the meaning, and also to loosen.

2) 光武帝 is the 世祖 or founder of the Eastern *Han*-dynasty.

3) A district in the N. W. of China, prov. *Šen-si*.

4) 事 下 三 府 is in the ori-ginal text. I have omitted the full-stop and translated 事 下, the affair went down to the *San-fu*; compare next page where the expression 事 下 四 府 appears without the full-stop between the two first characters.

was abandoned (lit. was lain down to sleep), till *Ma-yuen* came back again, and tried to forward his former memorial to the imperial court, which however was very difficult as he had to send it ten consecutive times. Now, at last, his dispatches were opened and explained (unfolded), and his meanings were wholly made known. The Emperor followed his advice.

The founder of the new dynasty began in A. D. 40 to bring again in circulation the 5 *tšu* coins, and the whole empire enjoyed its blessings.

不 劉 改 桓　Under the reign of the Emperor *Hwan-ti*
便 陶 鑄 帝　(147—168) the advice was given to alter the
乃 言 大 時　money and to cast large coins. But as *Liu-t'ao*
止 其 錢 議　said that this measure would be impracticable,

it was given up.

*Liu-t'ao*'s speech on that occasion is interesting, especially as his comparisons remind us of Mencius' manner of speaking. The following passage contains nearly the whole of it.

### SPEECH OF LIU-T'AO.

達 至 朝 年 民 不 議 能 府 鑄 故 人 ○
農 急 有 無 饑 在 曰 言 羣 大 致 以 時
殖 也 饑 貨 盖 於 當 之 僚 錢 貧 貨 有
之 議 故 不 民 貨 今 士 及 事 困 輕 土
本 者 食 可 可 在 之 陶 太 下 宜 財 薄
多 不 為 一 百 於 憂 上 學 四 改 薄 言

At that time there was a *Šang-šu* who maintained that the people were impoverished and in want, because the currency was too light and thin, which ought to be mended by casting great coins. The proposition went down to be deliberated on by the mint-college (lit. college of four mint masters). It was then that the very learned and eloquent scholar *Liu(T'ao)*, coming to the court, in order to give his advice, said. "The distress of the present times does not take its origin in the currency but in the fact that the people are suffering from famine, for the people may live a hundred years without a currency, but without food they cannot exist a single day, and therefore food is (at present) of the utmost necessity. Your councilors do not comprehend the first requi-

言冶鑄之便。故欲
因緣行詐。以¹⁾買
利國利將盡。取國
爭競夫欲民股者
皋要在止役禁財
則百姓不勞而奪
陛下欲鑄錢齊足。
以救其弊。此猶貨
魚沸鼎之中樓養
烈火之上水木鳥
魚鳥之所生也。本
之不時²。必致焦用
帝乃止。不鑄錢爛。

site of agriculture. The frequent talking of the benefits of melting and casting (money) is because they are desirous of an oppertunity to bring false coins in circulation, and in this way ¹) to capture the benefits which the soil yields, but as soon as those benefits are totally exhausted, those who appropiated them, will quarrel and fight. If you wish your people to live in a flourishing state and to increase in wealth, it is necessary, that they should be in a condition, in which they can quietly perform their duties, and are prevented from hankering after large profits; only then the people will enjoy a state of competence without care and troubles. As to the desire of your Majesty to cast money and to arrange the currency in order to repair its present vicious state, it is just the same as if you would rear a fish in a caldron with boiling water, or roost a bird on a hot fire. Water and wood are essential for the life of fish and birds. But in using them in a wrong way ²), you will surely cause (the bird) to be scorched and (the fish) to be cooked to shreds. Thereupon the emperor abandoned his purpose and the large coins were not cast.

We now approach to the end of the great *Han*-dynasty and Ma-twan-lin's informations regarding the last two emperors are of little economical value. There are, however, few places where the Chinese text is so difficult to understand as in the following piece which refers to the money of the emperor *Ling-ti*, who reigned 168—190 A. D.

1) 以 = 是以.

2) 不時 has here another signification as in the passage quoted from the *Tseu-li* See p. 22. It rather means here 非時, the wrong, the improper time. See for the different meanings of 不時, 無時 and 非時, J. J. HOFFMANN, Japanese Grammar. 2d Ed. 1876; page 129.

靈帝中平三年鑄四出文錢○錢皆四道識者竊言侈虐已甚形象乇見此錢成必四道而去及京師亂錢果流布四海

In the third year of the period *Tšung-ping* (186 A. D.) the emperor *Ling-ti* had coins cast with the design of the four outlets.

This money had on the reverse four ways (issues), the covert meaning of which, according to the saying of those who knew it, was that whenever extravagance and oppression were too heavy, the figure of those coins would be a prognostic from which it appeared that this money would have 4 ways to escape. And as the revolution broke out in the capital, that money did indeed stream and diffuse itself over the whole empire.

The following explanations of the just quoted fragment will, I hope, prove an acceptable digression to such of my readers as are students of the Chinese language. Ma-twan-lin is sometimes very obscure, and a great many difficulties are often to be surmounted before his meaning is thoroughly understood. 乇 is a character not to be met with in any Chinese dictionary. I first took it for 乖 to which it has a strong resemblance, but when I found the same character a second time in Mat. IX 3*a*, it was at once clear to me that in both places it stands for 兆, which has the meaning of 1° a prognostic; omen, 2° a million. — I came to that conclusion in the following way: The second passage, Mat. IX. 3 runs 韓愈拜京乇尹。 *Han-yü* was appointed Governor-General of the capital. The official title 京兆尹 ruler of the millions of the capital is often met with in history, (Morr. *in voce* 官 n°. 130) and the *Han-yü* in question was according to history indeed called 京兆尹 (de Mailla-*Hist. Gén. d. l. Chine* Vol. VI p. 439). Comparing the two passages of Ma-twan-lin, it is evident that 乇 is used for 兆, and that in the above quoted sentence, 兆 has the signification of prognostic, omen.

皆 stands for 背 the reverse of the coin, as is evident from a passage in a Japanese book treating of the same coins 此錢 今世尚ヲアリ 字ジ 畫ノ 明ヲ 澂ミ 背文四出. "On those coins on which the strokes of the characters are still visible, we plainly see on the reverse four outlets" — and that is the reason why that money is commonly called the money with the corners. 俗ヲニコレヲ 角錢 ト云フ.

If we look at the subjoined illustration of the reverse of the coin, Ma-twan-lin's meaning is quite clear. The four little strokes from the corners of the hole to the outer edge are the four outlets spoken of. — BIOT in loco p. 439 writes "l'Empéreur *Ling-ti* fit fondre quatre espèces de pieces nouvelles. L'une d'elle se voit dans la Musée de *Kien-long*". — We see how far he was from the right tract and was led astray, 1o. by the wrong character 皆 which made him take the object as a plural, 2°. by not knowing the meaning of 四出, and 3°. because the monogram 扗 was not explained. This passage may serve as an instance of the many difficulties which Chinese authors may cause us by using incorrect and wrong characters.

The emperor *Hien-ti* tried in the first year of his reign to improve the money, and establish it on another basis in consequence of which he suppressed the 5 *tšu* pieces and had little coins cast. In order to obtain the necessary quantity of copper, he confiscated copper statues, figures of the *Fei-lien* [1]), and many other objects made of copper. The money, however, was without governing principle,

---

1) *Fei-lien* 飛廉 is the poetical name of 風伯 the ruler of the winds. According to the "Rites of the *Tšen*-dynasty", sacrifices were offered to him. Cf. Mayers I. 137.

the design was badly made, and it was not convenient to the people in daily use.

These few lines would suffice to get an insight into the political history of that time. They are so many instances of misgovernment and arbitrariness. Already during the reign of the Emperor *Ling-ti* the imperial authority had been undermined by eunuchs and designing courtiers, and the time of the fall of the *Han*-dynasty was near. The emperor *Hien-ti* was to act the principal part in a drama that scores of times afterwards in all parts of the world would be represented by demoralized monarchs and their ambitious ministers. The leading personages are well known — a weak and effeminate prince and a majordomo who usurps the powers of the state and stirs the people to revolt, in order to dethrone his master and take his place. So also here. The Generalissimo *Ts'ao-ts'ao*, to whom the emperor had gradually deputed all his authority, abuses his power and involves China into a civil war. A descendant of the ancient *Han*-dynasty gains a battle over that general, conquers Western China, and assumes the title of Emperor, as the representative of the legitimate line. *Ts'ao-ts'ao* himself established his residence in the North and called himself king of *Wei*, but after his death his son also assumes the title of Emperor of China.

Finally, one of *Ts'ao-ts'ao's* former officers takes arms against the usurper and becomes the rival of his master. After much slaughter and bloodshed he succeeds in establishing himself in the county called *Wu*, south of the *Kiang*, where he also assumes the title of emperor. Hence it is that in Chinese history we read of the three kingdoms, viz. *So*, *Wei* and *Wu*.

# CHAPTER III.

## HISTORY OF THE MONEY DURING THE PERIODS OF DIVISION OF THE EMPIRE.

THE THREE KINGDOMS. — THE TSIN-DYNASTY RE-UNITES THE EMPIRE. — HWAN-HIUEN PROPOSES TO ABOLISH THE MONEY. — SPEECH OF THE PRIVY COUNCILLOR KUNG-LIN AGAINST THAT PLAN. — THE SAME QUESTION DISCUSSED IN ANOTHER PART OF THE COUNTRY. — DIVISION OF THE EMPIRE INTO NORTH AND SOUTH. — THE SOUTHERN EMPIRE, THE SUNG-DYNASTY. — A SESSION OF THE PRIVY COUNCIL AND ADVICE NOT TO COIN TOO LIGHT PIECES. — 'WRETCHED CONDITION OF THE CURRENCY DURING THE REIGN OF THE "DEPOSED EMPEROR." — VIEW OF THE POLITICAL EVENTS BY WHICH THE FOUR SUBSEQUENT DYNASTIES ROSE AND FELL. — ADMIRABLE SPEECH OF A MINISTER ON THE NECESSITY THAT MONEY SHOULD HAVE A REAL VALUE AND BE PERFECTLY COINED. — THE LIANG-DYNASTY. — INSTITUTION OF IRON MONEY; ITS FAILURE. — THE TS'AN-DYNASTY. — THE NORTHERN EMPIRE. — THE WEI-DYNASTY. — MONEY IS NOT USED AT ALL, THE PEOPLE ENFORCED TO USE IT. — DISCUSSIONS ON THE INSTITUTION OF A NEW CURRENCY. — NORTHERN TSI-DYNASTY. — ASSISEMENT INTRODUCED — GOLD AND SILVER MONEY OF THE FAR WEST. — THE SUI-DYNASTY RE-UNITES THE EMPIRE. — UNAVAILING MEASURES TO INTRODUCE A BETTER CURRENCY. — MONEY SUPERSEDED BY OTHER OBJECTS. — END OF THE SUI-DYNASTY.

Ma-twan-lin's informations as to the transactions of this period confine themselves to the measures taken by the three emperors, after they had founded their empires, and were sufficiently at leisure to think of the interests of their subjects. He first treats of the money introduced into the land of *So*, the present province of *Sse-tšuen*, by the representative of the ancient imperial line, who after having conquered this country had established the seat of his government in *I-tšeu*, then the capital of that part of China.

昭烈取蜀，鑄直百錢。○先主)攻劉璋，與士庶約，若事定，府庫百物，孤無取焉。及入成都，士庶皆捨干戈，赴諸藏取寶物。軍用不足，備憂之。西曹掾劉巴曰，此易耳，但當鑄直百錢，平諸物價。備從之，旬月之間，府庫充實。文曰直百。亦有勒為五銖者[2]。百亦。

As *Tšao-li* had seized on the land of *Šo*, he caused coins to be cast of a nominal value of 100. During the struggle of *Sien-tšu* [1]) for the scepter of the *Han* (lit. of *Liu = Liu-pang*) he had agreed with his officers and soldiers that whenever the affair was decided, the public treasuries should not be plundered, the people being unprotected; but no sooner had they entered the capital, than all of them, officers as well as soldiers, threw away their shields and spears, and hastened to the treasuries where they made themselves master of all the valuable objects. For the wants of the army was not even left enough, and (*Liu-*)*pei* [1]) was greatly concerned at this. — *Liu-pa*, the governor of *Si-tšao* said. — This evil is easily remedied, you have only to cast coins which have a value of 100 others and you will make the prices of all commodities on a level. (*Liu-*)*pei* followed that advice and within ten months the treasuries were filled (with money), the design of which was "Value 100". Also they happened to be made and engraved as the 5 *tšu* pieces [2]).

Secondly our author gives us some information on the economical condition of the medium of exchange in the northern kingdom of *Wei*, where the son of the generalissimo *Tsʻao-tsʻao* under the name of *Wen-ti* had assumed the title of Emperor, 220 A. D.

1) By 先主 the first ruler 劉備 *Liu-pei*, afterwards the emperor 照烈 of 蜀 is designated. In this little fragment the three different names are alternately used. See Mayers I. N°. 415 j². N². 88.

2) The meaning of this phrase is explained in *Kin ku-tsʻuen-ho-kien* Vol. I. p. 12a. (a work already quoted. See p. 24.

Note 3, where we read that the form of the 直百 五銖 perfectly resembled that of the of the *Han*-dynasty, and that they even happened to be engraved with the very characters on them, but in reversed order, the 五 being placed at the right instead of at the left side and the 銖 at the left instead of at the right.

He introduced a currency of articles of consumption, as grain, rice, etc., but after a short time it was clearly proved to be unsuitable.. The fragment is remarkable for this reason that the arguments against the fitness of the use of these commodities as a medium of exchange are the same as those which we find in economists of our time, as Mr. STANLEY JEVONS, and Prof. SUMNER, in his work "A history of American currency[1])."
It runs as follows:

乃 錢。省。錢 馬 以 薄 兢²)入ﾟ。帝 以 罷 魏
立 於 刑。非 芝 嚴 絹 濕 人 世 穀 五 文
五 是 若 徒 等 刑 以 穀 間 廢 帛 銖 帝
銖 爲 更 豐 議 不 爲 以 巧 錢。爲 錢 黃
錢。便。鑄 國。以 能 市。要 僞 穀 市。使 初
　 明 五 亦 爲 禁。雖 利。漸 用 至 百 二
　 帝 銖 以 用 司 處 作 多 旣 明 姓 年。

In the second year of the period *Hwang-tšu* (221 A. D.) *Wei wen-ti* abolished the 5 *tšu* pieces and ordered the people to market by means of grain and silks. Up to the time of the Emperor *Ming-ti* the money remained abolished, and during that time grain was used as such. But the cunning and false among the people gradually brought a large quantity moist grain to market with a view of making a larger profit, and they made a thin and sleazy silk to market with it. Although severe punishments were inflicted, the evil practice could not be checked. *Sse-ma-tši*, (the first general and minister at the court of *Wei*), and others gave the advice, that according to their opinion the use of money would not only enrich the country but also lead to a decrease in the number of sentences. When the 5 *tšu* pieces were cast again, it would, moreover, be convenient. Thereupon the emperor *Ming-ti* introduced the 5 *tšu* pieces again.

*Sün-K'iuen* 孫權 ³), the monarch of the third empire of *Wu*, who did not take the title of emperor before the year 229 A. D.,

---

1) JEVONS. "Money and Mechanism of Exchange," p. 25. 36. SUMNER p. 7.

2) 兢 is here used for 競.

3) On *Sün-K'iuen*. See Mayers. I. N°. 632.

.iutroduced iu the year 236 the so-called large coins oue piece of which had a nominal value of 500, and two years later he made money of a nominal value of 1000 copper pieces.

錢既太貴。但有空名。and such private persons as wished to That money was very dear but it had but an empty name, (the intrinsic value being in no proportion to the nominal). This raised the discontent of the people. On hearing that his people considered this currency as unsuitable, (Sün;-K'iuen diminished (the circulating quantity) and discontinued (further to make) it. He ordered it to be melted for implements. The functionaries (who had received it) did not issue it again, get rid of it took it to the treasury where it was exchanged at a proportional or a somewhat lower rate; and it did not happen that any one was treated in an unreasonable way.

人間患之。權息之。百姓

不以爲便。省勿復出也。鑄

爲器物。官勿復出也。鑄

私家有者。並以輸藏。

平卑其直。勿有所枉。

*Caetera desunt* and the next fragment informs us of the monetary system of the emperors of the *Tsin*-dynasty who reunited the three empires under their sway, after a separate existence of above 50 years.

The better to understand what follows, we have given a concise view of the political events which brought about the re-union of three kingdoms.

A minister at the court of *Wei*, the most northern of the three states into which China was divided, had conquered the western kingdom of *Šo* and driven away the last descendant of the great *Han*-dynasty. This minister himself was a descendant of the vassals of *Tsin* who reigned in ancient times, when the empire was divided into different almost independent kingdoms. To reward him for his services the emperor bestowed on him the title of *King* of *Tsin* 晉王. The son and successor of this minister usurped the throne and was the founder of the 晉 *Tsin*-dynasty

265 A. 'D. His great ambition was to consolidate the whole of China to one kingdom as it was under the *Han* and with this object in view he conquered in the first years of his reign the southern kingdom of *Wu*.

Ma-twan-lin's account of the money of the new dynasty could not be shorter. "The *Tsin* used the same money as the *Wei*-dynasty, and I have not heard that afterwards money was introduced, which bore a characteristic of being made by that dynasty."

Without saying any more he passes to the year 317, and says: "When the emperor *Yuen-ti* had crossed the river, he used the old money of *Sün*." 元 帝 過 江. 用 孫 氏 舊 錢。 This passage too requires a short historical elucidation.

*Min-ti*, the fourth emperor of the *Tsin*-dynasty, was besieged in his capital *Tš'ang-ngan* 長 安 by a Tartar prince from the North. The town being taken he was led away a prisoner, and had to suffer many humiliations, as to serve the prince at table, to walk before his horse as he went out hunting, etc., and when some faithful but rash followers of that unfortunate emperor, indignant at such treatment, marched their armies to the north in order to release their sovereign, the Tartar prince caused him immediately to be put to death. After the capture of *Tš'ang-ngan*, a relation to the *Tsin* family repaired with a great many followers to *Kien-k'ang* 建 康 (the present *Nang-king*) on the right bank of the *Yang-tsze-kiang*, and had himself proclaimed emperor under the title of *Yuen-ti*, as soon as the death of the emperor *Min-ti* was ascertained. *Kien-k'ang* was the capital of *Wu* at the time when it was a separate kingdom, and when *Yuen-ti* came there the currency introduced by *Sün-k'iuen*, the founder of that kingdom, was still in circulation. Ma-twan-lin

5

tells us that the emperor *Yuen-ti*, after having crossed the river (i. e. the *Yang-tsze-kiang*), did not alter or change the circulating medium. We omit the uninteresting account of the various denominations and sizes of that money, but merely state, that in spite of all the good cares and precautions of the humane and amiable prince, the money at last circulated in no sufficient quantity, and consequently became dearer and dearer when it was weighed against commodities. Equally uninteresting is the following passage — moreover rendered obscure by the use of a wrong character [1]) — in which we are told that the emperor *Hiao-wu-ti* issued a proclamation prohibiting the export of copper which speculators carried to the barbarious tribes of *Kwan-tšeu*, who made drums of it, and paid high prices for it. For says the emperor in his proclamation "money is the most important treasure of the country." 錢國之重寶.

And now we have come again to a part, in every respect worthy of our interest. It is a plea, delivered in the privy council assembled at court, important in an economical point of view as well as on account of the curious language, construction and historical details.

食 政. 洪 之 〇 可. 以 帛. 錢 議 立 與 安
次. 貨 範 義 孔 乃 爲 朝 用 欲 輔 中. 帝 元
豈 爲 八 曰. 琳 止. 不 議 穀 廢 政. 桓 元

In the reign of the emperor *Ngan-ti*, in the period *Yuen-hing* (402) the advice and desire of *Hwan-hiuen*, who at that time was (still) attached to the government (as governor of a province [2]), was to abolish the money and to employ grain and silks (as a medium of exchange).

---

1) Chinese students who may happen to read Ma-twan-lin's text, will easily observe that the wrong character spoken of is 意.

I should wish to supersede it by 息; the meaning of the sentence would then be plain.

2) *Hwan hiuen* soon after became a rebel and after having conquered a great part of the empire and dethroned the emperor, was defeated by one of the faithful generals of *Ngai-ti*. — 輔 means to join, to help, 政 the government. — 宰輔 is a cabinet minister.

贅。財。貨。聖　嘗　器。自　禁　是　用　者　貲。不
又　既　以　王　致　各　務　之　妨　力　乎。為　以
省　無　通　制　勤　綵　穀　可　於　若　用　交
運　毀　有　無　於　其　工　為　使　之　易
致　敗　用　用　錢。業。自　也。生　為　之　錢　百　之
之　之　之　之　故　何　今　之　業。則　姓　要　所

The council assembled at court were however of opinion, that this could not be, and thereupon the matter was dropped.

*Kung-lin's* advice (on this occasion) was: In the Great Plan, the part treating of the eight Objects of Government[1]) the commodities are second in rank to food (i. e. commodities rank second while food is the first among the objects of government). Who then shall not exchange for it (money) the wealth he possesses, as it is of the first necessity in daily use?

If the people are induced to occupy their (best) strength in making money, this interferes with the exercise of the trade by which they ought to live. To oppose this is allowed. At present the husbandman applies himself, heart and soul, to (the cultivation of) grain, the mechanic to his tools, and every one to what pertains to his trade. And where has it been seen that they have devoted their energy to money? For this reason wise princes always took care that a merchandise without utility of itself, was employed to circulate as a treasure which had a utility[2]). The facts that destruction of wealth arising from putrefaction and tearing did not occur, and that the damages caused by the continual passing from one hand to another were slight, were the reasons

1) *Hung-fan* „The great plan", is a chapter of the *Su-king*. (Part V, B IV). 八政 „The eight objects of government", See Legge. Shoo-king page 327. *Kung-lin* means by this that in the ancient times of the *Sang*-dynasty, the currency was already of so much importance to men that among the eight objects of government it ranked next to food, which was first in rank.
2) Utility is here, what is necessary to meet our requirements of daily life. A man can very well live without making use of the metal of which money is made, but without food, he can't go a single day. This again is what our Chinese Economist wants to express by his 用 and 不 用之貨. By making use of an ob-ject of first necessity as grain, to supply the want of a medium of exchange, you are diminishing the store which ought only be to used for food. Therefore it was a benefit to the people when the wise rulers of antiquity took care that a medium of exchange was made of a material which was of no strict necessity in the requirements of life. The argument was quite right in a country so densely peopled as China, where all that was produced by the soil was consumed by the inhabitants or put in store for coming times of distress. Cf. Matw. IX. 37a. The same idea is expressed by 反以天下有用之物 為無用。in the case mention is made of the adoption of grain as a medium of exchange.

而 兵 所 芝 嚴 制 巧 謂 手 拆 於 代 苦。
然 亂 以 以 刑 薄 僞 幣 耗 甚 衣 不 此
漢 積 省 爲 非 絹 之 著 棄 多 食 可 錢
末 久 刑 用 能 以 人 於 於 又 今 廢 所
是 用 錢 錢 禁 充 以 目 勞 分 者 以
也 之 之 之 也 貧 競 前 毀 以 也 嗣
今 於 不 不 是 魏 濕 故 截 爲 穀 功
既 廢 用 用 以 代 穀 鍾 之 於 貨 帛 龜
用 有 由 豐 以 以 緜 用 商 則 本 貝。
而 由 於 國 司 制 要 曰 之 販 致 充 歷

that the successive dynasties did not think it right to abolish the
copper money which succeeded to the suitable tortoise shells and
cowries (the primitive medium of exchange)[1]). Grain and silks are
the materials by means of which clothing and food are procured,
now when they are torn to pieces to be employed as a medium of
exchange, those silks will get damaged in no slight degree, and in the
hands of the merchants it (the grain) will get spoiled, and by (being
so) torn up and divided (both) will diminish in value, and finally be
destroyed, and this might be called to draw upon one's self a wretched
condition while one saw it with open eyes. It was therefore, that the
mint-master *Yiŭ* said that cunning people and cheats immoderately
moistened the grain to make profit by it, and fabricated a thin and
sleazy silk in order to increase their riches.

Under the *Wei*-dynasty (it was tried) to restrain (such offenders) by
severe punishments; yet the evil could not be sufficiently checked. For
this reason it was that *Sze-ma-tsi* thought that by employing money
again, the country would not only prosper but the number of punishments would greatly decrease.

The non-employment of money has sometimes been the result of the
confusion of war. The fact that (money) which had been long in use,
has been drawn back with a view to abolish it, has also occurred,
among others at the close of the *Han*-dynasty. But if the money is

1) Without the rhetorical inversion the phrase would run as follows. 歷代不可廢錢。所以嗣功龜貝。以其既無毀敗之費。又無省運致之苦一。嗣 Jap. ツグ。カサチル, is to heap the one on the other, to succeed, to continue. — 功 adjective attributive of 龜貝.

於 錢 況 之 之 據 而 棄 道¹ 相 或 度 廢
人。廢 又 怨 處 今 饑 物。資 倉 天 之。
乃 用 錢 惑。不 用 困。寶 通 庫 下 則
舉 穀。便 語 為 錢 是 假 則 充 之 百
朝 四 於 曰。富 之 此 有 於 錢。溢。穀 姓
大 十 穀 利 又 處 斷 錢 一 貧 或 以 頓
議。年 也。不 人 不 之 無 朝 者 周 亡
精 矣。魏 百 習 為 又 粮 斷 仰 靡 天 其
才 以 明 不 不 貧 立 之 之 富。下 下 利。
達 不 帝 易 來 用 弊 人 致 斗 之 今
政 便 時。業。久。穀 也。皆 便 之 儲。既

abolished now, after it has been in circulation, the people will suddenly
lose all their profit. As till now the grain (produced) in the empire
was weighed in order to circulate as food for the whole empire, some
store-houses are overflowing, while the store-houses of others do not
contain a single measure of provisions. Now if this is to circulate
as currency, the poor will be entirely dependent (lit. will have to look
up to) on the rich. Such a manner of acting is moreover wrong in
relation to the existing copper money. If it is abolished all at once
(lit. at a single morning), you cause the articles (which till now were
money), to be put aside, and this again causes the people who have
money but no stores of grain, to be in want and distress. Besides,
the abolishment will also give rise to trouble and mischief. It is moreover a convincing proof (against the proposed measure) that in the districts where at present money (as a medium of exchange) is used, no
poverty prevails, while in places where grain is used there is no wealth.
Also have the people long since learned to suspect and dislike sudden
changes. The proverb says: "When the profits do not amount to 100
per cent, I do not throw up (lit. change) my employment." Finally,
money is also much more convenient than grain. In the time of the
emperor *Ming-ti* of *Wei* (227—240 A. D.) the copper money was
abolished and grain was used (as a medium of exchange), I believe[2]), for
forty years. As it proved to be inconvenient to the people, a great council was assembled at court. Of all the superior talents and eminent
scholars who informed the government of their advice, there was not
one who was not of opinion that the use of money should be reverted

1). Cf. St. Julien. Syntaxe Nouvelle I, p. 80.    2) 矣.

之士。莫不以宜復用錢。下無異情。朝無異論。彼尚捨穀帛而用錢。足以明穀帛之弊。著於已誡也。愚謂救弊之術。無取於廢錢。朝議多同琳[1]之。故玄議不行。

to again. On the side of the people there was a general desire of it, and at the court the majority pleaded for it. The fact that all those wished to do away with grain and silks, and again to introduce the copper money (as a medium of exchange) is sufficient to set forth the unsuitableness of grain and silks. Agreeably to that precept of warning we must act. It would be stupid to say this unsuitableness might be made up by an artifice; better it is not to proceed to the abolishment of the money. The council assembled at court for the greater part agreed to (*Kung*)-*lin's* opinion and so it happened that *Hwan*-(*hiuen's*) advice was not followed.

The views and arguments of the following speech fully coincide with those of the preceding. Hence we have followed Ma-twan-lin's exemple and inserted it after the plea of *Lin*.

○前涼張軌。太府參軍索輔。言於軌曰。古以金貝皮幣爲貨。息穀帛量度之耗。二漢制五銖錢。通易不滯。晉太始中。河西荒廢。遂不用錢。

In the presence of *Tš'ang-kuei*, the Governor of the province of *Liang-tš'eu*, the officer of public administration *So-fu*, speaking said to him. (lit. to [*Tš'ang*]-*kuei*): "The ancients employed gold, shells, and skin-parcels as medium of exchange, and put an end to the spoiling of grain and silks by the constant weighing and measuring. The two *Han*-dynasties caused the 5 *tšu* pieces to be made and trade was not trammeled by it.

1) 琳之 = 琳之議.

2) 涼 *Liang* was a province in the remotest corner of the N. W. of the empire. *Tš'ang-kuei* is probably one of the governors who at the decline of the *Tsin*-dyn. made themselves independent. On a Chinese map of the empire during the division into N. and S., on the spot where the province of *Liang* is situated, the sentence is found *Tš'ang-kuei* occupied it 據之. Cf. Matw. VIII 37*a* where of *Ši-sze-ming* another rebel, who conquered part of the empire is also said 據 occupied (the Eastern provinces) — 太府參軍 was an officer of public administration. Cf. Morr. 官 137—139.

其 遂 準 軌 濟 宜 亂 .也 .衣 壞 市 數 .裂
利 .大 布 納 通 復 此 今 用 .女 易 縑 匹
行 .用 .之 .變 五 方 中 弊 工 .又 布 以
人 錢 .立 之 銖 .全 州 之 不 難 .旣 爲
賴 錢 制 會 .以 安 .雖 甚 任 徒 壞 .段

When in the beginning of the rule of the *Tsin*-dynasty the country
west of .the (Yellow) river was totally ravaged and cut off from the remaining part of the empire, no money was any longer used there. When
the .closely woven silk and hempen cloth was ripped up to make parts
of it, those pieces were spoiled, and it was difficult to make use
of them in the market. (The result was that) they had destroyed only
the women's labour (the tissue) which was furthermore unfit to be used
as clothing, and the bad .quality (of these stuffs) was excessive.

Though there are at present great disturbances in the provinces in
the middle of the empire, yet these parts are perfectly quiet, it would,
therefore, be reasonable to introduce here again the 5 *tšu* pieces in
order to further the uniformity in the. transactions (i. e. to bring more
uniformity in the commercial intercourse.)"

*Tš'ang-kuei* acted agreeably to this advice. He made it a rule to use.
money equalizing in value those pieces of silk. The money then had an
extensive circulation and the people enjoyed the profits' thereof.

EPOCH OF THE DIVISION BETWEEN SOUTH AND NORTH.

The condition of China during the reign of the *Tsin*-dynasty
was very miserable. Since *Yuen-ti* had removed his residence
to the new. capital, south of the *Yang-tsze-kiang*, the powerful
Tartar chiefs had pursued their conquest in the North, and established themselves in the ancient capital *Tš'ang-ngan*, where they assumed the title of emperor of China. So arose the Northern
Empire.

The southern empire, China proper, was weakened by intestine
war. The last monarchs of the *Tsin*-dynasty had neither the
power nor the ability effectually to oppose the .continual insur-

rections excited by ambitious ministers and chiefs. The minister *Hwan-hiuen* of whom we know that he had tried totally to abolish the money (See p. 66) had already conquered three fourths of the empire, and himself proclaimed Emperor by his army, when he was defeated and murdered by another powerful chief, called *Liü-yü* who as yet had remained faitful to his sovereign. *Liü-yü* restores the dethroned prince to his dignity, but perceiving how totally unfit he was to govern — for *Liu-yü* too was caught by the contagious disease of rebellion — he takes up arms against his master, captures the capital and causes the emperor to be put to death. For a short time an insignificant representative of the *Tsin*-dynasty occupies the throne, but fully convinced of his impotence, and fearful of his life, he abdicates in favor of *Liü-yü*, who now becomes emperor of the Southern Empire and the founder of the *Sung*-dynasty. This division into two empires has continued for above one century and a half, and during that time four different dynasties reigned in the North and five in the South. Ma-twan-liu first treats of the Southern empire, and then of that of the Tartar princes in the North. This part of our chronicle is especially remarkable for the excellent economical theories of money, advanced by the ministers in their memorials presented to the throne, or delivered in the assemblies of the emperor's privy council.

### THE SOUTHERN EMPIRE: THE SUNG-DYNASTY.

From Ma-twan-liu we learn nothing of the monetary system of the first three rulers of the new dynasty, whose reigns together lasted but four years, and as no money indicative of being made during that time is found, we may safely conclude that the emperor *Wen-ti* was the first that cast a currency indicative of that dynasty. In the year 430 he cast copper coins with a raised edge and the design of 4 *tšu*. They were equal in value to the old 5 *tšu* pieces. As these coins were easily to be distinguished from counterfeit and clipped pieces, the profits accruing from the fabrication of false money were very small, and the number of counterfeiters was reduced almost to a minimum. The coins of the next Emperor *Hiao-wu-ti* bore on the obverse the year-name *Hiao-kien* and on the reverse the indication of the value 4 *tšu*, but as it was probably too difficult by the method of casting coins in sand, to make a design on both sides the characters 4 *tšu* of the reverse were soon dropped [1]),

But these coins being the cause that counterfeiting was practised again on a considerable scale, the emperor, grieved thereat, asks the advice of his privy council and the speeches delivered on that occasion are important in many respects.

罪 銅 策 刑。鑄。典。應 將 不 公 貨 徐 尙
爲 贖 合 著 納 收 遵 大 有 私 薄 爰 書.
品。刑。宜 在 贖 銅 式 乏 革 俱 人 議 右
詔 隨 以 往 刊 繕 古 宜 造。弊。貧。曰.丞

The *Šang-šu* and councilor *Sü-yuen* gave his advice and said: "When the money is of a bad quality, the people get poor, and if once there is a general exhaustion, publicly as well as privately, it is too late to be mended. Now as great misery is about to befall us, it is a necessity and a duty, agreeably to the venerable precepts of the ancients, to draw back the copper (in order to) re-cast and better it, and to take ransoms instead of executing the sentences. It is written in the records of days gone by that it is meet to buy off the punishment with copper according to the circumstances of the crime. It is allowed (in the present

---

1) We omit the fragment of Ma-twan-lin VIII 18b—20a as it is rather too long and of little importance. It contains the advice given by a minister to make great coins of a nominal value of double the real, which was not adopted.

可之。所鑄錢形式薄小輪郭不成就於是人間盜鑄者雲起。雜以鉛錫並不牢固。既轉小鑿古錢以取其銅。錢嚴刑。人史官違長。官式。雖其銅。制相係而盜之。鑄彌甚品物免重者貫。人患苦輪者乃加禁斷格。薄小無輪以郭銅悉難得欲時議者又以顏峻曰議者將鑄二銖錢。顏峻曰謂官藏空虛宜更改變。天下銅少宜減錢式以救災

circumstances) to publish that this shall be so in future (in order to come by the necessary copper to cast money).

As the form of the money which is cast is thin and small, and as the raised wheel-shaped edges are not applied, the false coiners among the people spring up like clouds. They mix their false fabrication with lead and iron, consequently those pieces are not firm and solid. Also they clip the old coins to get possession of the copper. And when such money has circulated, though in a small quantity, the official form is lost sight of [2]) and though severe punishments are inflicted to check this, the functionaries and those who hold high offices, and (therefore) escape the punishment for their offense, and those who further belong to it, cast false money in very large quantities.

By reason of this the prices rise all at once and the people taste all the bitterness thereof. Now if you institute a standard coin of the kind (which may circulate as money), the increase of pieces which are either too thin or too small or without the raised edge will entirely be counteracted. At this time one of the councilors wishing to have 2 *tšu* pieces cast, as the transfer of copper was very difficult, *Yuen-siün* said: "Your councilor will think that as the treasury is empty, a change ought to be made in this, and as the quantity of copper in your dominions is small, the form of the money ought to be reduced (diminished) in order to meet the present wretched condition, and to relieve the pitiable people of the country. Indeed it would be stupid (in general) not to adhere to that opinion.

But that unbounded wish to have 2 *tšu* pieces cast renews the

2) Here we have in plain words, the "Theorem of sir THOMAS GRESHAM", that whenever bad money is circulating it drives out the good money. That also in Chinese society good money has not the power of turning out bad money, we have had many opportunities to observe.

弊。賑國吊人。思以謂不然。今鑄
二銖恣欲新細於官無解於乏。
而人姦巧大興天下之貨。將糜
碎至盡空。立嚴禁而利不可復絕。救
不過一二年間。其弊不可復。不
此其有一二也。今鉛¹⁾鑄獲利。得
見其頓得一二倍之理。縱復得懲
此必待彌一二年。又不可二也。人
大錢必之改。兼畏近日新禁。市井
之間必生紛擾。富商得志。貧人
困窮。又不可三也。況又未見其
利而泉弊如此。失筹當時。取諸
百代。上不聽。

subtile (money) in the empire without giving a solution to the miserable condition; on the contrary, by an extraordinary affluence of false coiners among the people, the currency in your empire will be totally debased and the quality will be bad in the extreme. In vain you are laying heavy restrictions, where the profits are so great you will not be able to root out the evil, and within the course of one or two years the condition will be miserable beyond redemption. And this may not happen. This firstly.

At present by melting and casting large profits are made (by the government). But I do not see a reasonable ground to gain at once 100 or 200 per cent, and granted, we shall make such profit, we shall certainly have to await the end of the year (before it is certain that such a profit is made), and that also may not be. This secondly.

The people will impede the change of the large money, and as they will fear that within a short time new restrictions will be issued, this will cause excitement and confusion in the market; the rich merchants will attain their object, and the poor people will be in want and distress. This may not be either. — This thirdly.

Besides, I do not see any profit (in the measure), but only hurtful consequences as those mentioned. Let us then for the present desist from this plan by which we would draw down (upon us) the censure of all generations." The Emperor did not listen to that advice.

The dangers against which the member of the privy council

1) 鉛 is used instead of 鎔.

had so earnestly warned, actually came over the country when the tyrant who is known in history only by the name of *Fei-ti*, "the deposed emperor," caused pieces of 2 *tšu* to be cast. Ma-twan-lin gives in his simple language a glowing picture of all the miseries of that time.

"In the year 465 A. D. the deposed Emperor" cast coins of 2 *tšu*, the design was *King-ho* 景和 (the year-name), the form that of the wheel-shaped small state coin. As soon as a piece was paid and accepted among men, it served for a model to copy. Also the size and thickness were entirely a failure, it was without the surrounding rim, and the pieces which were not filed out or clipped were called fetus (來子 lit. coming children). When they wanted to characterize the very light and thin pieces they called them *Hing-ye* 荇葉 i. e. weed-leaves. In the market they were generally made use of. In the first year of the period *Yung-kwang* (the same year 465), which was the commencement of the destruction of all that was good, they were largely counterfeited; hence there was an inexpressible confusion in the currency. One thousand coins piled together had only a height of three *tsün* (inches). Those corresponding in size to the last mentioned were called goose-eye-coins. 鵝眼錢 and those which were still smaller were called *Yen-hian* 綖環 (little rings of the thickness of a thread)."

商 椈 ．萬 不 手 入
買 斗 錢 ．復 破 水
不 米 不 斷 ．碎 ．不
行 ．一 盈 數 市 沉 ．
萬 ．一 十 井 隨

"If you threw them into the water they did not sink, and in consequence they were broken in the hands. In the market they were no more prohibited. A number of 100.000 of those pieces was no more than one handful; a *teu* (about 10 pints) of rice cost 10.000 coins; trade was brought to a stand-still."

1) See DE CHAUDOIR, Pl. III n°. 27—28.

The tyrant had not yet occupied the throne a single year when the courtiers and people rose in rebellion, and murdered him in his palace. His image was not placed in the ancestral hall.

"Under the reign of his successor *Ming-ti* only the circulation of the goose-eye-coins and of those which were as thin as a thread was prohibited; the rest remained in circulation. False 錢 唯 又 廢 官 coining was suppressed with severity. At 用 普 工。署 the state-offices (the mints) the workmen 古 斷。尋 亦. were dismissed, and soon after, coining was wholly discontinued, and only the different species of money, formerly in use, circulated.

Here end the informations on the money of the Southern *Sung*-dynasty, and the first fragment of Ma-twan-lin now following is a speech delivered by the prime minister of the first Emperor of the next dynasty.

The political history of these days is the same as that of so many other states, ancient and modern, in the lawless and rude times when submission to the sovereign lasted only so long as he had power to enforce his claim. The events which led to the successive changes of dynasty were in every instance the same.

A prince of feeble character, who is only interested in some of his female subjects, and a general who having crushed a rebellion, dethrones his sovereign on his return. Or instead of that general a first minister who in fact is sovereign while his Majesty devotes himself to the internal palace-policy. Such a minister is commonly so taken up with his admirable management of the state affairs that he heaps honors and titles on himself. One day he comes to the knowledge that he descends from an old race of independent vassals, powerful in the days of the *Tšeu*-dynasty, or perhaps earlier; and he thinks it quite in accordance with the venerable tradition of his ancestors to elevate himself to the rank of titular prince of that imaginary territory. A *placet* to that effect is addressed to the emperor who happy to have an opportunity to reward the faithful services of his minister, signs the petition. The first step leading to the imperial dignity is taken.

A short time after, another *placet* is presented, in which the faithful servant requests to be appointed king of the same imaginary kingdom. Again the emperor assents, because he has not the power to refuse. And so the second step is taken.

The third and decisive step is the *coup d'état*; without the knowledge or assent of his sovereign he assumes the title of "Son of heaven" and founds a new dynasty which he names after his imaginary kingdom. The dethroned emperor weeps and laments in his captivity that he should have lived to see that day, — as Chinese history often relates — but, as a rule, he need not complain long of it. His successor furnishes him with the means of making away with himself, and if it is contrary to the dictates of his conscience to take his own life, a kind hand is always ready to ease him of his scruples and to be responsible for the death of his late Majesty.

Such is, in the main, the history of the rise and fall of the four successive dynasties that have ruled over the Southern empire. And as to the condition of the people and the country amidst so many intrigues and court-cabals, the history of those days fully verifies the truth of the Chinese proverb 君臣不信國不安. "*When sincerity is wanting between prince and minister, the kingdom is in disorder.*"

As it would, therefore, be useless, to give a minute account of the political transactions which brought about the changes of dynasties, we shall confine ourselves to what we find recorded of the money under each of the three dynasties.

The speech on the necessity that money should have an intrinsic value, which now follows, may be considered as one of the most excellent models of economical reasoning, which Ma-twan-lin communicates to us in his "Examination," It has, therefore, been given in full.

KUNG-K'AI'S SPEECH.

盗 輕 而 更。之 可 非 貴。被 國 凱 四 ○
鑄 錢 難 弊。不 穀 是 水 之 土 年。齊
爲 弊 用 錢 在 察 穰 天 潦。關 書。奉 高
禍 盜 爲 患 輕 也。賤 下 而 閫。朝 帝
深。鑄。無 難 重 鑄 此 錢 糴 曰。三 請 建
人 而 累。用。屢 錢 不 少。不 歲 吳¹)孔 元

In the 4th year of the period *Kien-yuen* under the reign of the emperor *Kao-ti* of the *Tsi*-dynasty, the *Sang-su Kung-k'ai* very deferentially brought forward a proposition, saying:

The avenues and passes (leading) to the three divisions of the kingdom of *Wu* ¹) have during this year been covered with showers of rain, and consequently the purchase of grain cannot be dear ²). It is a fact that in the empire money is scarce, but it is not true that grains are cheap ³). Now this ought to be further inquired into (lit. this may not be left without inquiry). The wretched condition of the present cast money is chiefly to be attributed to the repeated alterations in the weight. The heavy currency excites discontent and is inconvenient in use, and that inconveniency in use is the cause that there is but a small quantity on hand. The light currency is of a bad quality, and is frequently coun-

1) 三 吳 Cf. Mayers. 11. 72.

2) The fields have been fertile, the harvest cannot therefore be poor.

3) He means: The harvest being abundant, the prices of grain might reasonably be expected to be low; yet the reverse happens. But the reason of this must not be sought in the want of grain, but in the condition of the medium of exchange. The currency is scarce, and besides of a bad quality. Hence the dearness of food.

所盜鑄。嚴法不禁者。由
上鑄錢惜銅愛工也。
銅愛工也者。謂錢欲令用
之器以通交易省務而易令
輕而數多。使省工而易
成。不詳慮其患也。漢
鑄五銖錢制度有廢與
百餘年。制錢其輕重與
不變五銖者其為輕重
得貨之宜也。以其輕重可
錢府方督貢金。大與鎔置
鑄重錢五銖一依漢法。
府庫以實。國用有儲。乃

terfeited, and its being debased is the cause that misery is deep. (The fact) that false coiners are not restrained by severe. laws, results from the way in which the money is cast on the part of government. Government is too sparing of the copper and grudges [1]) the expenses consequent upon the mechanical process. They who act up to such principles have a notion of money without (heeding its character as) an instrument in daily use to further exchange. Their purposes and desires are merely to make the pieces light and as numerous as possible. They take care that the mechanical process is as simple as possible, and the fabrication of the pieces easy; but they do not think and consider what are the fatal consequences of it [2]). Since the princes of the *Han*-dynasty have cast the 5 *tsu* pieces till the time of the emperor *Wen-ti* of the *Sung*-dynasty, more than 400 years have elapsed. In the way in which the money was fabricated, changes were frequently made (lit. there was abolishing and introducing), but the pieces kept their value of 5 *tsu*. And by adhering to that weight they could keep the fitness of a medium of exchange. By establishing mint-colleges and by taking care that the metal is of a superior quality, and by building on an extended scale founderies for casting money, while the money has a weight of 5 *tsu*, we will entirely act according to (those) rules of the *Han*-dynasty. Because the treasury will be well-stocked there will be

---

1) 愛 to grudge, See MENCIUS I. part 1. VII. 5. Dr. LEGGE, Chinese Classics II. p. 15.

2) The words with which that noble and intelligent Chinese minister so freely censures the uneconomical principles of the emperor's government are on a level with the following passage quoted from Prof. W. STANLEY JEVONS' latest work, Money and the Mechanism of Exchange, page 59. "*Ruding is then unquestionably right in saying that our efforts should be directed not so much to the punishment of the crime (of counterfeiting) as to its prevention by improvements in the art of coining. We must strike our coins so perfectly, that successful imitation or alteration shall be out of the question.*"

Admirable is also *Kung-k'ai's* definition of a currency as "the instrument in daily use to further the exchange.

量俸祿薄賦稅。則家給人  
足。頃盜鑄新錢也者皆效作  
已。布莭鑿。不鑄大錢也。若官錢小  
輕破於人使嚴斷莭鑿。官得小  
行。官錢缺無小周郭者。悉不塞兩。  
銷以爲大。利小貧民稱合之銖  
姦巧之路。大錢貨既均人。近  
則一。百姓樂業。市道無爭。  
衣食滋殖矣。時議者以爲  
錢貨輻小。宜更廣鑄。重其  
鈇兩。以防人姦。上乃使諸  
州大市銅。會上崩乃止。武

enough for the wants of the empire, if the salaries are liberal, and the duties and taxes small, the common people have enough to supply the necessities of their families. If there are for a time false coiners who imitate the new money, they cast no great coins but imitate the clipped pieces. And as then the (really good) state-money already circulates among the people, severe restrictions must be made against all coin that shall be clipped, too little or too small, cracked or without raised edge, so that (the false pieces) cannot circulate at all. And if the state money will have become small (in consequence of being clipped or worn), it must be weighed by *tsu* an *liang* (ounces) [1]) and melted to be made into great coins again. This is profitable to the poor and well-to-do, and the ways of the rascals and cunning are obstructed by it (i. e. false coining is made impossible). In the medium of exchange there will be a perfect uniformity and what is employed far off as well as near (the capital) is of the same sort. The people take pleasure in their occupations; in the markets and on the roads there arise no quarrels, and clothing and food are produced in abundance. Now your councilor is of opinion that as the quantity of the circulating medium is small, it is right to mint again a large quantity, and to take care that the pieces have their full weight, in order to prevent in this way the false coiners. And if the emperor takes care that copper is on hand in the great markets of all the districts, cabals (intending) the emperor's fall then cease [2]).

---

1) It is then no more used as money but according to its weight (*tsu* and *liang*), it is transferred and drawn back by the government in order to be recast.

2) 崩 has here an uncommon signification. Generally it means the death of the emperor; in my opinion it is here taken in the more general meaning of the emperor's fall; according to WILLIAMS it means also fall, ruin.

聊 鞭 兩 所 鑿 有 百 機 檽 觸 賤 土 帝
捶 代 受 解 由 所 杼 艱 貏 類 殆 表 時
質 一 必 復 人 以 勤 劬 莫 欲 日 竟
縶 困 須 完 間 然 苦 斜 不 兼 頃 陵
益 於 圓 者 錢 者 匹 直 知 倍 錢 王
致 無 大 公 多 寶 繰 數 茲 凡 貴 子
無 所 以 家 亦 三 千 稼 在 物 良

In the time of the emperor *Wu-ti* of the *Han*-dynasty (140 B. C.) *Ling-wang-tsze* deferentially offered a memorial in which was said.

"At present money is dear, and commodities are cheap and the dangerous desire to make a profit of 100 percent is the result thereof that we are pushing our horns against that which is good. Who does not know the hardships of sowing and reaping, and yet the value of a bushel of grain is but 1000 copper-pieces; who does not know the toil of the loom and spool, and yet a piece of silk has hardly a value of 300 copper-pieces. And in this must the reason be found that the money circulating among the lower classes is so frequently clipped. If it is thought desirable to make an end of such a condition for good and all, care must be taken that the money generally received shall be round and great. To receive back only one piece for the value of two pieces is more painful than being beaten with a whip and cudgel, or being imprisoned without knowing why. Even more than this (the grief at such a treatment), it makes that nothing is (henceforth) to be relied on [1])".

### THE LIANG AND TSAN-DYNASTIES.

In the beginning of the reign of the *Liang*-dynasty, money was so scarce that it was employed only in the capital and its immediate vicinity. The merchants who carried on an extensive trade with distant countries employed exclusively gold and silver bullion as medium of exchange.

The emperor *Wu-ti* supplied this deficiency of money by casting large quantities of all sorts of coins which, however, differed

1) 因於 comparative — 無所 without knowing the reason why — 質 | 縶 to tie and fasten, to imprison — 聊 *liaó* is used for 憀 of the same sound.

more in names than in value. We shall not follow Ma-twan-lin's account of the names, dimensions and weights of all these sorts, as those particulars have little interest if they do not contain some curious phrase or historical allusion, which requires to be elucidated.

Of one of those sorts of money is told that it was commonly called boy's money 男錢, as the people believed that a woman who carried this money about her, would be delivered of a boy. 云婦人佩之。郎生男也。

In the period of 520—27 the plan was suggested to supersede the copper money by iron money, in order to put an end to the speculations of some cunning traders who, taking advantage of the circulation of so many various sorts of copper money nearly equal in value, sought to make profit by continually exchanging one sort for another [1]). But now there arose another difficulty. Every one could easily get iron; and as the government itself could not resist the temptation to make large profits by the casting of money, false coining was greatly promoted; so that, when that iron money had been in use about ten years the circulating mass of it was like a mountain. 所在鐵錢遂如丘山。

陌。八嶺利。之姦貫。而復載者貴。物
名十以自以作。商誰計錢。以交價
日。爲東。破求因旅論數。不車易騰

The prices of all commodities rose rapidly. Henceforth exchange was effected by cart-loads of money without caring for the number (of the coins), and who quarrelled for a single string of 1000 pieces? Travelling merchants and rascals (imposed upon the people, and) with the purpose of gaining profit, they made their way through the mountain-passes into the East, where they brought them in the market at 80 per cent. The name was Eastern money. In *Kiang-Ying* [2]) they were worth 70

---

1) In the Vth Chapter the disadvantages of a double standard in China will be treated of.
2) *Kiang-ying* is the ancient name of the district of *Kiang-ling* 江陵 in *Hing-t'cu-Fu* province of *Hu-nan*.

五　年。盒　人　足　子　大　陌。師　名　土。東
爲　遂　多　不　陌。乃　同　名　以　曰。七　錢。
陌。以　至　從。詔　詔　元　曰　九　西　十　江
三　于　錢　下　通　年。長　十　錢。爲　郡
十　末　陌　而　用　天　錢。爲　京　陌。以

per cent, (and there) they were called Western money. In the capital they had still a value of 90 per cent, and were called there great money (or long money). In the first year of the period *Ta-Tung* (525) the emperor decreed that they should be in general circulation at the full amount of 100 per cent. He dictated this to his subjects, but they did not obey. A hundred of these copper coins fell lower and lower, till at the close of that period the worth of a hundred had come down to 35 (or 35 per cent).

In the beginning of the reign of the *Tš'an*-dynasty that ruled the empire after the confusions occasioned by the fall of the *Liang*-dynasty, the iron money did not circulate any longer. The new princes reverted for a short time to the old 5 *tšu* pieces which, measured against the still circulating goose-eye-coins had a relative value of 1 to 10. Another ruler of the same dynasty again committed the folly to introduce pieces of the weight of 6 *tšu* and a nominal value of fifty 5 *tšu* pieces. But soon the relative value was changed, so that they circulated together with the 5 *tšu* pieces at the same rate. As to this money Ma-twan-lin adds:

亡。行　崩。之　錢　與　人
五　遂　象。有　訛　皆
銖。廢　未　不　言　不
竟　六　幾　利　曰　便
至　銖　而　縣　六　乃
陳　而　帝　官　銖　相

The people did not think them convenient, and they told one another the false rumor that the 6 *tšu* pieces had not graced the image of the emperor. When shortly afterwards, the emperor died, the 6 *tšu* pieces were done away with for good, and the 5 *tšu* pieces continued to circulate till the end of the *7šan*-dynasty.

1) 盒多 worse and worse.

In the Northern empire the Tartar chiefs *Topa* had etablished themselves, and gradually had they modelled their policy on that of the conquered people who were their superiors in civilization.

One of their institutions was the casting of money which bore the characters *Ta-ho* (lit. great harmony) for its device; but, says the chronicle, "nowhere did it occur that it was employed".

For a long time the want of money seems to have been very slight, for Ma-twan-lin passes a period of eighty years without so much as touching upon the subject. During this time barter was the only means by which business was transacted, which is evident from a decree, issued by his Tartar Majesty *Hiao-wu-ti*, deciding that money should be used in his

錢 給 祿 內　empire and that the salaries of all the state-
二 錢 皆 外　officers should be reckoned by it at this rate
百 匹 準 官　that 200 pieces of copper money equalled a
爲 絹　piece of silk.

This decree was attended with the remarkable circumstance that the coining of money did not, as usual, become a preroga-

無 銅 就 人　tive of the crown, but that the people when-
所 必 聽 有　ever they wished to have money cast might
和 精 鑄 欲　go with their copper to the State-mint to
雜 鍊 之 鑄　have it coined; consequently the money was

made of pure metal and so it did not occur that it was either debased or mixed. This money had again the standard-legend of the Chinese coins, 5 *tsu*.

Notwithstanding all this the people had a dislike to money and did not want to use it in their dealings. Hence it is, that some privy councilors persuaded his Majesty to enforce the use of money as a medium of exchange, though they were of opinion that it should be left to the people what pieces they thought fit for this purpose. And says one of them: "The same money will not do for the different parts of the kingdom, for in the South and East money is a great convenience to the people, as they have employed it there already in former times; but in the high North, as for instance, in *Peking*, the Northern Capital, and in the far off districts and free states, where, till this day, no money is used, you cannot manage this affair in the same way, but it will be necessary gradually to accustom the people to it. The profit connected with the use of metallic money, compared with the simple mode of bartering goods, is indeed so great that it must be obvious to the people as soon as they can be gradually brought to employ it."

I may be allowed to quote a little fragment in which the excellence of the money as a medium of exchange is explained, if it were only to complete what elsewhere has been said on the same subject (page 67).

| | | | | | | | | | | | |
|---|---|---|---|---|---|---|---|---|---|---|---|
| 大 | 外 | 新 | 方 | 於 | 濟 | 不 | 不 | 爲 | 貞 | 而 | 布 |
| 小 | 全 | 鑄 | 鎮² | 此 | 代 | 勞 | 假 | 擔 | 裂 | 帛 |
| 悉 | 好 | 并 | 其 | 請 | 之 | 秤 | 斗 | 貫 | 之 | 五 | 不 |
| 聽 | 者 | 古 | 太 | 並 | 尺 | 斛 | 繦 | 難 | 穀 | 可 |
| 行 | 不 | 錢 | 和 | 下¹ | 便 | 之 | 之 | 相 | 錢 | 則 | 尺 |
| 之 | 限 | 內 | 及 | 諸 | 益 | 平 | 器 | 屬 | 之 | 有 | 寸 |

If silk is used (as a medium of exchange), it cannot be divided into portions (without spoiling it), and if it is grain, there is the difficulty of transport. If, however, money strung together is used, people have

1) 下 in time, i. e. henceforth.

2) 鎮 name of part of the country, a free-city or palatinate, see WILLIAMS. It frequently occurs in Ma-twan-lin's IXth. Volume.

nothing to do with false measures, or take the trouble to measure the exact number of feet (of the silk pieces) in order to make them fit according to the requirements of exchange. This is much more convenient than the other. So I submit it to your Majesty's consideration henceforth in all parts (of the kingdom) to circulate the *Tai-ho* money as well as the new coined pieces together with the old money, and without paying attention to their size, if they are good, internal and external (i. e. not clipped and not debased).

In the same fragment we find a report of an high functionary on the produce of copper in the different parts of the empire. Here we have an exact statement of the quantity of native copper and copper ore which was dug out of the different mountains and valleys.

The report ends with an urgent appeal to the central government to build founderies for casting money in those places where copper is found, and to submit the coining of money to a strict control. This advice was acted up to, and at the same time severe restrictions and punishments were instituted against false coiners, and rewards were promised to those who informed the government against the offenders.

陳 雍 臣 侃 書 一 斗 水 至 薄 者。初。孝
聽 州。頃 奏 郎 千。幾 浮。風 小。益 私 莊
人 表 在 曰。楊 秘 直 米 飄 乃 更 鑄 帝

In the beginning of the reign of the emperor *Iliao-tswang-ti*, the false coiners augmented again the quantity of debased coins, and it had come so far, that the false coins were whirled by the wind and floated on (the surface of) the water. A measure (*t'eu*) of rice rose to the price of nearly 1000 *cash.* The privy secretary *Yang-K'an* in a memorial to the throne, said as follows: "Your minister resided for a short time in the province of *Yung-tseu* [1]). According to an account (of those regions), the people together with the public functionaries cast 5 *tsu* coins. In order to promote the welfare of the people, that mean and vicious state (of things) ought to be changed". A decree, containing the Emperor's will (on this subject)

1) A province west of the *Hoang-ho* and North of the river *Wei*.

與官並鑄五銖錢。使人樂
為而俗弊得改。昔尚書理
八座不許。臣前今旨昔。下披
不殊。求取宜剖說。帝御為理
析。侃乃隨宜御史中從之。
乃鑄五銖錢。四民之業。尉錢高
恭之又奏曰改鑄王政所錢。
貨之項以本。救弊私鑄薄濫。
先自頃以來非一。在今銅官
司紕緷挂網得銅一斤。私
價八十一文。得銅一斤。
造薄錢斤餘二百。既示之
以深利。又隨之以重刑。得

went down (was handed to the council of the ministers of the crown). But the eight seats (the dignitaries) of the *Šang-šu* (the ministry, central board of administration) did not agree to it (and they expressed as their opinion) that at present one had rather rely on the principles of former times and that it would be sensible not to break with them. They tried to withdraw the imperial consent and decision to the foregoing memorial and proposed arrangement [2]) of the minister (*Yang-K'an*). But as *K'an* thereupon again in a very clever way lay open his arguments, the Emperor followed his advice, and caused the 5 *tsu* pieces to be cast.

On this occasion one of the imperial historiographers *Wei-kao-tien* also offered a memorial to the throne, in which he said: The medium of exchange is the basis (foundation) of business and of the commercial dealings of all nations. To amend a vicious state (of that medium of exchange) by making alterations in the fabrication of money is therefore one of the first duties a king has to perform in his government. During the present time private coining has brought over us a profusion of debased currency, and the officials who have to examine and stop (the circulation of) the bad coins do not suppress or lay hold of a single piece.

The prices of copper are at present such that one gets a pound of copper for 81 *cash*, while they who cast thin coins, make out of a pound more than 200 coins. This already shows how large the profit is. And though they are prosecuted by heavy penalties, and the number

1) 為理 = 當理.

2) 經 a regular series or arrangement.

3) 四民 the four peoples is here nothing but a plural, meaning the nations of the four regions of the earth.

通。刑　潤。料　鑄　小。復　以　切。欲　甚　有　罪
公　廣　直　錫　大　以　改　五　朝　不　榆　五　者
私　設。置。炭　錢。三　五　分　廷　沉。莢。銖　雖
獲　以　無　鉛　銅　錢　錢　失　此　之　之　多。
允。臣　利。沙。價　代　為　之。乃　貲　文。姦
復　測　應　縱　至　輕　小。彼　因　便　而　鑄
遂　之。自　復　賤。也。半　改　循　破。無　者
用　必　息　私　論　今　兩。復　有　置　二　彌
王　當　心。營　其　據　此　何　漸。之　銖　衆。
侃　錢　況　不　中　古。鑄　罪。科　水　之　今
計。貨　復　能　人　宜　四　至　防　上。實。錢
　　永　嚴　自　功　改　易　孝　武　不　殆　薄　徒

of those who incur punishment is large, the false coiners are still excessive in quantity. The money at present in use has only the device of 5 *tšu*, but it has not 2 *tšu* real worth, the pieces are as thin as elm-leaves, and if the best string extant is cut asunder and the coins thrown on the surface of the stream, they have hardly any inclination to sink.

Now this is the result of following the old way (lit. an existing stream). The supervisors who ought to provide against it, don't suppress it, and your Majesty's government loses sight of it. But in what degree are those (supervisors) to be blamed for it?[1]) In former times the emperor *Han-Wen-ti* diminished the money by one fifth (of its value) and had the pieces of 4 *tšu* cast. *Hiao-Wu-ti* changed these again for 3 *tšu* pieces and made half ounces of them Now all these princes converted the great currency into smaller kinds, and heavy money into light. And now it is argued that the present ought to be modelled upon the past, and that it is, therefore, allowable to make a change in the great currency.

Now when the price of copper is extremely low, the cunning among the people engross the raw materials, as tin, charcoal, lead, and fine sand, and in a pleasant way they find in false coining a means of subsistence for themselves. And if the result is that they cannot enrich themselves by it, they have simply undertaken something that yields no profit, and therefore without more thought about (the matter)

---

1) The cunning imperial historiographer expresses himself here very diplomatically. He dares not say, "to what extent is the imperial government to be blamed," and therefore mentions only the state-comptrollers, but from the sequel it appears very clearly that it was a home-thrust intended for his Majesty.

they will give it up, and that so much the more when severe punishments are largely instituted against it. If your servant is to give his opinion (lit. to sound) on this matter, it will positively be this, that the medium of exchange must continue to circulate, and that the money received by the State as well as by private persons be true and good. It is, therefore, desirable to act up to the plan suggested by *Wang-k'an.*

Now while several influential officers advice the Emperor to introduce again the 5 *tšu* pieces, there is an old servant who with all due respect and deference repairs to court, and offers a memorial in which he requests in a very pressing way to have the 3 *tšu* cast again, as in his opinion the 5 *tšu* pieces are too large to be used as a single and indivisible medium of exchange. He describes a great many facts in the ancient and modern history of China, to prove that the value of the money was always regulated with respect to the wants of the time being. The peroration of the piece is really so eloquent that, on reading it, one is inclined to forget that those opinions were delivered in the year 528 A. D., at the court of a Tartar prince in North China.

Having adduced his historical arguments, he thus continues: ·

不 也。何 何 可 則 軍 人 州 冠 而 莫 輕
以 且 妨 損 以 鑄 國 物 郡 難 變。不 重
錢 政 於 於 富 小 用 渝 未 況 隨 大
大。與 人 政。益。錢。少。沒。零。除。今 時 小。

"There is not a single piece, be it light or heavy, great or small, that has not undergone a change in the lapse of time. And in the present circumstances, now the disturbances of the (yellow) caps have not been crushed, while whole provinces and districts are ruined and the riches of the people are as scattered leaves, now the wants of the army and country are few, the casting of little money may contribute so much the more to an increase of wealth. And what injury will this cause to the government and what impediments to your people? Moreover the flourishing state of a reign is not the result of the money being large of size, no more than the decay of a reign can be attributed to the money being small of size; if only that which is received in public as well as in private (dealings) has a real value (i. e. if only the

卒。之。其 之 任 乏。請 於 古。臄。得 小。政
事 益。無 使 五 鑄 今 亦 既 所。唯 衰
未 詔 損。並 銖 以 矣'。宜 行 政 貴 不
就 將 國 用。之 濟 臣 效 之 化 公 以
會 從 得 行 錢。交 今 之 於 無 私 錢

intrinsic value is looked to) the government can change (the outward
form), without causing any trouble. With the ancients this was
practised already, and it would also be very proper, this should be
imitated by the present generation [1]). Your minister (the minister is
here *K'an*) now proposes, for the sake of the commercial intercourse
as well as to relieve the want (of your people), to have 5 *tšu* pieces
cast. If that plan is adopted, the 5 *tšu* and the 3 *tšu* pieces may
be in use at the same time, and this can be without any loss,
(on the contrary) the country will enjoy the advantages thereof". The
Emperor declared (his readiness) to act up to that advice, but (said)
that the affair could not at once be brought to a final decision.

So in the year 529 a decree was issued that the 5 *tšu* pieces
should be cast; of the 3 *tšu* pieces, however, no mention is made.
When afterwards the government wanted to know what the money
was worth, pieces of silk, representing a worth of 200 good
copper coins were taken from the treasuries. State-officials were
then sent to the different markets in the country to sell them
there. In some markets, says our author, those silks were sold
for 300 copper coins, and this was not because in those places
such silks were higher valued, but because the money was debased [2]).

1) Again an instance of what is said on
the force of the final particle 矣.

2) It is remarkable indeed that we find
also here an attempt to resolve a question
of Political Economy which for all times
has been discussed over and again by European Economists. Adam smith and after
him many other authors have sought for a
general measure by which the value of different commodities of all times and all
places might be compared. Smith after long
considerations adopted labour, and among

commodities, corn, the article most generally consumed, as such a common standard.
Now we see here that the Chinese used
silks to ascertain the value of money, as
they presume that silks at all places will
have a same value.
Cf. Adam smith, Wealth of Nations. Book
I. Chapt. V. Michel chevalier la monnaie.
Sect. II. Chap. II—V. Prof. t. m. c. asser,
Verhandeling over het begrip der Waarde
passim and page 282—287. Dr. s. van
houten, Verhandeling over de waarde,
page 129—139.

Herewith we are at an end of Ma-twan-lin's informations as
to the Northern *Wei*-dynasty,

## THE NORTHERN TSI-DYNASTY

In the North we now see the same drama acted that in the
South already so often and so successfully had been represented.
The prime minister, after having obtained the title of king of
*Tsi*, dethrones the last emperor of the *Wei*-dynasty, and is the
founder of a new imperial line known under the name of the
Northern *Tsi*-dynasty. As to the currency during its reign, the
money of the *Wei's* continued to be used, but as it was not in
sufficient quantities existant to meet the general want, several
functionaries began to make their own money which generally was
named after the district, were it was circulating. The effect of
this unwholesome condition was that all sorts of bad money arose.
For this reason, after having drawn back all copper money as
much as possible, the emperor caused it to be cast into 5 *tšu*
pieces, and to prevent the use of false money in the markets
there was a balance placed at the entrance of every market-
place, in the capitals as well as in the provinces and principalities, and every private person who used scales in the market,
was obliged to have them verified by the government standard
balance. Assizement thus took place.

A hundred copper pieces of 5 *tšu* were to have a weight of
1 pound, 4 ounces and 20 *tšu* (i. e. 500 *tšu*) in order to be
employed as a medium of exchange in the market; and money
greatly adulterated might not be used. One great advantage of
this measure was, according to the Chinese chronicles, that every
individual could now make money, if he liked; for provided his

pieces had the standard weight and quality, they were current in the market.

Another particular illustrating the despotic government of those times may not be omitted.

私 銅 止。惡 二 而
鑄 償。乃 雖 年 ·私
少 由 令 殺 間 鑄
止。此 市 戮 郡 巳
　　 利 增 不 有 與。
　　 薄。長。能 濫 一

. Notwithstanding the measures just mentioned the false coiners did not remain idle, and they seemed to carry on such a flourishing trade that their worthless coins overwhelmed the country. Many a one was put to death for the offence but it was impossible to suppress the evil, and then it was that the emperor ordered to enhance the prices of copper in the market, and as consequently the profits became less, the false coiners discontinued their occupation for a while.

What follows on the monetary institutions of the Northern *Tsi*-dynasty, is of little interest. Equally uninteresting is the subsequent history of the Northern *Tšeu*-dynasty. The only fact worth mentioning is, that under that dynasty the gold and sil-

而 金 或 河
官 銀 用 西
不 之 西 諸
禁。錢。域 郡。

ver coins current among the barbarous tribes of the far West were made use of in the provinces of China, west of the *Hoang-ho*, and that the public functionaries did not prevent it. What pieces they were is described by Ma-twan-lin in a note borrowed from the *Han-šu* (the annals of the *Han*-dynasty). As this note contains some linguistic difficulties, I have added the Chinese text to the translation, and have tried to explain its meaning as much as possible.

大月氏亦同鑄。　面。王死郎更人　王面。幕爲夫爲　以銀爲錢文亦　釋其仄。安息銀　爲騎馬加金幕　同。之錢與人頭國　也。烏弋山燕國　人面。其郎漫　文面。其騎馬幕爲　賓國以銀爲錢。　漢書西域傳。剼

In the Annals of the *Han*-dynasty, the chronicles having reference to the Western foreign regions, (is reported) that in the country of *Ki-pin* the coinage is made of silver. On the obverse is the design a man on horseback, on the reverse is the face of a man, but what properly makes the coin is the reverse. The money of the kingdom of *Yen* of *Wu-yi-šan* is similar to that of the country of *Ki-pin*; on the obverse there is the head of a man, on the reverse a horseman. Besides the sourrounding rim is left away in those gold and silver coins. In the country of the *Ngan-si* (the Parths) they make also their currency of silver, on the obverse is the face of the king, on the reverse is the face of a lady. When the king dies the coins are recast. In the kingdom of the *Ta-yue-ši* (the Scyths) it is just the same.

As the Chinese reader will be aware, a great many difficulties present themselves in this little fragment. *Ki-pin*, is *Cophine* or *Kaboul* a part of *Persia* in *Afganistan*. — 幕 taken in the meaning of the reverse of a coin, is not to be found in any Chinese dictionary, but the Japanese dictionary 字林 玉篇 *in voce* 幕 gives the explanation: *zeni-no ura* ゼニノ ウラ, the backside or reverse of a coin. — The phrase 其 止郎漫.也 is difficult to explain. 漫 is here also a technical term signifying the same as 幕, which appears from a sentence in another work in which also the coinage of foreign countries is treated of, and which was kindly lent to me by Prof. G. SCHLEGEL at *Leiden*. In this work entitled 格致鏡原 Vol. 35. page 18*b*, the following information is quoted. "*Tš'ang-yen* says:

目 漫 面 張　On the obverse of the coin, the figure of a
也。面 作 晏　horseman is made, on the reverse (*mo-mien*)
幕 作 騎 曰　is the effigy of a man. 漫 has here the same
音 人 馬 錢　sound as 幕 *mo*." But now that the meaning
漫。面 形。文　of that character is clear, 止 presents difficulties, it may be either 正, the real, the right side, or 址
the foundation; and we may translate: "what properly
makes the coin is the reverse," because the face of the
reigning sovereign is engraved thereon.

What is meant with the country of *Yen* 燕 of *Wu-yĭ-šan*
烏弋山 I don't know. The book above mentioned speaks of the
country of *Li* 離 instead of 燕國. As the coins bear the same
design as those of Kaboul, it is most likely another part of
Persia[1]). — 安息 are the Parths. — 大月氏 the Getae or
Scyths. Among the coins of Parthia, which are in the numismatical cabinet of the Leiden University, I have not found a
silver coin, answering to the description of our Chinese informant.

In professor GEORGE RAWLINSON's work "The sixth great
Oriental Monarchy, or Geography, History and Antiquities of Parthia, London 1873. p. 220, an illustration is given
of a coin struck during the reign of Phraataces, king of Parthia,
who reigned at the time of the emperor Augustus. On the reverse
of that coin he placed the effigy of his concubine *Mousa*, an
Italian woman offered to him as a present by Augustus. As
Prof. RAWLINSON observes 1° that that sovereign departed from the
practice of all former Parthian kings in placing her effigy on his
coins, and 2° that none of the other coins of later monarchs, of which
copies are found in the mentioned work, bear the design of a

1) See Addenda.

female head, it is most likely the coins of king Phraataces which are alluded to in the *Han-šu*. It also very well agrees with the time, as the *Han-*dynasty, in the annals of which thòse informations are found, reigned 200 B. C.—190 A. D. The legend around the head of the Parthian courtisane is a proof of her lord's fondness. It runs ΜΟΤΣΗΣ ΒΑΣΙΛΙΣΣΗΣ ΘΕΑΣ ΟΤΡΑΝΙΑΣ (Musa, the queen and heavenly goddess).

We silently pass the introduction of all sorts of coins bearing such grand inscriptions, as "the eternal money circulating throughout all countries," 永通萬國錢 and "the money of the five elements, spreading in great abundance;" 五行大布錢, their feeble metallic value was the cause that their little course was soon run. Specimens of these pieces may be seen in DE CHAUDROIR and in several Musea.

Of little importance to our subject is also the history of the *Suy-*dynasty. For though under this race of kings the two parts of China were consolidated again to one empire, the realm was in such a deplorable state of anarchy and confusion that to attend to the economical and commercial interests of the people was a thing quite out of question. And if some good measure was taken, the false coiners soon rendered it ineffectual. Two efforts to prevent the circulation of bad money are found in Ma-twan-lin's "Examination" Vol. 30 *a—b.*

乃 銅 壞 同 過．然．檥 外 檥．百 關．四 三
下 入 以 者．檥 後 相 來．從 錢 各 面 年．
惡 官．爲 則 不 得 似．勘 關 爲 付 諸 詔

In the third year (583) an order was issued that on the four fronts of the entrances to the market should be a specimen of a string of 100 cash, as these should be, in order to be transferred to another (to be legal

錢之禁。京師及諸州肆之上。皆令立榜置於樣。不中樣者不入於市爲准。十八年中詔漢王諒置十鑪鑄錢於并州。又江南人間錢少。晉王廣以為請於鄂州白紵山有銅鑛處鑄錢。詔聽之。於是詔立五鑪鑄錢。又詔蜀王秀聽於益州立五鑪鑄錢。是時錢益濫惡。乃令有司檢天下邸肆見錢。非官鑄者皆毀之。其銅入

tender). And on coming forth again through the entrances, people were obliged to see whether the money they carried about them agreed with the specimen, and then they got leave to pass on. The money which did not agree with the specimen was broken, and (lit. to make that) the copper was confiscated by the government.

Besides the restrictions on the bad money, it was regulated that over every lodging-house or shop in the capital as well as in the provinces, a list should be nailed up containing a specimen (of the coins) which were permitted (to be used), and that the pieces not coming up to that specimen should not be received in the market.

In the 18th year (598) (the emperor) ordered *Liang*, prince of *Han* to build five money-founderies in *Hing-tseu*. Also in *Kiang-nan* there circulated too little money among the people. *Kwang*, prince of *Tsin* then proposed to his Majesty to have money cast also in *Ngo-tseu*[2]), where at some places in the "White-hempen mountains" copper ore was found. His Majesty then ordered to build there ten money-foundaries. Further, he ordered *Siu*, prince of *So* to build five money-foundaries in the province of *Yik-tseu*[3]). Now, as at that time the money increased (in quantity), and as there came an abundance of bad money in circulation, he ordered the officials charged with this (duty) to exercise a strict control over the ready money[1] in the inns and shops of the whole empire, and to break all that was no state-money, and to confiscate

1) 見錢 is used here for the first time by Ma-twan-lin. It means visible, real, tangible money in contradistinction to the unvisible, imaginary paper-money which during the author's life in such large quantities circulated. This is evident from the antithesis of 見錢 and 飛錢 frequently occurring in the history of paper-money. In *K'ang-hi* and after him in all European dictionaries ready money is the only meaning given — 見 is used for 現 *hien*, meaning to appear, to be seen, *de facto*.

2) A principality on the *Yang-tsze-kiang*, prov. of *Hu-pe*.

3) A province in *Sse-ts'uen*, its old name was *So*.

官。而京師以惡錢
貿易。爲吏之所執。有
死者。數年之間。私
鑄頗息。大業以後。私
王綱弛紊。臣姦轉大
猾。遂多私鑄錢。
薄惡。每千宜重二
斤。後漸輕至一斤。
或以剪鐵鑱裁衣糊
紙以爲錢。相雜用
之。貨賤爲錢。物貴以
於亡。

the copper obtained in that way; and those who carried on their trade in the capital with bad money, and were detected in the act by the functionaries, were put to death.

So, for a great number of years, false coining diminished a little. But after the period *Ta·ye* (605—617), when the royal tie which held society together got loose and ravelled, and even state-ministers were false coiners and great rascals, counterfeiting at last increased so much, and the money which circulated, got so thin and bad, that 1000 pieces (originally) equal in weight to 2 pounds, gradually got so much lighter that they came down to a weight of 1 pound. Some cut little pieces of iron from their ploughshares, or they cut up clothes and paste-board to make money thereof, and promiscuously they employed all this. (The consequence was) that money was cheap and merchandise (goods) dear, and this lasted till the end of the dynasty (618).

The fall of the *Suy*-dynasty was near at hand. Taking advantage of the disturbed state of the country, *Li-yuen*, titular duke of *T'ang* drove away the reigning monarch, and founded the great *T'ang*-dynasty. His descendents ruled China for nearly two centuries.

# CHAPTER IV.

## HISTORY OF THE MONEY UNDER THE T'ANG-DYNASTY.

KAI-YUEN-T'UNG-PAO-MONEY. — ORIGIN OF THE NAIL-MARK ON THE REVERSE OF THAT COIN. — OPINION OF LATER TIMES. — FRAGMENTS OF THE ANNALS OF FALSE COINING. — FREE COINING DISCUSSED AGAIN. — THE ANNALS OF FALSE COINING CONTINUED. — REPORTS OF THE COLLECTORS OF SALT AND IRON-DUTY. — APPARITION OF PAPER-MONEY. — TYRANNICAL MEASURES TO OBTAIN THE NECESSARY COPPER. — RESTRICTIONS ON THE POSSESSION OF READY MONEY. — MA-TWAN-LIN'S CRITICISM. — BUDDHA RELIGION LAID UNDER REQUISITION AND FINALLY ABOLISHED IN ORDER TO CONFISCATE THE COPPER VESSELS OF MONASTERIES AND TEMPLES.

A better and brighter day dawned upon the Chinese empire with the accession of the *T'ang*-dynasty. The first emperors were energetic men, full of that spirit which animated the princes of high antiquity, a spirit which we learn from the writings of the philosophers and from the books which record the sacred history of old China. Many improvements, both political and social, they accomplished, and their best cares were devoted to the welfare of the country and the people.

Among the decisive measures which wrought a change in the wretched condition resulting from a maladministration and confusion of a long series of years, one of the first was to make a change in the currency. The 5*tšu* pieces which had been the standard coin for more than eight centuries, were held in such contempt that it was impossible even to retain the name; a coin entirely new was instituted bearing the legend of *Kai-yuen-t'ung-pao*, or current money of the newest beginning [1]). According to the testimony of many writers of different times, this money was uncommonly good, and it may safely be considered the best coin issued in the course of many centuries. The history of its rise, the importance which it has had, and the opinion on it of later generations, have again been related in the words of our Chinese authorities, and this time also there will be ample opportunity to give many an explanatory note on Ma-twan-lin's text.

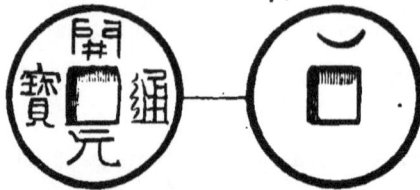

A diagram of this coin has been appended, because of the curiosity of the nail-mark on the reverse. The origin of this casual mark would little more interest us than so many other anecdotes woven as a "fringe to grave History's dress," were it not that since the issue of the *Kai-yuen* coin, this mark has spread all over the East, and for hundreds of years together it occurs on the coins of China, and even on those of Japan and Corea. It is highly probable that without knowing the origin of it, and merely following the bent of their genius to imitate anything and everything, the Japanese adopted this mark.

The historical record of the origin of the new coinage runs as follows:

1) It is not unnecessary to point out that in this case 開 元 is not the year-name of the period 713—42 as presumed by MARSDEN in his "Oriental Coins Pl. LVI j° Vol. 11, p. 819," but simply denotes that it is the coin which dates from the beginning of a new period in history. As appears from the historical quotations communicated below, this sort of coin was cast in 622, the year of the accession of the *T'ang*-dynasty.

閒 ○ 屬。盗 射¹⁾王 幽 中。兩。計 鉢 唐
生 高 　 鑄 裴 齊 益 置 得 一 錢。武
緣 祖 　 者 寂 王 等 錢 輕 十 鑄 德
環 初 　 死。一 三 諸 監 重 錢 開 四
錢。入 　 沒 鑪。鑪。州 於 六 重 通 年。
其 關。　 其 以 右 賜 洛。小 一 元 廢
製 民 　 家 鑄。僕 秦 并 四 兩。寶 五

In the fourth year of the period *Wu-te* (622) under the reign of the *T'ang*-dynasty, the 5 *tsu* pieces were abolished, and the *Kai-t'ung yuen-pao* money was cast. Ten pieces had a weight of an ounce, and the weight of 1000 pieces was estimated at 6 pounds 4 ounces (100 ounces). They hit upon the exact mean as for weight and size. A general money-office was established at *Lo-(yang)* (the capital of China under the *T'ang*), and likewise in *Ping-tseu, Yiu-tseu, Yik-tseu* and other provinces. (His majesty) gave the prince of *Tsi* and the prince of *Tsin* four money-founderies each, and *Pei-si*, a principal minister of the right side, one foundery for casting money [2]. False coiners were put to death, and their houses and property were confiscated.

In the beginning when *Kao-tsu* took the decisive step and mounted the throne of the *Suy* [3]), the people fabricated a sort of money of no

1) 僕射 *Pu-šai* lit. "Servant archer" Title of a principal minister 神宗以左右僕射爲宰相. The Emperor *Šin-tsung* made the left and right *Pu-šai* officers, his ministers of State. (MORR. in voce 官, 4).

2) According to a map of the Chinese empire under the reign of the *T'ang*-dynasty the provinces of *Ping-tseu* and *Yiu-tseu* are situated in the N. E. and *Yik-tseu* in the South part (now the prov. of *Yün-nan*.) There is also a *Yik-tseu* in the present prov. of *Sse-tš'uen*, it is, however, only to be found on a map of China of the division into N. and S. 秦 *Tsin*, is a little principality in the N. W. (prov. of *Kan-su*) 齊 idem in the N. E. prov. of *Šan-tung*. Hence it appears that in the most different parts of the realm money-founderies were established.

3) 高祖入關。 "When *Kao-tsu* took the decisive step and mounted the throne of the *Suy*." This rendering is a little free, but justified by the historical events which caused the accession of the prince of *T'ang* to the throne.

The emperor *Yang-ti* of the preceding (*Suy*)-dynasty, generally hated for his maladministration, having repaired to the south of his empire, the prince of *T'ang*, called *Li-yuen* (Cf. MAYERS n°. 381) marched with a numerous army to the capital *Li-ngan-fu*, and captured it. At the tidings that the emperor had been murdered in the south, he had *Yang-ti's* grandsons *Yeu* and *Kung* successively proclaimed emperor, but after a short time the two boy-kings were dethroned and murdered. As there were now no other descendents of the *Suy* line, *Li-yuen* made himself master of the trone, and reigned under the name of *Kao-tsu*. The new dynasty was named after the principality of *T'ang* (唐) of which *Li-yuen* was titular duke. —

輕小。凡八九萬。繞其半
斛乃鑄開通元寶。其文
給事中歐陽詢製詞及
書時稱其工。詢製詞三
體。其詞鄭虔云。篆隷¹)
後右。鄭虔日文德皇后云。次左
進蠟樣。會上後下。初
一甲跡。故錢上有皇后掐
每兩二十四銖以上則一錢文。
重二銖半以下則古錢比
今秤三之一也。則今錢
為古秤之七銖以土古
五銖則加重二銖以土。

more than a silkthread. in thickness; 80.000 or 90.000 of such pieces hardly filled a half-*hu* (bushel). Then the *Kai-t'ung-yuen-pao* pieces were cast. The characters occurring on that coin were made by *Ngeu-yang-siün*, under-secretary of the censurate.

The characters (words) and the writing accorded with the workmanship. The words were (written) in the *tšwen* and *li* writing, in three different writing-manners ¹). Of these words first came those at the top and then those at the bottom, moreover the left-hand came after the right hand (characters ²). *Kien-hoei-ts'ui* of *T'sing* says that when *Siün* showed a model in wax (of this coin), her august majesty queen *Wen-tek* reaching for it, left on it the impression of one nail, and that this. is the reason why at the top of (the obverse of) the coin there is the mark of a nail. An ounce is 24 *tšu*, hence a copper piece weighs a little less than 2½ *tšu*. Comparing the ancient weights with the present, the ratio is of 3 to 1. So that at the present time the money is somewhat heavier than 7 *tšu* ancient weight (2½ × 3), thus as heavy as the old 5 *tšu* pieces, plus a weight of a little more than 2½ *tšu*.

We see that the intentions of the government regarding the

入關 is lit. to enter a doorway. According to WILLIAMS 關 signifies also a Rubicon, an important point in one's life.

1) *Tšwen* is the seal, *li* the official-writing manner. Three different writing-manners. Cf. Matw. IX 4 *b*, where of a coin of the *Sung*-dynasty is said 作眞行草三體 the (legend) was made in three different writing-manners, strait-hand, running-hand and grass-writing, DE CHAUDOIR *in loco*. Pl. VI. 40—42 gives a diagram of each of them.

2) Right and left side are as in heraldry. Just as a coat of arms, a Chinese coin has its own right and left side and not that of the looker-on. See the diagram p. 100. What Matw. calls the left is as seen by us the right side. The same fact is obvious from Matw. IX 2 *a*.

issue of this new money were good in every respect, and the opinion of later times has been very favorable also. "This money is so excellent, says *Šui-ye*, (the author quoted page 16) "that as soon as the *T"ang*-princes began to cast it, it spread all over the empire; and even up to this day it is frequently met with," but, continues he, "under the *T'ang*-dynasty itself, these coins were not on hand in such large quantities". [Matw. IX. 42*a*]. This last remark explains much of the history that follows.

Also *Tung-lai* the other writer on money (See page 13) speaks in high terms of this money. He says [Matw. IX. 37*b*]: "From the *T'ang*-dynasty to the five dynasties it has not been necessary to alter the value of the *Kai-yuen-t'ung-pao* money once fixed, because with this money the exact proportions had been so admirably hit upon. 最 得 其 平。

But now the money was really so good, there was at once a great demand for it, and the Chinese, these matchless false coiners, found in this fact a fresh opportunity to exercise their occupation with double zeal, and to render the judicious measures of the central government ineffectual by melting the good money and to circulate it again mixed with other baser metals.

Mr. JEVONS says somewhere in his admirable work on money: "The annals of coinage in this and all other countries, are little more than a monotonous repetition of depreciated issues, both public and private, varied by occasional meritorious but often unsuccessful efforts to restore the standard of the currency". This is perfectly applicable to the history of the money under the *T'ang*-dynasty, as recorded by Ma-twan-lin in the last part of his eighth volume, and if I had no other task than to give an account of Chinese money, this short quotation would suffice to characterize the time which now follows.

Involuntarily I recall the time when I was preparing this part of the ·work, the many weeks ˉof incessant and dull labor necessary to get an exact view of the history of this period. All the time I felt as if I were wandering about in an unexplored desert where for miles together nothing remarkable meets the eye, and where the mind grows weary with an eternal and mournful monotony. Yet occasionally I found an oasis which I have not failed carefully to mark down. To these most fertile spots I intend to devote a few lines that he who goes out on such a wandering expedition after me may know where to find a resting-place, worth his while to examine more narrowly. I shall, however most earnestly try to make the passage through the dreary sands as short as possible. And might it appear to my reader that the bridges I have built here and there, to get over such places as were well-nigh insurmountable, are too light and dangerous, I kindly beg him to fortify the frail structure with some timbers of his own store.

In a short time false coining had so considerably increased that 40 years after its issue, the new money was abolished again, and the state-money was provided with a new legend in order to check the use of the false *Kai-yuen* pieces. When this measure threatened to become fatal to trade it was soon retracted. The swarms of false coiners increased again, nay, it came even so far that there were who made false money in vessels and on rafts in the middle of the river 有以舟筏鑄江中者. Then the government ordered that the circulating false money should be accepted, a measure which did not improve the matter, to be sure.

者 錫 官 爲 民 儀
沒 鑞 督 業。多 鳳
官。過 捕。詔 私 中
百 載 巡 鑄 瀕 江
斤 銅 江 錢 江

During the period *I-feng* (676—79) the people living on the river *Ping-kiang* [1]) made a regular employment of false coining. Hence it was ordered that a journey to that river should be undertaken with a view to examine the matter, and that the officials should set afoot an inquiry and persecution. What there was above 100 pounds of copper and tin (aboard a vessel), should be confiscated by the government.

Another measure to diminish the circulating quantity of bad money was, that grain and rice were taken from the state-granaries and brought to market, and the bad money was accepted as legal tender to an amount of 100 pieces to a measure. "To a measure, says our text, 100 pieces of false money were accepted as a part of the payment" 斗 別 納 惡 錢 百 文 [2]). The false coiners expiated their crime with their lives, and the accomplices (lit. those who supported and protected them) were persecuted and summoned before the judge". 私 鑄 者 抵 死。隣 保 從 坐.

Queen *Wu-heu* again tried another expedient to check the deeply-rooted evil in some degree. Henceforth it was not allowed to make payment in pieces strung together, but they must circulate loose, that the copper, tin, and iron pieces might be distinguished at once.

The haunt of the false coiners was the country called *Kiang-Hoai* 江 淮 大 甚, and they were so skilful and cunning that notwithstanding the repeated efforts of the government, the officials were unable to do anything against them.

Ma-twan-lin says:

---

1) In the North of China, province of *San-tung*.
2) The false coins were in this way reduced to a sort of change or token, which only to a certain amount were allowed to circulate as legal tender. It was thus a legitimation of false coins by the government.

相 豪 淮 往 偏 無 種 江
屬 歲 私 往 鑪 復 雜 淮
　 歲 鑄 藏 錢 以 以 偏
　 取 者 之 七 錢 鐵 鑪
　 之 京 以 八 形 錫 錢
　 舟 師 易 富 以 輕 數
　 車 權 江 商 一 漫 十
　 　 　 　 當

In the district of *Kiang-hoai* a large quantity of money was cast, even as many as 10 various sorts; it was mixed with lead and tin, light of quality, and spread in great profusion; often it had not even the form of money. A (good) piece of money was commonly worth 7 or 8 pieces of this money cast in large quantities. Rich merchants gradually collected the good money to sell it to the false coiners of *Kiang-hoai*. In the capital the quality of the money had remained still very good, but every year it was collected and transported by freights an cartloads".

And as a proof how far the Chinese were advanced in the art of making false money, our author says: "Some melted in a short time 100.000 pieces out of tin in the form of copper-money. 或鎔錫模錢．須臾千百．

After so many abortive attempts the imperial council was at a loss how to proceed, and an assembly of the Lords of the realm was called in order to advice his Majesty in this juncture. When they were assembled an imperial message again raised the question whether it were desirable to retract the existing prohibitions against the casting of money by private persons, and to leave it entirely free. In that case the state should have to exercise only a strict control over the money brought in circulation. Ma-twan-lin gives: 1 the imperial message. 2 two speeches, one defending the other attacking the proposal. 3 the imperial decision. Many passages of this fragment show us that notwithstanding the wretched social condition of that time the humor of the Chinese statesmen was not quite extinct.

開元二十二年三月二十一日敕。布帛不可以尺寸為交易。菽粟不可以抄勺貿有無。古之為錢。以通貨幣。本雖有官鑄。所入無幾。約給工計。本不勞費。而用者不瞻。公私之問。言其誼已移。事亦無異。今來時移事異。亦欲不禁私鑄。其理如何。公卿百僚詳議可否。秘書監崔汚議曰。夫國之有錢。時所通用。若許私鑄。

In the 22nd year of the period *Kai-yuen* (734), 3rd month 21st day an imperial decree was issued (in which was said) that pieces of silk might not be measured by a foot or an inch to serve as a medium of exchange, and that edible pulse and grains might not be used any more by handfuls and spoonfuls to barter what one had for what one had not. The reason why the ancients made money was to circulate merchandise and silks. Though at present the government casts money, what is paid for (by means of money) is not much, and though the generally received principle in the making of money is to economize the expenses of the fabrication, labor and expenses are as yet important, while the amount of what is provided for common use is not equal to the want, and perpetual complaints are made of the bad state of the money. What in the lapse of time has continued to exist without change? Formerly in the time of the reign of *Han-wen(ti)*, while free coining was already granted to the people, it was not prohibited by that sage prince, notwithstanding *Kia-I* thought it wrong. Those old times are past and gone, the present is before us. Living in other times and under other circumstances (lit. while the details of the events are different) it is desired that private persons are not prevented from casting money. How far is that right?

When in a general assembly of ministers and lords the question was discussed, whether it should be allowed or not, the privy councilor *Ts'ui-mien* spoke these words: "If we allow the money which is in common use in the empire to be cast by private persons [1]), the people will un-

---

1) lit: The actual money of the country, which at present is used, if we allow it to be cast by private persons. It is a rhetorical inversion which reminds us of Thomas Carlyle's style.

人必競爲。各徇所求。小如有

利漸忘本業。大計於貧。是以

買¹⁾生之陳²⁾。福規³⁾殷更貧。漢令。

太公創九府。將以殷乃有貪人。況

依法。則不成。違法爲盜鑄錢令者。

按漢書文帝雖除盜鑄他鑄巧者。

而不得雜以鉛鐵盜鑄錢令。

然則雖私鑄不容姦錢。

容姦則私鑄自息。者無利不

則爲法正等能謹於法而節

除。爲法自息。斯則除之與不利不

其用。則令行而詐不起。事變。

而姦不生。斯所以稱賢君也。

doubtedly make it in large quantities, and though the profit which every one tries to make for himself is but small, yet he will gradually leave his old employment in the lurch. And great, it may be computed, will be the poverty afterwards, and that was the very reason why *Kia-(I* the minister of *Han-wen-ti*) ¹⁾, thinking that such a proceeding would produce the seven blessings set forth by him ²⁾, remonstrated ³⁾ against it, and insisted on the revocation of the decree issued by the *Han* (emperor). The institution of the nine departments for the administration of the finances by *Tai-kung* was made with a view to sustain the poor. But (it will be said) if one does not succeed by acting in conformity to a rule, it may be of use to act against that rule. If we attentively look through the annals of the *Han*-dynasty we will see that though the emperor *Wen-ti* repressed false coining with severity and would not suffer the money to be mixed with lead and tin in order to adulterate it, (he managed it so) that private persons were allowed to cast money, but false money was not tolerated. Now, in that case, casting money yields no profit, and private persons cease casting of their own accord. In this case the restraint is perfectly equal to the non-restraint. When after the enactment of laws and regulations due care is taken that they are maintained, it is quite possible to cut off the road to such practices and to manage it so that (money) continues to circulate without the appearance of bad money. Such a proceeding alters the affairs, and causes that there is no false money fabricated. To effect

1) See page 31.

2) 陳, to set forth, to express carefully, to state.

3) 規 = 規諫.

今若聽其私鑄。嚴斷惡錢。官必得人。人皆知禁。誠漢政也。恐未侔皇唐。今若稅銅折役。則官冶可成。估度銅庸。私則無利。成而可久。簡而難誣。謹守舊章。無越制度。夫錢之為物貴。以通貨利不在多。何待私鑄然後足用也。左監門錄事參軍[1]劉秩議曰。與之在君。奪之在君。以人戴君如日月。親君如父母。用此術也。是謂人

this end is that by which a sage prince is characterized. Now if in accordance with the principle of free coining, we take severe repressive measures against the false money, so that the officials positively and surely shall seize every person (who violates the law) and that all shall know the restrictions, we shall indeed act according to the policy of the *Han*-dynasty, though I fear that even then we shall not quite act up to the old traditions of the illustrious *T'ang*. Now if the copper, received as taxes by the government (service), is held back, money may be made of it in the state-foundaries and if we accurately estimate the unit of value, private persons will not be able to make profit. It will be easy to distinguish them (those coins) in the long run and very difficult it will be to adulterate them. If we, moreover, take care that the old seals are upheld, and that we do not transgress the fixed measure and limits, the money will be an object which has its full value as a medium of exchange. As the profits derived from coining cannot be large in this way, what can we then further expect of the casting of money by private persons, as afterwards we shall have enough for general use?

*Liu-tsi*, an officer of the left palace gate and secretary to the board of control of government officers [1] said: "It lies with the prince to give and it lies with the prince to take. As the people honor their prince like (the light of) the sun and moon and as they are attached to their prince like to their fathers and mothers, the prince uses such expedients, and his being able to do so is (a visible proof of) his

---

1) For those official titles see MORR. in voce 官 76 j°. 138. The high officers at court where divided into those of the left and those of the right side. The left side was first in rank.

*Liü-tši* first reminds us of the manifold institutions of the ancient kings, he quotes the piece of *Kwan-tsze* already treated of page 10, with the intention to show that only the sovereign has a right to manage the monetary affairs of a country.

主之權。今之錢，即古之下幣也。陛下若捨之任人，則上無以御下，下無以事上，其不可一也。夫物賤則傷農，物貴則傷買，故善為國者，觀物之貴賤、錢之輕重。物重則錢輕，錢輕由乎重。物多則重重，重則作法收之，使少。少則重重，重則作法布之，使之輕。輕輕重之本，必由乎是。奈何而假於人，其不可二也。夫鑄錢不雜以鉛鐵則無利，雜以鉛鐵則惡，不重禁

power as the ruler of men. Now the present money is the medium of exchange of ·the lowest sort of the ancients. If your Majesty rejects it and thrusts it on the people, he who is at the head will no longer be able to govern those who are under him, and the subordinates will not be able to serve him who is set over them. This may not be. — This is my first objection.

When commodities are cheap, this is prejudicial to agriculture, and is the money base, it affects trade, hence it is the duty of a good ruler of the empire to excercise control over the relative value of commodities and the quality·of the money. Are commodities heavy (when measured against money) the money is light. The fact that the money is light results from the quantity of goods. Is it (the money) much (in abundance) a law must be passed to suppress it, and in this way to make that it becomes scarce, and consequently heavy; if it then gets too heavy again, a law must be passed to diffuse it, by which it is made light again. Surely, this is the fundamental principle by which the value of the money. is maintained. Now would you put this in the hands of the people? Such a thing · may not be. — This is my second objection. — If in casting money it is not mixed with lead or iron, it does not yield any profit, and if mixed with it, the money is bad. If the restrictions which cannot be made severer, are not yet sufficient to check ·and prevent it

---

1) 假於人 to transfer. — to put in another's hand. Another instance of 假 in this signification may perhaps be found in the passage on page 34; where I, however, took *kia* as an adjective of the compound 假貴. As far as I know, *kia* in the signification of to transfer occurs only connected with 於 The construction of the preceding sentence (on page 34), however, 以作兵器 allows us to take 假 there also as a verb.

111

不足以懲息。方今塞其私鑄
之路。人猶冒死以犯之況啟
其源而欲人之從令乎是設
陷穽而誘之入。其不可三也。
夫許人鑄錢無利。則人不鑄
有利者眾。則人去南¹)
衂者眾。則草萊不墾。又隣
寒餒其不。夫人之富溢。於
則不可以賞勸也。夫鑄錢
以威禁。故法令不行。人之
理皆由貧富之不齊也。若許
其鑄錢則貧者必不能為。臣
恐貧者彌貧而服役于富室。

(this mixing lead and iron with the copper) and that while at present the roads leading to private coining are blocked up, the people still continue to adulterate and run heedlessly on death in order to violate the law, how much more will this be the case if that source is opened and the people are desired to tread that way. This is making snares and pitfalls and enticing the people to run into them. This may not be either. — It is my third objection. — Further, if you grant the people (the privilege) to make money without their being able to make profit by it, they will cast no money; but if it yields profit, then they desert their fruitful fields¹) and are these deserted, thistles and weeds will not be ploughed up, and we shall soon come to cold²) and starvation. This may not be either. — It is my fourth objection. — If the people who then will cast money are rich and opulent, rewards and encouragements will be of no effect, and if they suffer want and poverty, threats and restrictions will be of no avail, and that your lawful orders will not be executed and that your people will not act according to reason and sense will be the consequences of this, that poverty and wealth are not in proportion, (that with the one wealth and with the other poverty will be the reason of the violation of the law). Now if you allow private persons to cast money, the poor, to be sure, will not be rich enough to do it, and then your servant fears that the poor will become still poorer and overawed by the power of the rich families. And if the rich families occupy themselves with it, they will steal the more. In the time of

1) 南 properly "south" is here used for fertile, as the south is "the region of heat and vegetation, where things get nourishment. See WILLIAMS in voce 南.

2) Because silkworms will not be reared.

富室乘之則益盜。昔漢文時。
吳濞諸侯也。財富埒天子。鄧通
大夫也。必俌王者。此皆鑄錢
所致也。必欲許其私鑄。是與
人利權而以¹⁾捨其柄。不可
也。陛下寔以¹⁾錢重而其傷本
贄而利寔。則臣願重而傷本
效患計。夫錢重者。猶²⁾言其
於前而冶不加於舊。又人公滋
重於銅。以之價頗等。故盜鑄
破重錢以爲輕錢。禁寬則行。
禁嚴則止。止則棄矣。此錢之
所以少也。夫鑄錢用不贍者

*Wenti* of the *Han*-dynasty free-coining was the cause that the feudal princes of *Wu* and *Pi* were as wealthy as the emperor himself, and that the treasures of the lord *T'ang-t'ung* were equal to those of a king. — All this were the results of the casting of money [3].

Certain it is that, if you wish coining to be granted to private persons, it is bestowing upon them an advantageous power, and it is giving that lever out of your hands. This may not be. — This is my fifth objection. —

Your Majesty, undoubtedly, still adheres to the opinion that it is hurtful when the money is heavy (dear) and that it yields little profit when the fabrication is expensive. Why then your servant wishes to tell you that you should leave off following such stupid calculations. The reason why the money is dear is that the number of persons (making use of it) is daily increasing in comparison to the number of consumers of former times, while the number of foundaries is not increased above the old number; besides, the state-money is heavy in proportion to the price of copper (which is now) rather higher (than formerly). Now this again is the reason that the false coiners break the heavy coins to make light ones of them. Are the restrictions on that money mild, it is brought in circulation, and are they severe, it ceases (does not take place) and then false coining will come to an end of itself. The reason why the money is now scarce, and why the quantity which is cast, is not in proportion to the want, is the dearness of the copper, and the copper is dear because it is in great demand for various purposes, for copper is still more suitable than iron

1) 以 = 以爲.
2) 猶 = 由.

3) Those princes revolted against *Han-wen-ti* (See Mat. VIII. 7a), — p. 35.

在乎銅貴。銅貴之由。在於㧈用者衆矣。夫銅器。以爲兵則兵。以爲器。不如鐵。以爲陸器。則不如漆。如禁之。人則無銅以爲器。則銅無所用。銅無所用則害。夫銅賤。布下則錢之用。盜鑄者無因而鑄。無因而鑄則公錢不破。公錢不破則人不犯死刑。錢又日增。日增則末復利矣。是一舉而四美兼也。伏惟陛下熟之。

to make arms, and better than lacquerware to make vases; without loss however you can forbid this. Why should your Majesty not prevent the people? If you forbid it, copper will not be so generally wanted, and this will cause the price to fall, and then you will be able to supply the want of money. Is that copper, moreover, not so widely diffused among the lower people, false coiners have no opportunity of making false money of it; nor does the state-money get broken, and the people do not violate the law any more and are not put to death. The money increases daily, and this again yields profit in the end. So a single act results in four successful consequences. I beseech your Majesty to consider this maturely.

His Majesty's sublime decision in this matter makes us strongly suspect that he has not listened at all to the sage counsel. Seven months afterwards another imperial decree is issued commanding that in great commercial transactions merchandise should serve as legal tender, while in smaller purchases in the market, partly money, partly merchandise should be employed. The decree reads thus:

其年十月十日。勅。貨幣將通用。以利布錢。兼本末。以是本貴末賤。爲弊。刀爲本。末爲賤。則深法。教之問。

In the same year on the 6th day of the 10th month an imperial decree was issued in which was said: If the medium of exchange becomes generally circulating, this will be an advantage in daily use, and while the silks have been the origin (of the medium of exchange)

8

罪。用。令千市綿布並口所自宜
蓮錢以買等。綾先馬有今有
者物土至其羅用交莊以變
科兼亦一餘絲絹易。宅後。革。

the copper money has become the end. What was cheap in the beginning has become dear at last, and this causes a state of wretchedness
which is very deep. If the laws dictates it to us, it is meet that changes
are brought about. Hence from this day forward when farms, dwellings, slaves and horses happen to be sold, use shall be made of the silks, silk
gauze, floss silk, and other varieties, formerly employed for this purpose.
For what further is sold in the market to an amount of 1000 cash and
a little more, both money and merchandise shall be used. He who acts
against it shall be tried as a criminal.

It need not be said, that the Emperor's ineffectual measures
did not improve matters of all. We again proceed to communicate the history of the miserable condition of Chinese society at
that time, as stated by the chronicles, but soon we shall have
reached the time that history is silent on the subject.

The ministers who commonly proved to possess more sense
than their royal masters did not lose courage yet. A short time
after the events mentioned above when the mass of bad money
threatened to ruin trade, the prime minister *Li-lin-fu* proposed
— a measure already practised before — to bring to market a
quantity of silks, and to sell them for bad money.

復復市以國兵
行之。門市忠部
舊明日。恩欲侍
錢。日行楊招郎
詔當鞭權楊

(He who made this known to the
people,) the vice-president of the ministry of war *Yang-kue-tsi*, desirous of
gaining power by means of public favor,
exclaimed, cracking a whip at the gates
of the market: "trade must come back,
and to-morrow it will be decreed that
the old money shall circulate again."

In the same way the government continued to cast money and
to exchange it for the false coins. The consequence was not that

the people ceased to make false money, but that the taxes must be made heavier, and that the false coiners enjoyed the profits arising from this measure.

In 758 *Ti-wu-ki*, vice-president of the board of finances and shortly afterwards prime minister, brings another hackneyed proposal on the carpet, viz. the institution of a currency which, as a Chinese author on money says, was only a equivalent [1]) for money as it consisted of coins as large as the circulating pieces, but which according to their legend were worth from 10 to 50 cash. The law having so often been changed within a short time, prices rose enormously; for a measure of rice 7000 copper pieces were paid, and on the roads hundreds died of sheer want.

The people had at last recourse to stones used for grinding rice, which had a fixed value, and for that reason were called money of an intrinsic value in contradistinction to the money properly so called, which had no intrinsic value. We read in Ma-twan-lin:

有 當 交 爲 磑
虛 錢。昜。寳 碨
寳 由 皆 錢。鬻
之 是 用 虛 受
名。錢 十 錢 得

Stones for grinding rice were received as money of an intrinsic value, and bartered for (real) money which had no intrinsic value (lit. hollow or empty money); they were (generally in use) to a value of 10 *cash*. In consequence of this, the money was called money of an intrinsic value, and money of no intrinsic value.

By way of a change we find now some statistical returns of what the people want to live on, together with an account of the money cast in the state-foundaries. The passage is remarkable as a counterpart of a similar account under the *Han*-dynasty (See page 48).

---

1) He uses the word 權 an equivalent, counterbalancing against. The
meaning must, however, be that it was a
representative equivalent, which ought to counterbalance the real, a token-money.

當時議者。以爲自天寶
至今九百餘萬王七制上
農食九人中農夫七人
以中農夫計之爲六千
三百萬人少壯相均人
食米二升日費米百二
十六萬二斛歲費四萬
千之三百六十萬斛五
倍之吉凶之禮再倍餘
三年之之儲以備水旱凶
災當米十三萬六千八
十萬斛以貴賤豐儉相
當則米之直與錢均也

At that time a councilor spoke: When we glance at the time elapsed from the period *T'ien-pao* (742) up to the present (763—65) there are more than 9.000.000 families. If your Majesty reckons that farmers of the first class procure food for 9 persons, and farmers of the second class for 7 persons, and you take the second class as standard (roughly calculated) it amounts to a number of 63.000.000 souls. If the weak and strong are taken together, one person consumes a quantity of 2 šang daily. Thus, 1.260.000 *hu* of rice are wanted daily. The annual necessary expenses (reckoned in rice) (for food of the people) thus amount to 453.600.000 *hu* (bushels [1])). We reckon for clothes as much again, and furthermore for ceremonies and sacrifices which take place both in days of prosperity and tribulations still as much again. Now there remains the three years' store which is intended to relieve the misery arising from inundations, times of drought and other calamities; this represents a capital of 136.080.000 *hu* in rice. If we take the expensive, cheap, rich and poor sorts promiscuously, we reduce the value of that rice to copper money [2]).

[1) A 升 šang is a little more than a liter. According to WILLIAMS, 1.031 liter. 斛 *hu* is here = 100 升. The measures in China have undergone frequent variations. From the calculation it appears that a year is reckoned at 360 days.

2) The councilor's meaning is, "By reducing this to money you can calculate how much money is wanted". An easy matter probably for his contemporaries who knew the price of a cup of rice, but for us this calculation is very difficult as the councilor does not state the price in money. His conclusion, however, is very uneconomical and he forgets that the money constantly circulates, and in that way performs the same service in exchange repeatedly, so that a people by no means wants a quantity of coined money as would be necessary to pay for what the whole people consumes a year. Regarding the same question, which our Chinese adept in statistics decides without hesitation Dr. ADAM SMITH in his "Wealth of nations" B. II. Chapter II observes: "What is the proportion, which the circulating money of any country bears to the whole value of the annual produce circulated by means of it, it is, perhaps impossible to determine. It has been computed by different authors at a fifth, at a tenth, at a twentieth and at a thirtieth part of the value."

田以高下肥瘠豐耗爲率。一頃出米五十餘斛。當田二千七百二十一萬六千頃。而錢亦歲毀於棺瓶埋藏以焚其問銅貴錢賤。有鑄以爲器者不出十年。錢幾盡。不足以周當世之用。諸道鹽鐵轉運使劉晏以江嶺諸州任土所出。皆重粗賤弱之貨。輸京師不足以供道路之直。於是積之江淮。易銅鉛薪炭。廣鑄錢。每歲得十餘萬緡。輸京師及荆楊二州。自是錢日增矣。

If we reckon high and low, rich and poor, good and bad fields together, a *king* produces 50 *hu* on an average, hence (the quantity of rice above mentioned, necessary to supply the want of the people) answers in lands to 27.216.000 *king*.

The quantity of money gets less every year by keeping it in money-boxes, by hoarding it up in treasuries, and by being destroyed by fire or dropped in the water; and if there is an interval during which copper is dear and the money is cheap, it is melted to make tools of it, and within a lapse of time of 10 years, the quantity of money is almost exhausted, and no longer sufficient to supply the want of the time being. The head comptroller of the salt and iron duties [1], *Liu-yen* (says) what is employed in the provinces of *Kiang* and *Ling*, and what is produced by the country of *Žin-tu* (as a medium of exchange) is a heavy, mean, worthless merchandise of a soft (unfit for money) substance.

What circulates in the capitals is not sufficient to supply the want of the outlying provinces. Besides in the provinces of *Kiang* and *Hoai* (where the false coiners are most active) the (still existing) money is gathered. (Hence it is necessary) to buy copper, lead, fuel, charcoal, and to cast money in abundance, so that every year more than 100.000 strings of copper money are circulated in the capital and as far as the provinces

---

The Chinese author proceeds with showing how much money there is actually in circulation, and how all sorts of influences combine continually to diminish this quantity which is already much too small. This leads him to the conclusion that it is desirable that the Government should cast money on an extensive scale.

1) The salt and iron duty was a kind of income-tax levied on every person or on every family since the reign of the *Tsi*-dynasty (479—502) There was a register of the tax-payers.

of *King* and *Yang-tseu* [1]). Acting according to this principle the money will be increased daily.

Of the statistical returns of the amount of money cast at that time the following extract will suffice.

The total number of money-foundaries was 99, distributed among the provinces. Every foundary was worked by 30 men. Yearly, in every foundary, there were fabricated 3300 strings of 1000 *cash* (1 string was worth about six shillings). The cost of each string was 750 cash, so that the profit of the state amounted to 33 per cent. In the whole empire 327.000 strings of copper money were fabricated a year. Some pages further we read that an adept in money-matters proposes that in the foundaries still to be built near the Red Cliff 紅 崔, the money should be cast in such a way that the cost of bullion, wages, and transport shall not exceed 900 copper pieces a string; then a trifle will float (will be the profit). 貫 費 計 錢 九 百。則 浮 本 矣。

Now we find a series of reports from the comptrollers of the iron and salt duties, who earnestly complain of the bad money which they commonly receive, and in consequence of which the taxes do not yield enough to provide for the wants of the State. Matters were worst in the districts of *Kiang-hoai*. Concerning this fact *Pao-ki* says: "When exchanging good for bad money we received a tub of tin, lead and copper promiscuously 並 鉛 錫 銅 盪. The influence thereof on the prices of commodities was enormous. Afterwards we still perceived a slight increase of bad money, and when we set afoot a strict inquiry in the several districts of this province, we found that in the mountains as well as in the flat country, there were subterraneous vaults containing

1) The provinces of *King-tseu* and *Yang-tseu* are situated west and east of the capital. The longtitude of *King* is 109° 44', that of *Yang* 117° east of Paris. The meaning is thus, throughout the whole empire.

money cast by private persons. The rascals and cheats who supplied one another with this bad money in order to bring it in circulation had been steadily on the increase. But now that the officials charged with this inquiry are aware of the real condition, and the way in which the false coiners dealt, they have instituted rewards and punishments in a very judicious way, and thus checked the increase of these evil practices."

Another provincial functionary states that in his districts the money which still contained an amount of pure copper was melted and made into all sorts of objects, and the profit gained in this way was so considerable that he feared that if no severe repressive measures were taken, the time would soon come when there was not a single good copper piece extant.

"Of 1000 good coins they extract 6 pounds of copper, and when they melt this mass to make it into instruments and other objects, a pound of copper obtains a value of 600 *cash*." So they make a profit of 260 percent. He therefore requested the central board of administration to make severer regulations against the melting of money. The Emperor's decision is remarkable. His Majesty decreed that his people should be at liberty to melt money but that the tools made of the copper might not be sold at a price exceeding 160 *cash* a pound. In this way he thought to be able to make this occupation so little profitable that people would soon take a dislike to it. — One or two years ago M. EMILE DE LAVALAYE, of Liege, gave a discourse in the Students' Literary Club DOCTRINA at Leiden. His subject was that the decline of the States in ancient and modern times was chiefly to be attributed to the insufficient knowledge of Political Economy of their rulers. The absurd regulations of the "sons of heaven" often remind me of the

spirited and captivating *causerie*, and I cannot but regret that the
learned speaker was not then acquainted with the history of
money in China. He would without doubt have found it a for-
cible argument in favor of his somewhat hasardous hypothesis.

All of a sudden there shone a light through the Egyptian
darkness which overhung the Chinese empire, but it was only
a dim and faint glimpse, which was visible to vanish immediately afterwards, and its existence was even too short to give a
satisfactory description of it. I mean the apparition of paper-
money. History says:

錢。禁 兆 之。方。以 軍 進 師。時 復 憲
與 尹 號 合 輕 諸 奏 委 商 禁 宗
商 裴 飛 劵 裝 使 院²。錢 估¹）用 以
買 武。錢。乃 趨 富 及 諸 至 銅 錢
飛 請 京 取 四 家。諸 路 京 器。少。

Under the reign of the emperor *Ilien-tsung*, because money was
scarce again, the use of copper tools was prohibited. In that time
travelling merchants who came to the capital brought with them the
money they had received in the outlying provinces, and deposited it
in a government-bank. Likewise did military and civil officers and rich
families, that they might travel unburdened through all parts of the
country. (Instead of their money) they received certificates of indebted-
ness (lit. corresponding billets); these bore the name of flying money.
The imperial governor of the capital *Pei-wu* proposed to suspend the
issuing of flying-money to the merchants.

Man wird sich nicht mit Börs und Beutel plagen;
Ein Blättchen ist im Busen leicht zu tragen.

says Goethe in his splendid satire on paper-money (Faust, Part II).
Our Chinese chronicle says in prose very much the same, and
surprising it is that an institution which would have proved to
be a great benefit to the Chinese society of those days, was

---

1) 估 = 買.　　　　　　　2) 院 is the word generally used for bank.

abolished without so much as even to mention the reason why.

Yet shortly afterwards this apparition is seen once more, but still dimmer than the first time, and then it disappears altogether to return more brilliant and more fully developed 150 years later under the reign of the *Sung*-dynasty.

A little while after the short-lived apparition of paper-money, in the year 809 the quantity of money circulating in the capital was uncommonly slight, trade was dead, 非交易 and the money still in circulation was no more in demand. 錢行衢路者不聞 Private persons tried to circulate silver money by working the silver mines in the *Wu-ling* mountains, but this was soon prohibited by government. Some high functionaries of the central board of administration then proposed to try once more paper-money.

Ma-twan-lin's communication is short:

貫 與 至 然 增 錢。鐵。部 商 頓 滯 飛 自
而 商 者。商 給 每 三 度 人 輕。藏。錢。京
易 人 復 人 百 千 司 支 於 請¹⁾物 家 師
之。敢 許 無 錢。絕 飛 鹽 戶 許 價 有 禁

Since the flying money was forbidden in the capital, the families had hoarded up the money in treasuries and the prices of commodities had somewhat fallen. (Some functionaries) ¹) suggested to allow the merchants to have their salt and iron appraised at the ministry of finances, and that on the flying-money (which they received in return) from the mint-college, they were to pay a premium of 100 *cash* on every 1000 string. But when there were among the merchants none that went there, it was allowed again to give the merchants, the full value when exchanging their strings (for notes).

As has already been said, no further mention of paper-money

---

1) The names of the offices and functionaries are omitted. The names of all public functionaries of ancient and recent times are to be found in the Rev. MORRISON's Dictionary of the Chinese Language *in voce* 官. It is a pity that the whole long list, which forms a volume by itself has been put together without a practical method or arrangement.

is made. Probably the credit of the state was so shaken that the people did not venture any more upon paper-money.

One tyrannical measure now succeeds the other. A decree was issued ordering that nobody was allowed to possess more than a certain amount of copper money, and those whose treasure of copper money exceeded this sum were obliged within a fixed time to exchange it for government products; state-officials residing in the market for that purpose. But as the merchants tried to make some profit by that exchange, a full year had elapsed and the decree had not been carried into effect. Severe measures were then taken to execute the laws.

十二年敕自今文武
官僚不問品秩高下
并公卿郡縣主中使
至士庶商旅寺觀坊
市所有私貯見錢並
不得過五千貫如有
過此許從敕出後限
一月市別物收貯如
限內未了更請限亦
不得過兩月限滿違
犯者白身[1]人處死於
是競買地屋以變其
錢而高貴大價

In the 12th year (817) an imperial decree was issued that from that time forward all civil and military officers without any distinction of rank, together with all functionaries charged with the government of provinces and districts down to the subalterns and soldiers, all merchants, monasteries and temples, hamlets and market-places might not possess more than a sum of 5000 string in ready money. When there were whose fortune exceeded that sum the decree allowed them a month's time to lay out their money in the market. If (after that time) there were who had again received and hoarded up money, they requested a second respite, if they had not been able tot get ready in the first, but this last respite might not exceed two months. When those respites were past, such private persons [1] as had violated and transgressed the law

---

1) 白身 = 白徒 private persons Cf. K'ang-hi's dictionary in voce 白.

were put to death. Then the people bought on a large scale farms and houses to convert their fortune (into landed property) and precious things fetched high prices.

Now Ma-twan-lin takes up the pen in order to show the folly and uselessness of those last regulations. Since his criticism on the financial system of the *Tseu*-dynasty he has been silent, except some explanatory notes to elucidate the texts he quoted. But now that no voice is heard of the ministers or learned men of the time to pronounce judgment on such arbitrariness, he addresses us himself, and in a few lines he gives an excellent critical review of the absurdity of such measures.

流　盫　立　故　田　不　可　限　豪　徒　産　者。○
通。蓄　法　必　者。亦　也。民　強。欲　以　不　按
初　錢　以　須　志。甚　限　名¹)兼　設　均　能　後
不　者　限　上　於　乎。民　田。并　法　貧　制　之
煩　志　其　之　吞　然　蓄　猶　之　以　富。民　為
上　於　頃　人。併　買　錢。云　徒　限　而　之　國

When we observe those who afterwards governed the country, they were not able to regulate the wealth of the nation in such a way that they made the condition of the poor and rich equal, and they tried in vain to invent means to check violent and oppressive actions. What regards the bringing of all into one hand, it was to be tolerated, when the people were prevented from bringing the fields under their names ¹), but to prevent the people from hoarding up money, is that not a little too bad? For he who buys land intends to engross all, and therefore those who are at the head of the affairs should surely make regulations by which this enormous possession of landed property (lit. *King* and *Meu*, both superficial measures) is restricted. Those, however, who hoard up money have made up their minds to make it stream and to circulate it. In the beginning the rulers of men did not trouble their heads about the enactment of laws teaching the people how to exert

1) 名 name — is here in the position of a transitive verb with 田 as its ob- | ject. I have not found another instance of that particular use of the noun.

擾之驅不取樂鑪錢立錢其之
耳門之必誰聞逐重蓄重懋人
。而徒設無也利錢物物遷立
重開法是人者輕之輕也法
爲告禁心棄之。限之。以
煩訐以正我正所然故教
許正。。所藏。以

themselves to turn over their capital. Now because the money is heavy and commodities are light (because money is scarce and commodities abundant) they have put a limit to the hoarding up of money; but the fact that there is such a proportion between money and merchandise (lit. that money is heavy and merchandise light), is for those who possess ready money and are greedy of gain, an intelligence at which they rejoice. For who does not cherish in his inmost heart the thought, what others cast away I take. Verily, it is not necessary to make prohibitions by law to force them to this. This only opens the door for accusations and complaints, and causes needless vexations in a high degree.

A few more pages of our chronicle we have to wade through before we are at an end. But all is barren from Dan to Berseba. Fresh regulations on the possession of a certain amount of copper money were issued. Whereas in the foregoing parts we have often seen that among the ministers of State and the high functionaries many an enlightened councilor succeeded in preventing the bad measures which the government was about to take, of the addresses which in these days are presented at court the one is still more absurd than the other. As there was nowhere any longer money on hand, the attention of the government is directed to the temples of Buddha, with their bulk of metal statues, tools and vessels. So the following decree was issued:

太和三年詔佛像以鉛錫土木爲之飾帶以金銀鍮石¹)烏油藍鐵唯鑑磬²)釘鐶鈕得用銅餘皆禁之。

> In the third year of the period *Tai-ho* (829), it was ordered that the Buddha-figures and ornaments should be inlaid with lead, tin, clay, or wood, and to make the girdle either of gold, silver, brass¹) or steel blued and polished. Only for mirrors, gongs²), nails, rings and buttons, copper might be used.

The attention of government once directed to the temples, it was not long before religion itself was laid under requisition.

Because the Empire was in want, the service of Buddha was abolished by the Emperor. Our chronicle says:

及武宗廢浮屠法永平監官李郁彥請以銅像鐘磬鑪鐸皆歸巡院州縣銅亦多矣。

> The Emperor *Wu-tsung* having abolished the so-called *Feu-tu*-(Buddha) service, *Li-yeu-yen*, the director of the mint in *Yung-ping* proposed to have all the copper statues, mallet-bells, gongs and clapper-bells confiscated by the body of itinerant officials. In the several districts of the empire a large quantity of copper would certainly be found.

But enough of this. Intestine division and anarchy increase more and more. However brilliant and glorious the beginning of the T'ang-dynasty had been, the end was most miserable. Our history is silent on the last 40 years of the existence of this imperial line. In what way a new creation sprung forth from this chaos will be shown in the next chapter. With the end of the rule of the T'ang-dynasty Ma-twan-lin closes his eighth volume.

---

1) 鍮石 a sort of brass resembling gold. It is imported from Persia.

2) 磬 a musical stone, suspended on a frame, one of the eight musical instru-ments, says MEDHURST, was struck in the temples to call the people to prayer. A gong is properly an instrument used in the army, a brass drum 鑼.

# CHAPTER V.

HISTORY OF THE MONEY UNDER THE SUNG-DYNASTY.

THE 5 IMPERIAL FAMILIES. — FREE COINING AND ITS EFFECTS. —. A CONFLICT BETWEEN CHURCH AND STATE. — SPEECH OF THE EMPEROR AND REPLY OF AN ECONOMIST BELIEVER IN BUDDHA. — THE SUNG-DYNASTY, NEW REGULATION OF MONEY-MATTERS. — THE HISTORY OF THE DOUBLE STANDARD IN CHINA. — THE ECONOMICAL INNOVATIONS OF WANG-GNAN-SI. 1° STATE ADVANCES TO CULTIVATORS OF LAND. 2° PROHIBITIONS AGAINST THE EXPORT OF COPPER SUSPENDED. — AN OLD WAY TO PAY NEW DEBTS. — CRITICAL OBSERVATIONS ON MONEY BY TUNG-LAI OF THE FAMILY LIU.

Many years were yet to elapse before the end of the reigning dynasty was near, and China was delivered of the weak and despotic descendants of the duke of *T"ang*.

But the fall of this dynasty made, if possible, matters worse than ever. The chief generals did quarrel and fight among themselves; anarchy and confusion run riot, and the country was lacerated as before by civil war.

Within the time of 53 years (907—960) there reigned five different imperial families; two of these were of Tartar origin. In these times of commotion and bloodshed, the monetary history is confined to the abolishment of the existing and the introduction of all sorts of restrictive measures, which were as thoughtless and tyrannical as those described in the preceding chapter. The following are some loose fragments which give an insight into the political and economical state of affairs and which also in a grammatical point of view are the most remarkable parts of Ma-twan-lin's book.

法。今鑄銅除永廢文。許府。鑄貲。晉
後錢器。鑄遠銅左鑄無無泉天
祇雜四錢冶。環錢問。聞。貨福。
官以年外。為讀仍公宜為三
鑄鉛勑不許之以私令為年。
造。錫以得百天應三銷詔
私缺天接姓福有京鎔曰。
下小下便取元銅諸則國
禁違公別便寶者道甚家
舊條私鑄利。鍊。久並州添所

In the third year of the period *T'ien-fu* under the reign of the (later) *Tsin*-dynasty (938), a proclamation was made in which was said, "A heavy medium of exchange constitutes the wealth of a state. And though a quantity (of coins) are cast equal to the number of woodworms, even then it will be (a thing) unheard of that there will be coined too much. It is, therefore, proper to issue a decree that in the three capitals and in all the country-towns [1]) everyone without questioning whether he be a public or private person, shall be allowed to cast money according to his being possessed of copper." The legend of this money was. "First treasure of the period *T'ien-fu.*" These words were read in a circle (beginning from the top) to the left [2]). In all the provinces the people were allowed to take possession of the copper-foundaries which were not used since a long time, and to open them immediately for the purpose of melting copper ore. It was ever of the highest importance that, as henceforth the government did not enjoy the profits any more, besides the casting of money, the permission did not include the casting of copper tools [3]).

In the fourth year (940) an imperial decree enacted that henceforth the money should be cast by the state exclusively, because in the whole empire everybody had cast money which was adulterated with lead and tin, which was bad and small, and (because) the people had disobeyed the prescribed regulations. Private persons were since that time checked again by the old restrictions.

1) lit. in all the towns of districts and provinces. 道 and, as we shall further see, 路 are both used as denominations of political divisions of that time.

2) Cf. page 102 on the signification of the left and right side of a coin.

3) lit. With this was not connected the separately casting of copper tools.

Notwithstanding the imperial decree (See Chapter IV p. 125) the people had remained faithful to the creed of their fathers, and when under the Later *Tšeu*-dynasty (951—60) there was again a great want of money, Buddhism was once more laid under requisition. But this timé it was ordered that all persons throughout the kingdom should sacrifice to their country their Buddha figures, and what copper vessels, utensils, etc. they might be possessed of.

On occasion of a levee at court this measure is made public by the emperor himself in a remarkable speech which he delivers in order to remove the religious scruples and misgivings which his faithful subjects might have. The address of the Emperor is followed by a reply of one of the high state-officers, who does not only prove to be a stanch adherent of Buddhism, but also develops his economical objections to such a policy in a very sensible and frank manner.

亦 身 以 雖 佛．佛 像 奉 苟 以 佛 卿 上
非 可 布 頭 志 耶．者．佛 志 善 爲 輩 謂
所 以 施．目 在 且 豈 矣¹．於 道 疑．勿 侍
惜 濟 若 猶 利 吾 所 彼 善．化 夫 以 人
也．民．朕 捨 人．聞 謂 銅 斯 人．佛 毁 曰．

The emperor addressing his attendance, said: "Noble servants of the crown! It is not my intention to raise doubt among the people by the confiscation of the Buddhas. Buddha indeed makes men better by leading them into the right path, and when our will is directed to the good, we must honor Buddha. But are those copper statues really what is called Buddha? Moreover I have heard that (the tendency of the doctrines of) Buddha is to benefit the people. And though your face is still opposed against these figures being spread and sacrificed (i. e. when your feelings are [against it) (be not afraid, for) as long as Our Imperial Self has the power to promote the interests of his subjects, there will be no reason to pity (them).

1) Remark 矣.

猶 尙 不 毛 必 之。所 像 禁 者 止。之 致
是 欲 敢 尹。矣² 錢 敬 是 銷 能。惟 而 堂
也。除 犯 神 韓 之 畏。也。錢 若 爲 行。胡
銷 佛 法³ 策 愈 不 尙 銅 而 世 人 禁 氏
錢 者 曰 六 拜 可 且 像 毀 宗 所 之 曰。
爲 亦 是 軍。京 銷 毀 人 銅 欲 難 而 令

· *Hu-ŝi* coming up to the audience-hall, spoke as follows: To command a thing and to have it carried into effect, to prohibit a thing and to cause it to cease, he alone may do who is compelled to it in behalf of the people. Now if (the emperor) *Ŝi-tsung* should wish to prohibit the melting of copper money and (to command) the breaking of the copper statues, it would be such a case ¹). Those copper figures reverenced and feared by the people, though you break them now, .yet it is sure according to my conviction ²) that the result will not be that a sufficient quantity of copper money can be melted. ·

When *Han-yü* was appointed imperial governor of the capital, and he was at the head of a well disciplined imperial army, he has not ventured to violate those laws ³), and it is said that he too wished to abolish Buddhism. This too was a similar case (to the present) ⁴).

1) Then it would be in the interest of the people that such a thing happened. "The king cannot do wrong". — *Hu-ŝi*'s words justify this interpretation. He says, pursuing the thread of his discourse after some digression, "but I am not aware that his Majesty wishes to prohibit it".

2) Subjective opinion of *Hu-ŝi* expressed by 矣 is clear here. So also at the end of this fragment.

3) The law 法 signifies here Buddhism 毛 = 兆 Cfr. page 58.

4) The following may serve as an explanation of the historical allusion, and the meaning of the speaker, that, what the most vehement antagonist of Buddhism and the most powerful man of his time has not dared to undertake, may no more be ordered by the present ministers.

韓 愈. *Han-yü*, a statesman and philosopher under the *T'ang*-dyn., was renowned for his antagonism to the religion of Buddha and his undaunted fidelity to his prince. In 819 A. D. he presented a remonstrance against the public honors with which a finger-bone of Buddha, a relic to which supernatural influences were attributed, was to be conveyed to the Imperial palace. *Han-yü*'s diatribe against the alien superstition is, according to MAYERS, still renowned as one of the most celebrated of state papers, but it only roused the Emperor's wrath against the author who was banished to a remote region in the South of China.

An extract of the remarkable remonstrance, as it is found in DE MAILLA, Hist. Gen. d. l. Chine Vol. VI, p. 433, runs as follows: "Buddha est une idole des pays "occidentaux à la Chine. Votre Majesté, "par les honneurs et le culte qu'elle lui "rend cherche à se procurer une longue "vie et un règne heureux et paisible. Parmi "les anciens rois, il y en a beaucoup qui "ont joui d'une longue vie, tandis que le "peuple vivait dans une paix constante, "cependant il n'y avait point alors de Bud-"dha; ce n'est que sous l'empereur *Ming-ti* "de la dynastie des *Han* (58—76 après J. "C.) que sa doctrine s'est repandue dans "l'empire, et depuis cette époque, les trou-"bles et les guerres se sont succédés, en-"trainant à leur suite les maux et la dé-"cadence des familles impériales. De tous

器其利十倍。錢所以權百貨。平低昂。其鐖之也不計費。不謀息今而銷之。可不禁乎。雖然銷而為器。錢雖毀而器存焉。若夫散而四出。舟

When money is melted to make tools of it, a tenfold gain is made by it. And is it now allowed (so people argue) that the money which serves as an equivalent for all other merchandise, whether its value be on a par, high or low, and that is cast by the government without reckoning the cost and without regulation when it shall cease, is melted without any prohibition [1])?

Notwithstanding it is a fact that it is melted and that tools are made of it, the money though gone, these tools remain!

Now if these tools are scattered over the four frontiers of the empire, (if they are) transported by freights and cartloads, carried into foreign countries, and come back again to the southern Barbarians, what then

"les princes des dynasties posterieures il "n'y a en que *Wu-ti*, de la dynastie des "*Liangs*, qui ait occupé le trône pendant "quarante-huit ans, et que n'a-t-il pas fait "pour obtenir de Buddha la paix et la fé-"licité? Il s'est vendu jusqu'a trois fois et "s'est fait esclave dans un de ses temples! "Et sa recompense fut de mourir misérable-"ment de faim. Cependant, il ne faisait, "disait-il, continuellement ces actions, si "peu convenables à un prince, que dans "l'espérance du bonheur qu'il attendait de "Buddha, et il n'en a été que plus mal-"heureux.

."Buddha n'est qu'un homme originaire "d'un royaume des barbares de l'occident "de la Chine, qui ne connaissait ni la fi-"délité qu'un sujet doit a son prince, ni "l'obéissance d'un fils à l'égard de son père. "S'il vivait encore, et qu'il vint à votre "cour, tout ce que votre Majesté pourrait "faire, serait de le recevoir avec magnifi-"cence, de lui faire quelques présents et "d'envoyer le reconduire jusqu'aux frontières "de l'empire, sans que vos peuples y eus-"sent le moindre part. Cet homme, ce "Buddha est mort depuis longtemps, on a "présenté a votre Majesté un os desseché, "qu'on dit être de lui, aurait elle dû "le recevoir dans son palais? J'ose donc "lui demander, qu'elle fasse remettre cet "os entre les mains des censeurs de l'em-"pire, afin que le faisant passer par l'eau "et par le feu, on abolisse ce culte si per-"nicieux. Si Buddha est tel qu'on le dit,

"qu'il ait le pouvoir de rendre les hommes "heureux ou malheureux, je consens que "tous les maux qui en pourront arriver "tombent sur moi, tant je suis persuadé de "son peu de pouvoir".

Under the Emperor *Mu-tsung* he was restored again to his high office, and was appointed generalissimo of an army with which he crushed a rebellion in the North of the Empire (DE MAILLA Hist. gén. d. l. Chine tome VI p. 439. etc.). When by his efforts peace was restored *"Mu-tsung, lui donna un emploi, dont la jurisdiction s'étendait sur tous les soldats, ce qui leur inspira tant de crainte qu'aucun n'osait manquer a son devoir"*. This *Hu-si* expresses by 神策六軍 where he says: Even he, the vehement antagonist of Buddhism, when appointed commander-in-chief of the whole imperial army durst not violate the law, and abolish the statues of Buddha.

左右神策軍 The right and left army of divine stratagems. Name of an army, which distinguished itself ou the Western frontiers of China. It continued to be a honorary appellation till the time of the *Kin*-dynasty. MORR. in voce 官 n° 84.

1) Yes, it is allowable, is the meaning of *Hu-si* with this question; for when the money is melted, the tools remain hence no wealth is lost.

遷車轉。入於他國歸¹⁾
於變夷。其害豈特爲
害而已。而不聞世宗
禁之。則不以泉貨貿
遠方之寶。可知已錢
之散也。以貿遠方之
寶於也。上好之下效
之。隳是關防不嚴。法
制日壞。眞錢日少。僞
錢日多。以不貴之價。
靡有限之錢。雖萬物
銅。陰陽爲炭。亦且不
給。區區器像。又何濟

constitutes the proper loss, (lit. what of that loss is then specially the loss), and if you can tell me that, I am satisfied (lit. and stop there, *nihil amplius*).

But I am not aware that the emperor *Ši-tsung* has prohibited it (the melting of money)²). Now if the treasures of far off countries are not exchanged for currency, may I know how the money is spread? Why, it is indeed because the treasures of distant countries have been exchanged for it³).

[*The speaker now abruptly leaves this subject and proceeds with stating the reason why the want of money should be attributed to no other cause than the badness of the quality*].

What the great ones are fond of, the lower orders like to imitate (i. e. government makes the money bad, and the people follow the example). In addition to this, the official seals are not well sunk, and the legal regulations (respecting the coining of money) are violated. The money which has its full intrinsic value becomes scarcer every day, whereas the false money increases daily.

Truly, when it (the money) has no more the price (value) of a precious object, and (when) the money which has certain limits, is no more extant, were all creation of copper, and the whole world (lit. all that

1) 歸 Come back to the Barbarians i. e. the native copper which we have received from the Barbarians, comes back to them made into all sorts of tools. Copper was also imported from Persia.
2) These words should have been spoken in the beginning of the speech, but in consequence of his meditations on "the Mercantile System," the speaker had lost the thread of his argument, and takes it up to drop it immediately afterwards.
3) He means to say — You, ministers, think that the money, if spread among the people, gets lost because it is melted, and that this is prejudicial to the country and the people. But you are mistaken; we get in return the treasures of distant countries and you are misled by the fact that it does not go away in the form of coined money with which these treasures are bought, but in the form of copper tools. But the people melt it, and make tools of it because the Barbarians give ten times more for a quantity of copper in the form of arms and tools than in the form of coined money. *Hu-ši* is an admirable economist, but it is a pity his reasoning is not a little clearer.

上　可　國　不　具　嚴　而　人　後　庶　乎。
矣。流　之　廢。在。密¹。又　之　可　無　故
於　錢。則　鼓　法　中　關　共　蓄　欲。惟
地　眞　中　鑄　制　防　寳。生　然　至

is light and dark) of charcoal, it would nevertheless be impossible to supply what is wanted. And how could the few tools and Buddha figures bring about a change in this. Therefore, only when without cupidity the utmost disinterestedness is observed, we shall succeed in producing for the people a common treasure which has an intrinsic value. Moreover, if care is taken that the seals are well sunk, and the legal regulations are maintained, and the casting (of money) is not discontinued, the money of the Middle Kingdom shall really be able to stream throughout the most exquisite of countries.

### THE SUNG-DYNASTY.

The people and the army, impatient of the perpetual change of princes and families, had got such a strong dislike to their insignificant rulers, often mere infants, that they had already long looked out for a leader firm and energetic enough to restore order and peace in the confused realm. And when they thought to have found such a man in their favorite general, they were quite ready to rise in his favor and drive away the reigning sovereign. An opportunity to carry out this bold resolution soon presented itself. After the death of *Ši-tsüng* a child having become emperor under the regency of the Empress-dowager, the *Liao* Tartars had taken advantage of this circumstance to invade China and extent their territory. To check the further progress of this formidable foe, a numerous army was sent out under command of the idol of the people, the generalissimo *Tšao-kwang-yin* 趙匡胤. One evening when the army lay

---

1 嚴密 lit. to keep diligently.

encamped near the capital and the commander was soundly asleep, he was roused by a stir without. On leaving his tent he saw a clamorous crowd of officers and soldiers who had just returned from a public meeting in which their general had been proclaimed Emperor; and before he was but half apprised of the cause of all this noise and uproar, the yellow mantle, the emblem of the imperial dignity, was thrown over him and he was hailed as "the Son of Heaven." The new-made emperor returned immediately to the capital where he was enthusiastically welcomed by the people. The boy-king abdicated of his own accord and the revolution was accomplished without the least violence, without so much as even the shedding of one drop of blood. *Tai-tsu* was the name of the emperor and the dynasty was called the *Sung-*dynasty after the district of *Sung-tšeu*, of which he had been governor. When hearing that the renowned warrior had ascended the throne, the Tartars lost courage and retired into their own dominions. The new emperor immediately applied himself to remove the evils which had arisen in the last reigns and was careful in adopting all such measures as promoted the welfare of the people.

Among others the monetary system was completely re-organized. A new sort of copper money was made, bearing the legend of "Current treasure from the beginning of the *Sung-*dynasty." 宋元通寳. The decrees by which people were forbidden to possess more than a certain amount of copper money were annulled, and in different parts of the country copper-foundaries were built, bearing such promising names, as "The Eternal Prosperity," "The Eternal Peace," "The Long Repose," "The Flourishing Country," "The treasures-producing Mint," and iron-foundaries styled "Beneficial to the People," "To the support of all," etc.

The two most remarkable events, however, recorded in the history of the money were, 1° the introduction of the double standard, and 2° the issue of paper-money.

As to the former, I have carefully collected all the passages in the Chronicle referring to this subject in order to be able to give a complete history of the double standard in the Chinese Empire.

Paper money forming one of the most interesting subjects in the history of Political Economy, a separate chapter has been devoted to all the matter relating to this currency under the *Sung*-dynasty.

### THE DOUBLE STANDARD.

The want of a sufficient quantity of copper very probably gave rise to the use of iron money. This new currency was first made by private persons at the close of the period of the "five imperial families," and during the reign of the *Sung* it was circulated in large quantities by the government without however superseding the existing copper money. It was principally in the western provinces of 四川 *Sse-tš'uen*, 陝西 *Šen-si*, and in the eastern tea-districts of 福建 *Fu-kien*, that this iron money was employed in large quantities. The legal ratio was such that 10 ironpieces had the value of 1 copper coin, 以鐵錢貿。凡 十當銅錢一。but it is evident that those pieces of the different metals were not equal in size. For we read, "that the Emperor built three state foundaries for casting iron money, and that a string of the money made there was to have a weight of

12 pounds and a few ounces in order to correspond in worth with a string of copper money weighing 5 pounds exactly." The calculation occurring in another fragment [Ma-twan-lin IX 7*a*] varies, though the relative values are nearly the same.

○凡鑄銅錢。用劑八十八兩。得錢千重八十兩。十分其劑。銅居六分。鉛錫居三分。有奇贏。鑄大鐵錢用鐵二百四十兩。得錢千重百九十二兩。此其大法也。

"In the casting of money a composition of 88 ounces was commonly used, and the thousand coins made of it weighed 80 ounces. Of the 10 parts of which that composition consisted were 6 parts of copper and 3 parts of lead and tin. Of all these there was an overplus (i. e. a little more of each of the three sorts of metal was used in order to make up the 10th part). In the casting of iron money 240 ounces were used, and the thousand coins made thereof weighed 192 ounces, this was the general rule." $(80 : 192 = 5 : 12.)$

This copper money contained 3 pounds and 10 ounces of pure copper, and 2 pounds of alloy. The alloy was composed of 1 pound 8 ounces of lead and 8 ounces of tin; and about 8 or 10 ounces were lost in the process of making it. From this account it appears that the relative worth of the two metals was about as 1 to 3.5 and not as 1 to 10 as we should presume from the above citation (p. 134). Ma-twan-lin, it appears, feared obscurity from these contradictory passages, and therefore he says in a note, that the little iron pieces, 10 of which were worth one cash, had been abolished, and that at the same time the relative value of iron and copper money had been altered, as the iron money circulating in the province of *Sse-tš'uen* of the nominal ratio of from 10 to 1, in weight, gave a ratio of 25 pound of iron to 5 pound of copper; accordingly a real ratio of from 5 to 1. This had not been done to depreciate iron money, but simply as a measure of utility, because the magistrates of the districts where iron money circulated, had perpetually complained that the money was so heavy that it was not possible to make use of it, and — says one of them — "if it was made a little lighter of weight, it would have this advantage that one might easily equip one's self for a journey" 錢輕則 行者易齎。 The weight of this iron money was likewise the cause that paper money was frequently used in those districts, as we will see in the next chapter.

In consequence of the use of two sorts of metal as currency, the Chinese got in greater difficulties than any European government has ever been on this account. The objections to the use of the double standard, if stated by a thorough Chinese, would be of quite a different nature from those which French and English economists have raised in a great number of books during the last 30 years. Were it not that seen from a Chinese point of view the question presents some new aspects interesting enough, I certainly should not venture once more to treat of it.

We have not as in Europe to do with two precious metals like gold and silver which drive each other out of the country as soon as either of them is overvalued, and oblige the governments to buy back the runaway servant at a high price of their neighbors; in China foreign trade had in this respect very little influence on the prices of bullion. The great drawback, however, was this, that the intrinsic value both of iron and copper was so little that it was not possible to estimate a constant legal ratio between them. Further, what lately, wherever in Europe the double standard is adopted, has been effected by the free market of foreign countries, was done in China by the false coiners.

These persons speculated on the relative value of the two sorts of money, which constantly varied, and they always coined the cheaper currency in order to exchange it for the dearer; and the difference was not 2 per cent, as in the Netherlands from 1816—1839, or even less, as in France up to 1869, but generally from 100 to 200 per cent, and this caused that the depreciated currency circulated at a high premium, or was peremptorily refused in the market. It is also remarkable that in order to remove the difficulties of a double standard, the Chinese financiers at length took the very same measures as afterwards were taken in Europe; they instituted again the single standard under the flag of the bimetalic system.

All along the western frontiers of China, from the southern provinces of *Yün-nan* and *Sse-tš'uen* to the North-western province of *Šen-si*, a numerous army was constantly kept in the field to resist the warlike Tartar tribes who perpetually invaded the Middle-Kingdom.

Great sums of money were required to provide such a host with provisions and arms, but the large supplies of money were not sufficient to meet the ever increasing want. Some magistrates of those parts then suggested that at those places in the mountains where considerable quantities of metal were found, forges and foundaries should be erected. This plan was acted up to. But now it occurred that in some districts the mountains contained much iron and hardly any copper, and as each of the magistrates of these districts wished to have some money at his disposal, they sought and obtained the permission of the Central board of administration to cast iron money. Ma-twan-lin says on this subject:

行。鐵錢悉幣致關中。數州錢雜小
錢而江池饒儀虢州。又鑄小
大錢。朝廷因勅江南鑄大銅鑄
州東竹尖嶺大銅錢而陝西復采儀
河勅³）中軍贊州。未幾三司采儀罷以
於晉澤二州貴。亦以三當十。以鐵
錢及奎促河東。又一鑄大鐵錢小
奎等奎請因晉州²）一積當大鐵小十。
小錢與軍行。大錢請一當當小錢十。與
永興¹）軍范雍請鑄大銅錢鑄
既而陝西都轉運使張奎知

*Tšang-kuei*, the head official for the transport of government goods, in the province of *Šen-si*, and *Fan-yung*, the civil magistrate of the headquarters of the army in the district of *Yung-hing* ¹), had already proposed to cast large copper coins which were to circulate together with the small coins, (in such a way) that one large piece should be worth 10 small pieces. (*Tšang*)-*kuei* and others had also suggested, there being plenty of iron in the district of *Tsin-tšeu* ²), to have money cast there, and when (*Tšang*)-*kuei* was obliged to go to *Ho-tung*, he had in the provinces of *Tsin* and *Tse-tšeu* large iron coins cast, one of which was again worth 10 small coins, in order to meet the expenses of the army encamped in *Kwan-tšung* ³). A short time afterwards the mint-college reported that east of the *Hoang-ho*, the casting of large iron coins had been discontinued, and that in *Šen-si* (thus West of the *Hoang-ho*) the people again ran after the yellow copper of the mountains of *Tšu-tsien-ling*, in the district of *I-tšeu*, where the foundary, "the Universal kindness", had been built for the fabrication of large money.

In the name of the government it was, therefore, ordered that in *Kiang-nan* large copper coins should be cast, and that in the districts of *Kiang-Tsi-Sao-I*-and *Kwo-tšeu* small iron coins should be cast, and

1) Prov. of *Sse-tšuen*. 知 lit. to know, is the title given under the *Sung* and subsequent dynasties to a civil magistrate appointed governor of a district. 知 … 軍 lit. knowing the military affairs

was the title of the same official in the headquarters of an army in field.

2) In *Ho-tung*, prov. of 山西.

3) 關中 *Kwan-tšung* is an ancient name of the province *Šen-si* and adjacent parts of *Ho-nan*. MAYERS, II. 309.

that all these (coins) should be carried to *Kwan-tsung*, where the money of those different districts should circulate together.

In this way there circulated four different varieties of coins, two of copper and two of iron. The relative value of the two copper varieties as well as that of the two iron, was as 1 to 10. The casting of the larger iron coins, however, was soon discontinued. If we inquire into the metallic worth of these coins, it appears that the government had again been misled by false theories, and but too soon would suffer the consequences of it.

大約小銅錢三可鑄當十大銅錢一。故民間盜鑄者眾。錢文大亂。物價翔踊。公私患之。

On the whole, of three of these small copper coins, one large copper coin could be cast, which then obtained a worth of 10 small pieces. Consequently there came among the people a great many false coiners, and in the currency there arose a great confusion. (The result was that) the prices of all articles rose enormously, and both with the government and with private persons this caused great uneasiness.

A still greater difficulty was the relative value of iron and copper money. A magistrate suggested that the worth of the iron money in *Ho-tung* should be as 2 to 1 little copper coin, but after a year it was thought necessary to make 3 iron coins equal to one copper coin, and in private dealings it frequently occurred that 5 iron coins were given for 1 copper coin.

To resume what has been said, there were circulating together: 1° large copper pieces of a metallic worth of 3 and a nominal value of 10 small copper coins. 2° small copper coins which generally commanded *agio*, when circulating together with the small iron money. 3° small iron money which had no constant value.

As such a condition proved to be untenable, various measures were suggested to bring about a change. Among others an assayer of the mint-college 三司度支判官 proposed as medicine, to melt copper and iron together, and to make the weight of a coin cast of that mixture, equal to that of the circulating copper money, and to determine the proportions so "that one piece 贏。皆居三而 contained three parts of copper and six 有六分銅 parts of iron, and of both metals a little 奇分。鐵居 more for the remaining 10th part". In this way, "he was convinced", as good a currency might be made, while the cost of fabrication should be less and the profits of the government larger. The fun of the whole thing was that when this worthy assayer made a trial in his mint to cast money in this way "the workpeople 無之。工多鐵 took a dislike to it, as the iron was too 成。後人不澁 hard of nature and therefore too difficult 卒苦就。而 to work, while the quantity (i. e. the real value) did not come up to what it should be; soon afterwards it was, therefore, not made any more" (Mat. IX 7a).

Very sensible, however, was the advice given by a committee, appointed by the emperor to make an inquiry of the advantages and disadvantages arising from the use of the double standard. This committee consisted of the mint-college 三司, together with Ts'ang-fang-ping 張方平 and Sung-k'i 宋祁, two men of high reputation in those days [1]), and the cabinet-minister Ye-tsing 葉清, who before being a minister had been member of the mint-college, and has held that office after his resignation. The report of this committee suggests: 1º to fix a better ratio between the value of large and small copper money, and 2º to determine the relative value of copper and iron money. A deputation of

1) Cf. MAYERS, I. 9 and 639.

two members of this committee went to his Majesty, as soon as the report was ready, and spoke about these words:

"Your Majesty when instituting the large copper money had thought to derive great profits from it. So it promised to be in the beginning, but when afterwards, in consequence of the little metallic worth of that money, the prices of all articles rose, that wrong proceeding at last made reprisals on the government, 終取償於上。 and by this you have lost in the end more than you had gained in the beginning. And even though your Majesty 縣官雖有折當之虛名，乃罹虧損之實害。救弊不先自損，則法未易行。 were inclined to reduce the present money which has an empty name to its real standard, and were willing to put up with losses, as by repairing the bad condition you will not escape to suffer the loss yourself, yet we fear that this new regulation will not easily be brought in execution".

"Now we would recommend you to make the value of one 大銅錢一當小銅錢三。 piece of the large copper money equal to three pieces of the small copper coins, in the different districts where both sorts are in circulation".

"The reason, however, why at present the false coiners do not exclusively occupy themselves with the casting of iron money, is that they can gain more by casting the large copper pieces. But as soon as the exact ratio between the copper coins is restored, they will cause new confusion, because they will then make small iron money. To prevent this likewise we would furthermore 以小鐵錢三當銅錢一。 suggest to you to make it a general rule that three pieces of iron money shall be equal in value to one (small) piece of copper. Moreover do we advice you to cease the building of state-foundaries on such a large scale."

The emperor consented to all this and made use of the advice given. The government went even further by estimating the relative value of the large and small currency of both copper and iron as 2 to 1. False coining was entirely discontinued, and the manifold complaints of suffered wrong, made since a long time, were not heard any more.

The apprehensions of the committee that the new regulation should cause difficulties proved to be well founded. For the Western parts of the country were choked with iron money which now, it is true, had obtained a certain worth in relation to the copper money, but which, on account of the little stability of its worth, proved to be unfit to serve together with the copper money as a measure of value. They experienced the fatal consequences, but missed the right understanding which would needs have led to a satisfactory solution of this knotty question. In order to get rid of the great mass of circulating iron money, the government determined to buy one pound of this iron money at 40 pieces of the new copper coin which was reduced to a value of 2 cents 折二錢; but enacting this law they committed the fault not to stop the circulation of iron money as legal tender. What now happens is communicated by a head-official for the government transports in a report to the central board of administration: "For 40 copper coins", he says, "we get one pound of bad iron money, and 1000 pieces of small copper money may be exchanged for 1000 iron pieces of a value of 2. A thousand small iron pieces contain 6 pounds of iron, and if people cast 2000 pieces of it, and exchange them for 1000 copper pieces, the goverumeut, iu my humble opiuion, sustains a considerable loss". (This is prefectly right; the loss amounts to more than 50 per cent, for 1 pound of iron = 40 copper coins, thus 1000 copper coins are worth 25 pounds of iron, and if 12 pounds of iron made into 2000 small iron pieces, are exchanged for copper money, 1000 copper coins are received for it).

"It is a wretched condition because the iron pieces reduced to a value of 2 cents are bought and sold in bullion at half the price which they have as coined money". That the difficulties of the double standard

其 錢 折
半。才 二
　 易 大

were not solved as yet, appears further from the statements communicated by the historiographer *Tseu-yin* iu his report to the Emperor.

又 後 貨。不 餘 官 利 而 用 問 路。奉 御
作 來 起 在 賈。中 倍 民 一 其 伏 使。史
折 減 初 其 民 積 又 間 當 本 見 經 周
二。為 元 數。中 聚。訪 溢 二 末。溢 由 尹
巳 折 以 緣 收 有 聞 鑄 鐵。鑄 永 言。
於 三。一 上 藏 數 得 者。錢 是 錢 與 臣
國 近 當 件 者。百 所 費 易 錢 不 秦 去
家 歲 十 錢 猶 萬 在 少 得 法 少。鳳 冬

The imperial historiographer *Tseu-yin* spoke as follows: "Your servant set out on a journey in the winter, when he was sent on a mission. When passing through the districts of *Yung-hing*, *Tseu-* and *Feng-tseu* he has secretly observed that false coining is not inconsiderable, and when inquiring into the cause and effect. it appeared to him that it was because the decrees regulating the relative worth of the money (lit. the money law) made 1 piece (of copper) equal in value to 2 pieces (of iron). The iron money is easily to be had, and the false coiners among the people make a double gain at little cost. I have also set afoot an inquiry, and I am informed of the amount of money treasured up by the functionaries; it amounted to a quantity of about 1.000.000 string. What is saved by the people is not so much. When in the beginning the relative worth of the money was estimated

重貨。十損其八。若更作一文行
用。即又損一分。所以不當輒有
奏請。若即改鑄之法。或只仍舊作
折二錢。欲即民間盜鑄定錢。亦更不可
止絕。臣望作折二鑄起自今不
別行改一文行用。須揀選
後。只作一文用。則盜鑄者。冒所
獲之不充所費。而自然無復。冒所
禁作過歲省重碎。
獲泉貨流通之利。且約官中所
有。止就四百萬貫言之。若以二
為一。即猶得二百萬貫之數致
力簡省。便可得用。

they began in the very first times with making 1 piece equal to 10. Then it (the value of 1 piece) was lowered and reduced to a value of 3, and last year it was changed again and the value reduced at 2. So, on the heavy medium of exchange instituted by the government, people have already suffered a loss of 8 parts on the 10. Now if you again make (a change) so that the pieces circulate and are employed at the worth of 1, you will again cause a loss of one part (to the present owners of the money). In what way. you should not make such sudden change, the memorial will suggest to you.

If you, when recasting the money, continue as before only to make pieces which are worth 2, you shall not be able to succeed in checking the making of false money among the people. But now your servant wishes you to cease making those pieces of 2 *càsh* when you cast money, and then not to have them (the now circulating 2 *cash* coins) separately recoined so, nor is it then necessary to sift and pick them out (to withdraw them). But if from this time forth you begin by making only pieces of 1 *cash*, and by bringing them in circulation, then the profit gained by the false coiners will not even be so great that the cost of fabrication can be defrayed by it. From that time the violation and transgression of the laws will not occur again.

The annual decrease (of money) will be considerable and visible, but both agriculture and trade will reap the fruits thereof that all articles stream and circulate. And, furthermore, if the money treasured up by the government amounts, for instance, to about 4.000.000 string, and those coins which are worth 2 are made into pieces only worth 1, then, obtaining 2.000.000 string, it is true that the power (i. e. the wealth) of the state will have been condensed and curtailed (but on the other hand it is also true that) it will be very convenient in use.

The measure which at length was resorted to and which solved the question in some degree at least, was to regulate the circulation of iron and copper money in such a way, that in some parts of the empire only copper money and in others again only iron money should be employed, by which the speculations on the relative value of the two metals, if not entirely, at any rate was prevented in the main.

Ma-twan-lin has the two following passages bearing upon this reform, and the fact that a period of more than a century has elapsed between the events he communicates (1075—1191) may serve as another evidence that the regulation, by which certain districts were bound down to the use of a certain sort of money, was the measure which was attended with the best results in the given circumstances. [Matw. IX 14a—15a and 23b].

無 之 深 條 沿 本 交 錢 北 曰。還 蘇 戶
由 所 重。法。邊 朝 易。幣。界 臣 論 轍 部
止。在。而 雖・禁 銅 並 公 別 切 事 北 侍
本 勢 利 極 錢 錢。使 私 無 見 宜 使 郎

The vice-president of the ministry of finances *Su-tse* [1]), who as envoy had returned from the north, speaking about the condition (of the money in those parts), and what ought to be done (to work a change in it) said: Your servant has carefully observed that on the northern borders especially, there is a want of medium of exchange [2]). In all commercial transactions of private persons as well as of the government, the copper money of our present dynasty is exclusively employed. Notwithstanding the restrictions and laws are very severe, by which the export of copper along the frontier is prohibited, yet the profit it yields (to export copper) is so great a power that there exists no means to stop it.

1) Cf. MAYERS I. G24.
2) He speaks of the Tartars and not of

the Emperor's subjects. Cf. page 148, where a passage is quoted alluding to the same fact.

朝每歲鑄錢以百萬計。而所在常患
錢少。蓋散入四夷勢當爾也。謹按陝河
北河東陝西三路。鐵錢數極多。與銅錢並能
西鑄二鐵錢萬數鐵錢十五。僅緣
行。而民間輕賤鐵錢與銅錢等。
比銅錢十。而官用鐵錢與銅錢雖有小
此解鹽鈔法。久遠必敗。河東雖有嘗
鐵錢。然數目極少。河北一路則未並
鼓鑄臣等嘗聞議者謂可於三路諸州
鑄鐵錢。而行使之地止於極邊諸州
極邊見在銅錢。並以鐵錢兌換般入
近裏州郡如此。則雖不禁錢出外界
而其弊自止矣。

If we consider that the amount of the money fabricated by our dynasty is 1.000.000 string yearly, and that perpetual complaints are still made that the money is scarce, it must be attributed to this that it is imported and spread among the Barbarians. Let us closely examine (the condition) of the three provinces of *Ho-pëk*, *Ho-tung* and *Šen-si*. In each of them the ground produces iron. Now we see that at present in *Šen-si* the number of tens of thousands of iron coins worth 2 *cash* which are cast there, is very large, and that it circulates together with the copper money; but that among the people the iron money is thought light and base, so that 15 pieces of iron money are made equal in value to hardly 10 pieces of copper money, while by the government the iron and copper money is employed on a par. In consequence of this the law of the issue of receipts for salt (on the part of the government) shall surely become a dead letter in the long run [1]. Though there is small iron money extant in the province of *Ho-tung*, yet the number of pieces is very little. Only in the province of *Ho-pek* no money has been cast as yet, now your servant and others (likewise) have been told that somebody whose advice was asked, had said that, iron money might be cast for those three provinces together, and that the districts where this

1) Because the government in the payment of these bills gives copper and iron money at the same ratio, and the people, when paid in iron, will consequently lose 50°/₀. For this reason they will furthermore refuse to accept the salt receipts which may expose them to such a considerable loss.

money was to circulate and be employed should be only the provinces situated along the extreme frontiers. The ready copper money circulating on these extreme frontiers should be entirely exchanged for iron money. (This copper money) was then to be conveyed with boats to the adjacent interior provinces, and if that advice was taken, the miserable condition in which (the medium of exchange) is at present, would soon be at an end, without having directly forbidden the export of money abroad.

臣僚言。江北公行。以銅錢一貫准鐵錢四。之當時一銅錢當四鐵錢。江北者。自乾道以來。悉以鐵錢收換。或以銅錢一貫換會子一貫。收換之銅錢。悉赴行在。及江南沿江州軍。及建康鎮江府。解赴行在。委官檢察。於江之南北。置各庫。以銅鐵錢交換。凡沿江私渡。及交換。徑路嚴禁透漏。極邊。

The functionaries stated that north of the *Kiang* the relative worth was such that 1 piece of copper money was equal to 4 pieces of iron money. This was put a stop to. Since the period *Kien-tao* (1165—74) the copper money circulating north of the river was then already entirely exchanged for iron money; or 1 string of copper money was exchanged for one *Hoei-tsze* [1]) of 1 string. The thus collected copper money was sent to the provinces where it was still circulating, and in the districts of *Kien-kang* and *Tsin-kiang* [2]), and the other districts and encampments situated on the river, in custom-house offices, at ferries and boat-stations, the officials charged with this (duty) exercised a strict control. Moreover, both north and south of the *Kiang* state-offices were established where one sort of money might be exchanged for the other. Generally, when private persons sailing along the river, went from one bank to the other, and when they passed through the districts situated on the extreme frontiers, the passage and outflow (lit. the oozing through) of copper money was checked by severe measures.

What is further recorded as to the relative value and the use

of money of the two metals we find inserted in the chapter on

paper money, but upon the whole it is so short of interest that,

---

1) 會子 *Hoei-tsze* bond, is the name of a credit note. Cf. Chap. VI. p. 186.

2) *Kien-kang* (ancient name of *Kiang-ning-fu*) and *Tsin-kiang-fu* are both situated south of the *Yang-tsze-kiang* 116° and 117° east of Paris. The *Yang-tsze-kiang* thus was the line of demarcation of copper and iron money.

though not entirely solved, we may easily conclude to have come
at the end of the question. The Chinese saying:

命程只有八合米
走盡天下不滿升。

"If a man's fate is to have only eight-tenths of a pint of rice,
though he traverse the empire all over, he cannot get a full
pint," is perfectly applicable to the Chinese government of that time.

In speaking of the disadvantages of the double standard we have said
that the influence of the free market, the greatest drawback of the bi-
metallic system in the present time, was of very little importance for
the China of those days. Independently, however, of the existence
of the double or single standard the export of money to the Barbarians was, especially in the latter part of the 11th century, enormous.

Their perpetual wars and constant intercourse with the Chinese
had taught the Tartar tribes to appreciate the use of money,
and as they did not make it for themselves, it was natural that
they tried to get it from their neighbors who, in spite of the
severest prohibitions instituted by the government, always found
means to supply them with the quantities of money they required.

We have already seen it from the passage quoted on page 145,
[Matw. IX 14a] which, though not very clear, is wholly explained by the following little fragment which is appended to the
report on the paper money of the Tartars [Matw. IX 28a].

中 錢 北 奏 濱¹⁾元　In the period Yuen-yeu (1086—94) when
國 幣 . 界 事 . 使 祐　Ying-ping¹) the envoy returned from the
錢 惟 別 亦 遼 間　Liao-Tartars, he also states in the report
云 . 用 無 言 回 潁　of his doings, that at the Northern fron-
the Middle Kingdom is in use. there.　tiers there is especially a want of money and that only the old money of

¹) Litterary name of 蘇轍 Su-tse who lived 1039—1112. Cf. MAYERS I. 624 and above, page 145.

If we consider how in our times, now the gold standard has been more generally adopted in Europe, the Asiatic countries have become the market for the superfluous silver, it will be easy to understand, how, in the times mentioned, the comparatively small amount of money flowed to the western countries where it was greedily sought after.

If the process by which the money was made had been better, and if the Chinese had known the art of striking money, the same circumstances which now proved to be fatal to the country might have been attended with the greatest benefits; but from the different minute informations given by Ma-twan-lin, it appears that the making of money was a troublesome and laborious work, every little piece being cast separately. The way in which the copper mines were worked was moreover far from perfect.

According to a statement given by Ma-twan-lin in particulars [IX 12b—14a] it appears that about the middle of the 11th century more than 5½ million string of money were fabricated a year in the whole empire; of these about 900.000 were iron money. By this proportion between copper and iron it ought not to be forgotten that moreover the quantity of money, and especially of the cheaper iron, which was thrown into the market by the false coiners, must have been enormous.

A second statement of about the year 11 0 shows that since that time, however, less money, only 4 million string, was cast in the empire [Mat. IX 20b—21a.]

Owing to the war the foundaries in the Western provinces had produced hardly any money, and accordingly they had been shut up for a while, for, though they had no work to do, the great number of officials retained their offices, and for this reason the cost of fabrication was so heavy that the government paid 2400 *cash* for the fabrication of one string of 1000 *cash*. Another reason why there was less money circulating, though not stated, must have been the gradually increasing issue of paper money.

About the close of the 11th century two measures were taken which in our eyes deserve high praise, but which, applied to Chinese society, proved to work in an opposite direction. These measures introduced by the learned but too theoretical prime-minister *Wang-ngan-ši* 王安石 were: 1o. The system known as 青苗, the state-advances for the cultivation of fields, given to such people as were too poor to defray the necessary outlays. 2°. The suspension of all restrictions on the export of money abroad.

Ma-twan-lin only notices these subjects in passing, and in such terms that it is evident he attacks not the system but the man. And indeed a man who abolished the time-honored institutions of his country, introduced all sorts of novelties, and taught his countrymen new-fangled ideas, such a man was a monster in the eyes of the true-born Chinese [1]).

To show the real worth and honorable intentions of the minister we shall, besides quoting those allusions to this subject scattered about our chronicle, communicate to our readers what we have found elsewhere regarding this system of state-advances.

DE MAILLA tome VIII p. 266, says that the minister *Wang-ngan-ši* proposed this plan to the Emperor in order to meet the wants of the people, and also to take care in the interest of the state that no fields should remain uncultivated. In the capital a central office should be established, from which agents should

---

1) The same *Wang-ngan-ši* tried to introduce a system of universal militia enrol- | ment. MAYERS I. 807.

be sent into the several provinces, who in spring-time advanced to people who were too poor, the seed which, taken from the state-granaries, was to be returned in autumn with a certain gain proportionate to the harvest. This means would produce that all the field suitable for cultivation yielding their fruits, there would be abundance of food among the people while the wealth of the state would be increased by it. Of this plan so excellent of itself, MAYERS says: I. 807. "Whatever benefit might have accrued to the agricultural classes from the system of government loans, was wholly neutralised through the rapacity and villany of the underlings and satellites into whose hands the disbursements of the advances and the collection of interest lapsed, distress and impoverishment taking the place of the expected advantages to the people, whilst on the part of the state vast sums were irrevocably lost."

In consequence of this after having been displaced by another, that unlucky minister saw after a short time his whole system condemned and rejected.

MAYERS says of him: During his life he shone, on the confession of his most vigorous opponents, as a celebrated scholar, and as a man who by the brilliancy of his genius blinded his faults.

The first of the fragments alluding to the system of *Wang-ngan-ŝi* is part of a speech delivered by *Tŝ'ang-fang-ping* [1]), in which he says that the quantity of money in the empire is insufficient for the wants of the people and points out the several causes which have occasioned this want. [Matw. IX 10*b*].

---

1) The same official that was a member of the committee which adviced the government as to the measures to be taken in order to avoid the dangers resulting from the use of a double standard. Cf. page 140.

今乃歲納役錢¹⁾七萬五千三百有零貫，散青苗錢八萬三千六百貫，累計息錢一萬六千六百餘貫，此乃歲輸實錢三千餘貫。又弛銅之禁、邊關之法，開則泄於四夷，內則縱行銷毀，鼓鑄有限，壞散無節，錢不可得。

Now they received, (it is true) on behalf of the government-service ¹), (a sum of) more than 75.300 string in money, and the 83.600 string lent as advances for the cultivation of land, yielded a sum of more than 16.600, compound interest, but of all this no more than 3000 string was received yearly. The restrictions on the export of copper abroad, and the laws on the selling of copper were also suspended, so that it is spread abroad to the Barbarians, while at home they connive at its being carried to the foundaries and being broken. While the coining of money has its limits the destruction and diffusion is unlimited, and the result is that the money is no more to be had.

The second fragment reads as follows:

自王安石為政，始罷民為銅禁，姦民日銷錢為器。邊關、海舶不復譏²），錢之出，國用日耗。又青苗助法，皆徵錢，民間錢荒。故方平極言之。

Since *Wang-ngan-si* had the reins of government in his hands, he began by suspending the restrictions on the melting of copper. Now villains melted the money daily to make tools of it. And when the export of copper along the stations of the custom-house officers on the frontiers, and in vessels across the sea was not controlled ²) any more, the money wanted for the use of the country diminished greatly. Likewise the method of supporting by state advances for the cultivation of land, demanded much money. Of all this the result was that among the people there was a great want of money. Hence it is explained what (*Tš'ang-*)*fang-ping* said at the end of his speech.

The third allusion we find in the beginning of Ma-twan-lin's

1) 役 the government service; 役錢 money on behalf of the government service.

2) 譏 means to blame, to reprove. I have, however, taken it here in the meaning of 察譏 to examine, to inspect.

VIII[th] Volume, in his own criticism on the transactions of the *Tšeu*-dynasty, and the way in which they had regulated the interests of the state advances, in those times supplied by the 泉府, (the collector of taxes) to the people for sacrifices and mourning.

於義皆無所當。然
息為休息之息。以
為生息之息。或以
解此語者。或以息
誤天下者。而後儒
為息之說¹。行青苗
自王介甫注國服

Even *Wang-kie-fu* (nom de plume of *Wang-nan-ši*), estimated the total sum of interest in proportion to the wants of the country, when he committed the error to introduce the method of state-advances into China, and of those of the commentaries of subsequent scholars who treat of it, some say that he made accrue interest on interest, others that he did not take compound interest (lit. that he let rest interest on interest). However as regards propriety all this is not as it should be.

Finally we have given a single fragment discussing the second measure of the unhappy minister: the suspension of all restrictions on the export of money. [Matw. IX 14*a*].

共用之也。
貨寶與四夷
而已。是中國。
每貫收稅錢
錢出外界。但
回。沿邊州軍而
海舶飽載而出。
關重車而此
錢禁以年削邊
寧七年。除
言者謂自熙

Somebody who made a communication on this head ²) said that since the 7th year of the period *Hi-ning* (1075), when the restrictions on the export of money were entirely suspended, in consequence of these measures, heavily loaded wagons passed the frontiers through the passes, and sea-vessels heavily freighted sailed out. In the districts and encampments situated along the frontiers the money went abroad. Only a certain tax was levied there on every string and that was all. This resulted from the fact that the medium of exchange of the Middle Kingdom was generally in use among the Barbarians.

When the time will have come that Western civilisation has penetrated into China and the sons of "the Empire under Heaven"

---

1) 說 = 稅.　　　　　　　　　2) lit. The speaker said.

read *Wang-ngan-ši*'s history in the light of the science of Political Economy, the impartial critic shall appreciate the good principles of the rejected system, and say after a Chinese sage:

"The prescription was good but the medicine bad."

Vast supplies of money were continually wanted. The war devoured treasures and the paper money which for a time had supplied the insatiable demands, began to lose its credit.

In addition to this there were the export abroad of coined bullion, and the influence of the false coiners; for China too was to obey the economical law that as soon as the quality of the money becomes bad, the quantity must be increased to restore the balance and to meet the demand for the requisite quantity of currency. Reading the history of the second part of the 12th century we might fancy to have got back to the days of the *T'ang*-dynasty: — decrees were issued prohibiting the possession of more than a certain amount of copper; monasteries and temples were despoiled of their treasures, and that good examples might not be wanting, the emperor himself ordered the officers of his court to take 1500 different objects made of copper from the imperial treasury, and to sacrifice them on the altar of the country. These measures enriched the country with 2.000.000 pounds of copper.

故 重 能 民 問 按
為 而 流 問 所 此
此 不 通．錢 行．即
末 能 縣 少 皆 唐
策 廣 官 而 是 元
耳．鑄．貧 不 以 和

"If we consider these facts, [says Matw. IX 21*a*], "we see here the same (excess) as under the reign of the *T'ang*-dynasty in the time of the period *Yuen-ho* (806—821). All this was the result of this that among the people money was scarce, and consequently could not circulate, and that the expenses of the government were heavy, while it had not the power to increase the fabrication of money. For that reason they passed to such extreme measures.

The further informations are devoid of interest. The government continued to cast pieces of 2 *cash* and to take care as much as possible that the money remained in the country, but no law could stop the outflow, and the cunning merchants knew how to keep up their prosperous, though illegal, trade.

Ma-twan-lin's last fragment [1]) dates from the year 1210, the third year of the period *Kia-ting* under the reign of the emperor *Ning-tsung*. At that time money was cast, which had a metallic worth of 3 and a nominal value of 5 *cash*.

Then there was a councilor who feared that this profit enjoyed by the government would cause a great increase in the number of false coiners, and that consequently the value of promissory notes would fall. Another councilor, however, was of opinion that it was highly desirable to make the money light; for though this might not act as a check on false coining, the promissory notes must necessarily get a higher value, because as soon as the money was bad, these notes would be in great demand, and consequently rise in value. Our clever economist, however, forgot that those notes, exchangeable for that debased money, must needs get lower in value at the same time.

We conclude this chapter with a critical view of the learned *Tung-lai* of the family-name of *Liu*, as read at the end of the IX[th] volume of Ma-twan-lin [2]).

In the part not quoted, he tells us how, in the beginning of the *Sung*-dynasty, they had adhered to the right principle of

---

1) We omit the part referring to the 小平錢 the little peace-money, which afterwards was instituted, and circulated for a long time. It seems to have been good, but nothing interesting is communicated beyond its institution.

2) The subsequent part of the essay of which the beginning is quoted page 13 ssq.

casting money of a quality as good as that of the *Kai-yuen* money in the times of the *T'ang*-dynasty. But when the continuous wars drained the resources of the country, so that the scarcity of money became very great, those good principles were lost sight of. He then proceeds as follows.

起。私鑄不敢起。則歛散若不得利。則私鑄不敢若不惜銅則鑄錢無利。鑄錢不可以惜銅愛工。利之大者南齊孔顗論多。利之小者。權歸公上。不知權歸公上。鑄錢雖以鑄錢所入多為利。殊取鑄利論財。計不精者。但錢。以權輕重本末。嘗思大體。家之所以未設可用。當時務之要得多不後錢雖多。然甚薄惡不

Afterwards the money though abundant in quantity, got very thin and bad and (consequently) unfit for use. At that time (the government) only strived after obtaining much money, but the fundamental rules (lit. the highest rules of propriety) were not thought of. The reason why the state has instituted money was to measure the beginning and the end of light and heavy (of weight), and it did not occur that they took profit out of it as long as they (really) considered it as a precious object. But those who reckoned the coins so that they were not pure, only thought that whenever that which was gained in coining was much, profit was made. But surely, they did not understand the importance thereof that the money came back again in the possession of its full value (lit. just and excellent). What is gained in the fabrication of money, however much it may be, is only a slight profit in comparison to the great profit that it comes back (to the government) still in the possession of its full value.

The theory of *Kung-I* of *Nan-tsi* regarding the casting of money is, that it is not allowed to be sparing of the copper or to grudge the workmanship, for as soon as the copper is not spared, the casting of money is without profit, and if no profit is to be made, the false coiners do not care to arise, this again is the reason that the money comes back in its full value as it was cast, when it is withdrawn as well as when it is issued again, and that it does not answer to an inferior

歸公上鼓鑄權不下分。此其薄
利之大者。徒徇小利。皆可以便爲
惡。利如此姦民務之。孔四散。乃爲
錢。不出於公上。利之南齊顗乃
是以小利失大利。利之論。或者
之言。乃是不可易之論。紛或
自綠錢薄。以惡錢。論者紛紛
是立法以禁惡錢。或是以錢
爲國賦。條目不一。皆是不
其本而齊其末。若是上之人
不惜銅愛工。使姦民無利。乃
是國家之大利。泉布之法。總
而論之。如周如秦如漢五銖

part of the whole). Now this is the greater profit (of the two). If, on the contrary only the smaller profit is aimed at, the money becomes at once light and bad, and if this is so, rascals try to imitate it, and everybody is able to do this, because the principle is neglected to make it pure and of its full value; the supposed profit spreads (now) in every direction, and so by (the pursuit of) a smaller profit the greater is lost.

This is what *Kung-I* of *Nan-tsi* has said and it is a theory which admits of no change [2]). Various persons have since because the money was bad, constructed theories in which there is neither rhyme nor reason [3]). Some thought that the remedy lay in this that a law should be enacted to stop the bad money; others were of opinion that, as money was about the same as the produce of the soil, the objects of which it consisted might not be of the same sort at all time. But all these theorists have not tried to comprehend what the origin and reason (of the institution of the money) has been, nor have they been able to understand the object of it, and that this would have been the greater profit of the government, when they who were at the head of the affairs had not been sparing of the copper and had not grudged the workmanship, and by this had caused that false coiners could make no profit.

If we consider in particulars the regulations according to which (in different times) money is made, perhaps those regulating the 5 *tsu* pieces

1) The profit is hollow and is spread in the four (directions).

2) *Kung-I* of *Nan-tsi* is obviously the same as *Kung-Kai* whose speech is treated of on page 79. The Chinese have frequently different names. See MAYERS. Introduction to "the Chinese reader's Manual".

3) 紛 | confused, disorderly.

4) 條目 properly a list of the articles.

可衣。至於百工之事。皆貧以 之錢之爲物。饑不可食。寒不可 財利之用。在於貿易。推本論 行者也。一時則所論利害。 鑄錢。皆一時矯枉之論。不可通。 廢錢。或見財貨之少。欲得多。 之蠱也。或見財貨之多。欲 幣。王莽以龜貝爲貨幣。此是財貨 之權也。如漢武帝以鹿皮爲 財。第五琦鑄乾元錢。以足軍市之錢 如劉備鑄大錢。以此是錢 此是錢之正。若一時之所鑄。 如唐開元。其規或可以爲式。

of the *Tseu*, *T'sin*, and *Han*-dynasty, and those regulating the *Kai-yuen* pieces of the *T'ang*-dynasty, may serve as examples, as these sorts have had the real (value) of money. If we mark the money made for a certain time, as when *Liu-pei* cast the great currency in order to meet the want of a medium of exchange for the army and in the market [1]), or when *Ti-wu-ki* caused the *Kien-yuen* coins to be cast [2]), these sorts were equivalents for money (i. e. tokens). When *Wu-ti* of the *Han*-dynasty made a medium of exchange of white deerskins, and *Wang-mang* of tortoise shell and cowries, these were the wood-worms of the money [3]).

At a time when they saw that there was a great abundance of money, some wished to have the money abolished, others, when seeing the great scarcity of the medium of exchange continually wished more money to be cast. All these theories were erroneous and wrong, and only prevailed for a certain time, and may not be applied as a general rule.

At present (also) the theories of profit and loss are very common, and the profit and utility of the money consist in the exchange effected by it. If we penetrate to the foundation in arguing (on the value and meaning of money, we arrive at the conclusion) that money is an object that in a time of famine cannot feed (us), in a time of cold cannot clothe us, but coming to the service of all occupations, all sorts of precious things may be procured by it. Hence it may not be bad! If this is so, although the vitality of the earth is spent to the

---

1) *Liu-pei* 220 A. D. the first emperor of the kingdom of *So* during the division of the Empire. Cf. p. 62.

2) *Ti-wu-ki*, a prime-minister under the *T'ang*-dynasty, 758 A. D. Cf. p. 115.

3) By this expression he probably means that these sorts of money would increase as rapidly as woodworms propagate. Cf. p. 127 were the same expression occurs.

為生。不可缺
者。若是不可力
既盡。穀帛有
餘。山澤之藏。
咸得其利。錢
雖少不過錢
重。錢雖彼重
此相權國家
之利。亦孔顥
之論。要當尋
古義。識經權
然後可也。

last, there is still a surplus of grain and silk, and what is hoarded in mountains and in moors, all this gets its importance (lit. profit.)

Though money is scarce, provided it have its full value, the fact that the real and nominal value are on a par, is the profit of the government. This is also the theory advanced by *Kung-I*. It is a necessity and a duty always to strive after the old and just, and if one knows to manage the money in such a way, that it is an equivalent for a real value, then matters will go right [1]).

1) 識經權 The terseness of this phrase renders it almost unintelligible to one who is no Chinese. 權 signifies here the exact counterbalancing, the precise ratio between the nominal and real value of money.

# CHAPTER VI.

## PAPER MONEY OF THE SUNG-DYNASTY.

ORIGIN AND DENOMINATIONS. PRIVATE BANK IN SSE-TŚ'UEN, ITS INSOLVENCY AND INSTITUTION OF A GOVERNMENT-BANK. — WAY OF ISSUE OF BILLS OF EXCHANGE BY THE STATE. — RECEIPTS FOR GOVERNMENT PRODUCTIONS USED AS MONEY. — RESERVE FUNDS. — TERMS OF REDEMPTION. — HISTORY OF THE BILLS OF EXCHANGE, AND BILLS OF CREDIT. — THE SOUTHERN SUNG-DYNASTIE. — BILLS OF THE PROVINCE OF SSE-TŚ'UEN. — HOFI-TSZE AND FRONTIER-BILLS. — BILLS OF THE DISTRICTS OF HOAI AND HU. — TYRANNY, OVERISSUE AND DEPRECIATION. — CRITICISM AND NOTIONS ON PAPER MONEY BY MA-TWAN-LIN, TUNG-LAI AND ŚUI-SIN.

———oo◦○◦oo———

A history of the development of the Chinese people compared with that of other nations, ancient and modern, which have existed and still exist in all parts of the world, would be an interesting subject indeed.

A great many points of comparison and resemblance would be found in the course of the development of the human mind, which in the history of those different nations have ultimately led to the same results.

And as the Chinese people existed and had already a history before that of other peoples commenced, and the Chinese people has continued to exist, and its history uninteruptedly goes on from age to age, when that of other peoples ceases and disappears, these points of comparison, only slightly modified, present themselves to us over and over again. But for the very reason that the Chinese people at one time had the start of all other peoples in civilization, we find such ideas and institutions as are only the fruits of a rather high stage of intellectual development, with the Chinese generally earlier than elsewhere. So also with the history of the rise, the progress, and decline of paper money; for the Chinese had already suffered all the misery arising from an overissued and depre- ·ciated paper currency when it was hailed in Europe as the inven- tion of the philosopher's stone for which had been sought so long. At what time we are to fix the first appearance of paper money, or rather of a representative currency is difficult to say. The white dear-skin parcels of *Han-wu-ti* were a similar kind of money, and in treating of them (See page 39) we have seen that the Chinese chronicle already refers to the circulation of a similar currency in olden times, about which history is silent, at least as far as Ma-twan-lin records it. A little work on Chinese money begins its account of the 楮 鈔 lit. bills made of the bark of the 爲 以 伯 軒 mulberry-tree, with this information: "*Pĕ-* 楮 布 陵 轅 *ling*, minister of *Hien-yüen*, began to make pa- 幣。帛 始 臣 per money of silk shreds." *Hien-yüen* is one of the names of the emperor *Hoang-ti*, the third emperor of China •mentioned in history, who is said, to have reigned about 2697 B. C. Such vague reports are of course, of no value whatever.·

The first trustworthy appearance of paper money we have in the reign of the *T'ang*-dynasty (See page 120) but, even then, we do not perceive the least method or systematic development in the institution.

Not until the reign of the *Sung*-dynasty we see this system

11

fully developed, but what originally was a blessing bestowed on China became a "bane of bliss and source of woe" by the stupidity and cupidity of the government.

Before treating of this institution, it will perhaps be well to mention the different denominations with which the Chinese have tried to express their notions of the now well-known and current technical terms: credit, assignment, paper, bond, bill of exchange, reserve-funds, time of redemption, etc.

1°. Flying money 飛錢 *fei-tsien* (See page 120) was the simple and natural denomination assigned to it, when the Chinese began to appreciate the great advantage that it was not heavy like the strings of copper and iron *cash.* It is remarkable that about the same idea suggested itself to ADAM SMITH when he wished to give his readers a notion of paper money, where he speaks of "commerce and industry, as it were, suspended upon the Daedalian wings of paper money [1])." But the Chinese idea exactly tallies with that expressed in GOETHE's Faust where Mephistopheles plays the trick upon the emperor to give him a paper currency, and the Marshal apprising the emperor of the effects of the new institution says:

---

1) ADAM SMITH compares the metallic and the paper money to two ways, one of which is a highway on the surface of the earth, the other a way through the air. The few lines which contain his metaphor follow here, to show that SMITH even in his allegorical comparison was much more practical as to the conception of the difference between coin and paper money than our Chinese authors. See Wealth of Nations B. II. Chap. II. Edition of M'CULLOCH, page 141. "The gold and silver money which circu-"lates in any country may very properly "be compared to a highway, which, while "it circulates and carries to market all the "grass and corn of the country, produces "itself not a single pile of either. The ju-"dicious operations of banking, by providing, "if I may be allowed so violent a meta-"phor, a sort of waggon-way through the "air, enable the country to convert, as it "were, a great part of its highways into "good pastures and cornfields, and thereby "to increase very considerably the annual "produce of its lands and labour. The "commerce and industry of the country, "however, it must be acknowledged, though "they may be somewhat augmented, cannot "be altogether so secure, when they are "thus, as it were, suspended upon de Dae-"dalian wings of paper money, as when "they travel about upon the solid ground "of gold and silver."

Unmöglich wär's die FLÜCHTIGEN einzufassen;
Mit Blitzeswink zerstreute sich's im Lauf.

2°. Convenient money 便 錢 *pien-tsien*, was another denomination which we meet with in the very first fragments referring to paper money.

But more remarkable than these are two other denominations which arose not until the institution had reached a higher stage of development, and which were intended to express the thought of the Chinese at the sight and use of such a simple shred of paper circulating as money. They are 1° 錢 引 *tsien-yin*, 2° 稱 提 *tš'ing-t'i*.

1° 錢 引 *tsien-yin* is the term the Chinese use to express their notion of *credit*; 引 *yin* properly signifies the bending of a bow, the stretching of the string. If we hold to this primary signification, it is clear how the Chinese have come by the secondary meaning, as it is in fact a stretching of money, money which becomes money only after a certain lapse of time, when the string is let loose; thus credit. The simile could not be chosen better. Very exactly it describes the suspension which is created by credit, and which does not terminate before payment takes place, or, to make use of the same figure, when the string is let loose. The (*ob-*)*ligare* and the *solvere* of the Roman civilians was a similar figure. BIOT *in loco* [1]) has taken this word in another meaning when he speaks of 錢 引 signifying *Introduction de monnaie métallique*. It is true that, as all dictionaries tell us, the character 引 means also introduction, but this too is already a secondary signification of the character, as the bending of the bow is the introductory

1) Journal Asiatique. Sept. 1837, p. 229.

act to shooting. Besides, what would be the meaning of *In-troduction de monnaie métallique* in the institution of paper money which is the very opposite of metallic money? Perhaps the history of the Austrian Metallicken ran in the mind of the learned author when he wrote that explanation. Henceforth, in the translation of our Chinese text, I shall render the character by the term **bill of credit**, as it commonly occurs in the meaning of the bill which is the bearer of the debt; as for instance in 川 引 *tš'uen-yin*, meaning (bill of) credit of the province of *Sse-tš'uen*.

2°. Still more peculiar is the second term 稱 提 *tš'ing-t'i* by which the meaning of promissory note is designated; and by which the nature of paper money is so perfectly expressed. The character 稱 means **corresponding to, counterbalancing, weighing against**; 提 signifies **to carry or hold in the hand**, and also **to bring forward**. The two characters combined mean therefore **to counterbalance a real possession**. The first time Ma-twan-lin uses the expression (IX 25a) it serves to explain the nature of the receipts issued by the state for government productions "These receipts," says the author, "could unobservedly help 稱 陰 可 (to supply the deficit in the state finances) as they 提 助 以 **counterbalanced the actual possession**" (of those articles yearly stored up by the state).

But the same combined expression occurs further as a noun which is either subject or object of a sentence; for instance in Ma-twan-lin, IX 29a, where we read 以 稱 提 失 職 "in consequence of (the bills) **weighing against a real possession** they lost their office," and a little earlier 而 重 刑 用 假 稱 提, "and the making use of false (bills) **weighing against a real possession** was severely punished. The real meaning of that compound expression is the assignats of government money or government productions, and we may safely translate it by assignments, checks, or promissory notes. Eight or nine passages have I found in Ma-twan-lin, where this word is employed, but to avoid needless repetitions they will further be treated of when they occur in our chronicle.

For the bit of paper itself (a meaning not conveyed by the characters above treated of) there exist several terms which are employed alternately. Of most frequent occurrence are: 1°. 鈔 *tšao*, a combination of the radical 金 *kin* metal and the phonetic element 少 *šao*, scarce, which according to the explanation given by Klaproth in "*Le Journal Asiatique*," (1822) would mean *manque du métal (monnayé)*. ·2°. 楮 *tšu* which is the name of the *Broussonetia-papyrifera* [1]), and refers to the material of which the bill was manufactured, a fibrous substance forming the inner coat of the bark of the *Broussonetia*. 3°. 牒 *pai*. ·4°. 票 *p'iao*. 5°. 書 *šu*. 6°. 劵 *kiuen*. 7°. 簡 *kien*. 8°. 帖 *t'iĕ*, etc., all of which have the signification of tablet, billet, document, slip of paper, card, etc. They occur alone or in combination of other terms which make the meaning still clearer, and most of them will often be met with in the sequel of this chapter.

Lastly, there are three more words used interchangeably for different varieties of paper money, and in this case we are fortunate enough to have in English equivalent terms of the same characteristic meaning. They are the words 交子 [2]) *Kiao-tsze*, bills of exchange; 會子 *Hoei-tsze*, agreements, bonds; and 關子 *Kwan-tsze*, frontier-bills, which last were a sort

1) See HOFFMANN et SCHULTES, "*Noms indigènes d'un choix de plantes du Japon et de la Chine*," n°. 94. THUNBERG, "*Flora Japonica*," page 72—77. SAVATIER, *Livres Kwa-wi* p. 77.

· 2) 子 is often added to names of things, as a formative of a noun.

of promissory notes used in the armies encamped on the western frontiers of the Empire, and with which the caterers for
the army were paid. The government, as it said, made use of
these receipts, in order to prevent the enemy from taking possession of the metallic money in case the camp might be plundered.
The true reason why those frontier-bills were frequently employed was, as history informs us, because this was the easiest
way for the government to pay its debts contracted in behalf of
the army.

In Plutarch's Life of Lycurgus we read: "He (Lycurgus) first
abolished all gold and silver currency, and ordered to make use of
a single iron money, and to this he gave a great weight and
dimension, together with a slight intrinsic value, so that the equivalent of ten minas required a large depository in a dwelling,
and a yoke of oxen to transport it 1)."

It is very doubtful whether this part of Lycurgus' reform was
really beneficial to the Spartans, and whether they would not
have soon made an end of it, if their attention had not been
entirely absorbed by warfare and public meals. — In the western part of China where nature and circumstances had blessed
the inhabitants with no less inconvenient a currency than the
Spartans' received from their legislator, the people were cunning
enough to substitute the πολλοῦ σταθμοῦ καὶ ὄγκου νόμισμα by a
more portable medium of exchange. They established a bank where
the heavy iron money was deposited and exchanged for the light
paper which was generally current in those parts. But let us

---

1) Plutarchus Vit Lyc. Capus IX.
Πρῶτον μὲν γὰρ ακυρώσας πᾶν νόμισμα
χρυσοῦν καὶ ἀργυροῦν μόνῳ χρῆσθαι τῷ
σιδηρῷ προτέταξε και τούτῳ δὲ ἀπὸ πολλοῦ σταθμοῦ καὶ ὄγκου δύναμιν ὀλίγην ἔδω-
κεν, ὥστε δέκα μνῶν ἀμοιβὴν ἀποθήκης τε
μεγάλης ἐν οἰκίᾳ δεῖσθαι καὶ ζεύγους ἄγοντες.

hear how the Chinese author in his simple way describes the origin of this institution.

初蜀人以鐵錢重，私爲券，謂之交子。以便貿易。富民十六戶主之。其後富者稍衰，不能償所負，爭訟數起。寇瑊嘗守蜀，乞禁交子。薛田爲轉運使，議廢交子則貿易不便，請官爲置務，禁民私造。詔從其請，置交子務於益州。

In the beginning the people of the province of Šo (the ancient name of the prov. of Sse-tš'uen) had made bills without the knowledge of the government, as their iron money was so heavy. They had called them *Kiao-tsze*, (bills of exchange). Because they were convenient in trade, sixteen wealthy families had united to manage the issue of the *Kiao-tsze*. But when the wealth of those families gradually diminished, and they were no longer able to redeem what they had bound themselves to (lit. what they had loaded upon their backs), many quarrels and lawsuits ensued. *Kwan-tsin* who had been a magistrate in the province of *Šo*, urgently requested to prohibit the people the use of the *Kiao-tsze*, and *Pi-tien* who then held there the post of officer for the transports, adviced to abolish the *Kiao-tsze*. As this, however, would paralyze trade, it was suggested to establish an office for the issue of paper money on the part of the government, and to prohibit the people to make (bills) for themselves. According to this proposal a decree was enacted, to establish a bank for the issue of *Kiao-tsze* in the province of *Yĭk-tšeu* (in *Sse-tš'uen*).

The two following passages which in Ma-twan-liu's "Examination" precede the above quoted fragment, give some information as to the manner in which in the beginning the paper money was emitted on the part of the government, the quantity which was brought in circulation during the first 50 years, and the way in which it became legal tender.

太祖時，取唐朝飛錢故¹⁾事，許民入錢京師，於諸州便換。其後慢州便入錢，京師乃用指射，自此之閑諸州當多益，度其用移或者錢，以送輸皆錢。○先以是許商人入他物，錢而左藏庫，先以諸州錢給之。乃商旅先經三司，投牒乃輸於庫，所由司計一緡私刻³⁾錢二十。開寶三年，置便錢務，令高人入錢。

During the reign of the emperor *Tai-tsu* (960—976), the old institution of the *T'ang*-dynasty, the flying money, was reverted to again. The people were allowed to deposit their money in the capital. As they (the bills) were in all the provinces convenient in exchange, it was afterwards decided also in the outlying parts, and in the provinces indifferent what were the boundaries, to allow and even to point out that they should be issued. Since this last (increase) the usual quantity (of ready money) in the capital augmented more and more, as the money from all the provinces was carried thither. Those (bills) which circulated (in the market) must be accepted instead of money. Sometimes by them other articles were transferred in daily use [2].

Before this time (probably under the *T'ang*-dynasty) when the merchants were allowed to deposit their money in the left state treasury, in order to receive afterwards the money current in all the provinces, (i. e. the paper money) they were however obliged to have carried the money to the exchequer before the three functionaries who were at the head of the establishment, issued the bills, and on this amount the functionaries charged a premium of 20 *cash* a string [3]. In the third year of the period *Kai-pao* (970) a government office for the issue of convenient money was established. The merchants who deposited money, had to apply to the office for the issue of bills, and the same day they had to take care that the money was conveyed to the left government treasury,

---

1) 故 = 古.

2) The meaning of this seems to be that the receipt which commonly ran: "for so much copper money," if required, might also run for so much iron, silk, salt or other articles for which they might be exchanged at the government treasury, because elsewere the same articles were deposited.

3) 私刻 to cut out for themselves (out of the strings), not for the state, which would be 公. Literally the phrase reads: "of which the functionaries reckoned on a string of 1000, a cutting out or deduction of 20 *cash*" — thus a premium of 2 per cent.

169

者詣務陳牒即
日鞶致左劝庫
給以券仍券諸
州凡商日人付券
至當日給人不券
得住滯遵者科
罰自是毋復停
澥至道末商人
便錢一末商人
餘萬貫百七十
增增一天禧末
三萬貫百一十

in order to receive the bills in return for it. Furthermore an order was sent into all the provinces that generally as soon as the t r a v e l l i n g - b i l l s [1]) of the merchants arrived, they should immediately be accepted · and transferred, and that no stop might be put to them. He who was disobedient to this order should be punished with a fine. Since that time they were neither stopped nor refused. At the end of the period *Tši-tao* (995—998) the quantity of "money convenient to the merchant" amounted to 1.700.000 string, and at the close of the period *T'ien-hi* (1017—1022) in consequence of a continual extension, this was increased by an amount of 1.130.000 string.

All these, however, were vague reports, and of a regular system there was no question as yet. Ma-twan-lin seems even to have quite lost sight of the paper money, as after these three fragments he devotes many pages exclusively to the metallic money. Suddenly [Matw. IX 18*b*] he begins a new chapter, entitled 交子. Bills of exchange, in which all informations on the issue of those bills from 1021 to the beginning of the next century are successively communicated; though without the least comment. We have given the whole of it with a verbal rendering, but to the better understanding of some allusions and expressions a few introductory words will be necessary.

Before the bills of exchange were brought in circulation, the Chinese seem to have had another sort of paper currency, in some

4) 齊券至 I have translated by the travelling bills arrived. 齊 means to prepare things for a journey, but also, to offer, to send. Hence it might also be translated by: when the bills presented by the merchants arrived.

respects resembling our dock-warrants and bills of lading, bills conferring authority to receive a certain amount of government products, as salt, alum, tea, iron, etc. These were transferred from hand to hand like money, and had great credit with the people, as the lands and manufactories belonging to the state yielded a large quantity of productions; especially in the encampments where that last sort of bills was made use of to pay the purveyors who in their turn transferred them to their creditors. And so they circulated till at last they fell into the hands of a merchant who was in want of the articles the bills authorized him to receive, and consequently realized them at the government granaries[1]). When, however, besides these produce-receipts, there came other bills which could be exchanged for real money, and which did represent not only a certain sum and often a fractional sum as the produce receipts, but were to be had of any amount and for even sums, they were generally preferred when payments were made, and it was not long before merchants and traders refused to accept the produce-receipts and compelled the government to shut in some encampments the offices for the issue of these notes. We read however that, in the time when the paper money was depreciated, those offices were opened again.

In the second place I wish to notice the way in which the payment of bills was guaranteed by the government, and something about the time at which they were redeemed. The principle, that a bill should be convertible at any time, the Chinese have never known, and from the beginning we see that only at prescribed intervals the bills could be exchanged for specie. A term of three years was

1) An allusion to this we find already in the second of our fragments referring to paper money (See page 168). From some vague allusions it also appears that the government discounted those bills and paid them in money, at places where no commodities were stored up. Cf. for instance p. 146 note 1.

generally adopted. So the first series of bills of exchange was emitted to circulate for a period of 65 years; every three years there would be a fixed time at which the holders could demand specie payment for their bills. The fund which in the first time of the issue of bills seems really to have been deposited at a ratio of $^3/_7$ of the amount of the bills then issued, was very characteristically called 本錢 *pun-tsien* lit. basis or fundamental-money, capital.

Surprising it is that Ma-twan-lin does not give the least information on these triennial times of redemption, but supposes his readers to be acquainted with the term 界 employed by the Chinese for time of payment due, which frequently occurs in the fragments he borrows from the annals and chronicles. This forms an additional difficulty in Ma-twan-lin's text, and though by comparing the several passages all doubt is soon solved, yet I have thought it desirable to give the explanation as it is found in the Chinese encyclopedia 原鐘致格. Vol. 35 pag. 21*b*, where we read the following phrase, after the origin of the paper money has been explained.

於是設質劑之法、一變一絕。以三年爲一界而換之。始祥符之辛亥、至熙寧之丙辰六十五年。凡二十三界。

"Thereupon they instituted the law of checks, every bill of exchange was of one string, every three years there was a time of falling due in order to pay them back (convert, exchange them). Beginning from the year 1011 [1]) to the year 1076, thus during 65 years there were 23 terms (or intervals) [2])."

It appears, however, that the people were so much in want

---

1) 劗劑 check, signifies the two halves of a written agreement or bond of which each contracting party retains one. *K'ang-hi* says 劗劑券也.

2) A great difficulty in the text is occasioned by this that the word 界 constantly occurs in the same fragments both in it's primary and secondary meaning.

of this "convenient money" that at the prescribed intervals hardly any bills were presented. The consequence was that the government became improvident, and the increasing wants of the army induced it at last to use the reserve-fund deposited in the bank. This is evident when we compare Ma-twan-lin's fragments, and it also explains what follows the sentence just quoted from the Chinese Encyclopedia. "Though they were uncommonly convenient, yet it happened (in 1076) that they could not be exchanged." 雖至巧有不能易。

The above information will be sufficient to understand the fragments bearing upon the issue of bills of exchange which now follow[1]).

### THE KIAO-TSZE OR BILLS OF EXCHANGE.

置 鐵 公 二 法。如 立 熙 四 萬 以 天
潞 錢 私 年。 官 僞 寧 十 六 百 聖 交
州[3]勞 共 以 印 造。元 紹 千 二 以 子。
交 貲。苦 河 文 罪 年。爲 三 十 來。
子 詔 運 東 書 賞 始 額。百 五 界[2])

Since the period T'ien-šing (1023—1032) the Kiao-tsze were limited to a fixed amount of 1.256.340 string.

When in the first year of the period Hi-ning (1068) there appeared for the first time forged (bills), (it was enacted) that this offence should be punished according to the laws of the forgery of state seals.

In the 2nd year (1069) it was ordered that in the district Lu-tšeu[3]) a bank for the issue of Kiao-tsze should be established, because in the province of Ho-tung the transfer of iron money to the government as well as to private persons involved so much trouble and cost.

---

1) Whenever Ma-twan-lin begins a new fragment, the Chinese text will commence with a new line.

2) Here, for instance, 界 is used in its common signification of to limit.

3) Lu-tšeu is the same as Lu-ngan-fu prov. of Šen-si, Ho-tung.

務。明年漕司言以其法行。則鹽[1]礬不受。有害入中糧草之計。奏罷之。四年。復行於陝西。永興軍[2]鹽鈔務罷。文彥博言其不便。未幾竟罷其法。五年。交子二十二界將易。而後界給用已多。詔更造二十五界者。用一百二十五萬。以償二十三界之數。變子之有兩界。自此始。九年。以措置熙河[4]財利孫迴。言商人買販牟利於官。且損鈔價。於是罷陝西交子法。

Next year (1070) the officer, charged with the transport of grain, asserted that in consequence of this law (by which bills of exchange were instituted), alum and salt were not accepted [1]), and that by this the state revenues and the estimate of the expenditure (lit. rations and forage) of the army were injured; he adviced to abolish them.

In the 4th year (1071) they were again in circulation in the province of Šen-si, and in the encampment in the province of Yung-hing [2]) the bank for the issue of salt-receipts was suspended. Wen-yen-po had said that these receipts were not convenient, and shortly afterwards the decree (by which they were instituted) had been retracted.

In the 5th year (1072) the 22nd term of redemption of the Kiao-tsze was come, and ·as there were a great many in circulation (to be converted) at the last interval [3]), an order was issued to make other Kiao-tsze of 25 terms to an amount of 1.250.000 string in order to honor with these the number of the still circulating bills of 23 terms. Since that time date the Kiao-tsze of two different terms of redemption.

In the 9th year (1076) the decree by which in Šen-si the bills of exchange had been instituted, was revoked again, because Šün-kiung who was at that time appointed in the districts of Hi- en Ho-tšeu (to collect) the treasures and profits (i. e. taxes), said that the merchants made profits by their trade at the expense of the government. Besides the value of the bills was already injured.

---

1) Salt and alum, i. e. salt and alum-receipts; they were not so current as the bills of exchange.
2) In Sse-tš'uen.
3) The 23rd term was the last of the first series issued, see p. 171

4) 熙州 is the name, under the Sung-dynasty, of the district of Lin-t'ao-fu prov. of Šen-si; 河州 was a part of Lin-t'ao-fu.

更新二法引<sub></sub>大崇十書增路人紹
張交十以自觀寧緡放造乏以聖
之子倍助元元元。百十交用元
成乃而兵年年。四五請子年
都一當價廷復十萬更通成
漕乃舊損取行萬緡印行都
司舊者費湟陝六是製於路
奏者及較廓西千歲詔陝漕
交之更天西交三通一西司
子四更聖寧²)子百舊界而言
務。故界一籍為四額。率本商
　。年界其子。
　逾錢

In the 1ˢᵗ year of the period *Šao-šing* (1094) the officer for the transport of grain in the district of *Tšˢʾing-tu* (prov. of *Sse-tšˢʾuen*) reported that the merchants circulated the bills of exchange in the province of *Šen-si*, and that on account of this his district was in want of them. He thus suggested to have new ones coined. Thereupon there came an order to make an increase of 150.000 string for the time of one term. As also in this year the full amount of former days had remained in circulation, the number of the issued bills was 1.406.340 string [1]).

In the 1ˢᵗ year of the period *Ts'ung-ning* (1102) the bills of exchange circulated again in *Šen-si*.

In the 1ˢᵗ year of the period *Ta-kwan* (1107), the bills of exchange of the province of *Sse-tšˢʾuen* were changed and made into bills of credit. Since the emperor had conquered *Hoang-tšeu* and had enlarged his dominions by the annexation of *Si-ning-fu* [2]), he had ratified this law in order to meet the expenditure of his army.

Compared with the first limit of the period *T'ien-šing* (1023), the number of circulating bills was certainly twenty times as much, and consequently their value was injured the more.

When they had come to a year of payment of the new bills, one (of these) had the same worth as 4 old ones (one new bill was exchanged for 4 old ones), and this was reason enough to extend it (the number) again. The officer for the transport of grain in *Tšˢʾing-tu-fu* reported that he had already changed the name of "Bank for the issue of bills of

---

1) 1.256.340 Cf. p. 172.
　　150.000
　‾‾‾‾‾‾‾‾
　1.406.340. Thus a very small number had been redeemed.

2) 湟州 and 西寧 are both parts of the empire N. W. of the province *Šen-si*.

已改爲錢引務。欲以四十三界。引準書放數仍用舊印行之。使人不疑擾自後並更爲行錢引從之。又詔陝西河東署引直五千至七千而成都纔直二三百豪右規利害法。轉運司覺捕扇惑之人準法以行。民間貿易十千以土令錢與引半用言者謂錢引雜以銅鐵錢。難較其直增損錢隨其直增損。詔令以銅鐵聞奏。所用分數比計作銅錢。

exchange" into that of "Bank for the issue of bills of credit". Now he wished to adjust (i. e. to increase, to supply to a fixed quantum) the number of the notes which were (already) emitted with bills of 43 terms, and when the old seals were made use of to bring them in circulation, the people would not be brought in doubt and anxiety, and then credit bills might be made anew. The emperor followed that advice.

There came also an imperial order (relating) to the number (to be employed) in Šen-si and Ho-tung. The limit of the value of a bill of credit was from 5000—7000 *cash*, but in Tš'ing-tu-fu (the value was so reduced that) they had hardly a value of from 200 to 300 *cash*. Kio-pu, an officer for the transports, a short-sighted muddy-headed fel-low, proposed as a judicious means of arranging this dangerous state (of affairs) to make it a rule in circulation that when among the people business was transacted to an amount of 10.000 *cash* and more, it should be ordered that half this sum should be paid in money and the other half in credit bills. Speaking about it he said, that when the bills of credit were used together with the copper and iron money, it would be difficult to compare the increase or decrease of their value, and that when it was ordered by law that, what in the future would be stipulated for in iron and copper money, should be paid partly in bills, they would have a value corresponding to that of metallic money. The advice given in this report was listened to.

1) 豪右 an excellent, clever (way). 一規 ... 法 is about the same as the immediately following expression 準法 | a regulator. 一利害 when not used as opposites, they mean sharp and injurious, formidable, dangerous.

觀中不蓄本錢而增造無
三十六萬緡新舊相因大
大凡舊歲造一界。備本錢
從之。
仍之。嚴禁止害法不行之人。
取便行使。公私不得抑勒
引或量支見錢一二分²任
下請給增不支支見一錢
通流增給不支支見一錢並支
民心不疑。價例。乞先相轉易。
益必官司收受無難自然。
一貫、今每道¹⁾止直一百文。
知威州張特。奏錢引元價

*Ts'ang-t'eu*, a magistrate of the district of *Wei-tseu* communicated in his report that of the credit bills, which originally had a value of 1 string, at present each bill ¹) had but a value of 100 *cash* (He thought however) that as soon as it was certain that the officers would have no objection to accept them, the minds of the people would no longer be suspicious, and that they might be transferred again from hand to hand in trade, and that the general circulation would increase, and raise the value to the legal rule (i. e. to the original value of issue). He requested (the government) to set the example (of going in the right path), and from this time forward to invite the high and the low to accept them, by making henceforth no longer payment in ready money, but to pay entirely in bills of credit, or in the payment of ready money to charge a deduction of from 1 to 2 (tenth-parts), with the purpose to make that, being considered profitable, they would be accepted and employed. Nobody, public or private person, would in that way be obliged to experience constraint or restriction ²). But it would be necessary strictly to control those persons who should thwart the plan and refuse to circulate the bills. This advice was followed.

Generally, when formerly the paper money of the first issue was made, the deposited capital of 360.000 string ³) had been furnished. But in consequence of the new bills and the old ones circulating together, in the period *Ta-kwan* (1107), no reserve-fund had been deposited, and the coining of new bills increased beyond all limits,

1) 每道 each piece. 道 is a classifier of written documents, papers and dispatches.

2) 抑一勒 lit. to press down with the hand, and to rein in, both borrowed from the taming of a horse.

3) This deposit is somewhat above ³/₇ of the amount of the bills issued in that time. Cf. p. 172.

免　卿　建。之　不　江　路。南　京　寧　數。紹。藝。
馬。里　蔡　以　行。浙　惟　京　東　間。錢　當　至
也。京　爲　趙　湖　福　師　西　行　引。錢　引
故　之　禑　挺　廣　建　諸　淮　於　崇　十　一

till at last a bill of credit of a string of 1000 was worth but 10 *cash.*
The bills of credit circulated during the period of *Ts'ung-ning* (1102—1107) in the districts east and west of the capital, in *Hoai-nan*, and in the imperial residence. Only in *Fu-kien*, *Kiang-tše* and *Hu-kwang* they did not circulate. *Ts'ao-ting* is of opinion that they did not circulate in *Fu-kien* because that province was the birth-place of (the prime minister) *Tsai-king* [1]).

From the fragments in Ma-twan-lin's "Examination," which inform us about the southern branch of the *Sung*-dynasty, it appears that especially under the emperor *Kao-tsung* 1127—1163 the issue of paper money was expanded in the most reckless manner, and that in this way the foundation was laid of the wretched condition to which the state finances were reduced at the close of the *Sung*-dynasty, a condition only to be compared with that of France when the blow had fallen and the full light shone upon the ruins caused by the splended but destructive fire-works of JOHN LAW.

A short historical introduction will be necessary to understand the monetary history of that time. Up to this time the Tartars had incessantly harassed the Chinese, but after the consolidation of the Empire under the *T'ang*-dynasty they had not been able to do much harm. In the beginning of the 12th century, however, having taken advantage of the confusion of China, they had come pouring in from the northern regions. About the years 1125—27

---

1) *Tsai-king* was a prime minister of the emperor *Hoei-tsung* who greatly contributed to the bad condition of the empire by his unadvised way of administering the government affairs. MAYERS. 1 749.

they had settled themselves in great numbers on the *Hoang-ho* and in *Kai-fung-fu*, the capital of China, and from that time they kept the country in awe and were the actual masters of the empire. At last they imprisoned the emperor *Hoei-tsung*[1]) and his whole family, and when his son and successor *Kin-tsung* humiliated himself so far as to go to the hostile camp and to beseech of the Barbarians the deliverance of his father, he too was made prisoner, while his family and the treasures found in his palace were seized upon a short time after. With these rich spoils, consisting of two emperors, two empresses, the consort of the future emperor, all the male descendants of the *Sung*-dynasty, and a very numerous train of attendants, the Tartars marched back to their own dominions.

A younger brother of *Kin-tsung*, the carried off emperor, who in the south commanded a company, being the sole representative of his line was proclaimed "Son of Heaven," and, as formerly the Emperor *Yuen-ti*, he fixed his residence in the south at *Kiang-ning* or *Kien-kang* on the *Yang-tsze-kiang*, which he made the capital of the empire, awaiting better days and preparing to deliver his imprisoned relations. A sad one is the history of this prince who for a long series of years struggled with disappointments, saw his best schemes frustrated and missed the grand aim of his life. With great zeal he devoted himself to his arduous task, but he wanted that energy, that indomitable will which alone would have been able to accomplish his bold plan; moreover he tasted the sad experience that the men he trusted in most, proved to be mere flatterers and traitors.

1) This emperor had abdicated in favor of his son.

After six years' captivity his father died in the foreign country; twenty-two years later death delivered also his ill-fated brother. Exerting himself to the utmost to rescue them, *Kao-tsung* was obliged to keep a numerous army in the field and to devise a hundred various means to provide for the necessities of his soldiers. The country got exhausted and overwhelmed with paper money that after all sorts of desperate plans of redemption and conversion became totally worthless. The wretched prince seeing his relations die in captivity without being able to deliver them, his people miserable without having the power to relieve them, felt no longer proof against his wayward fortune and abdicated in behalf of his adopted son. He retired into seclusion for the rest of his days, and, after 26 years, he died at the age of 84. His successors were as unlucky as himself, the war against the Tartars devoured the entire revenues of the state, for besides the expenditure of the army, heavy tributes must be paid to the victorious enemy. The issue of paper money was continually expanded, many provinces had their own bills; high-sounding names were invented to entice the people into accepting new issues; it came even so far — and here again we have a remarkable point of resemblance to modern history — that, when the people had no more faith in the old paper currency, bills literally bearing the name of **silver and gold metallics**, were issued with the promise that they would be convertible into those precious metals, deposited in the treasury for this purpose. How far the Chinese government has been able to fulfil that promise will be learned · from the chronicle.

Ma-twan-lin has a few lines relating to paper money, delivered by the emperor *Kao-tsung* himself. The one points to the necessity to have a reserve-fund in order to maintain the credit of the notes, the second expresses his Majesty's opinion that it is the duty of the officials to uphold that credit with the money in their cashes when there is danger of a depreciation of the bills. The latter anecdote is surely more a proof of his Majesty's simplicity and good-nature than of his sagacity. The passages read thus: [Matw. IX 30a and 31b].

高宗紹興三年六月。詔四川引自祖宗¹)六以來。先計引數封椿本錢。以權輕重。故錢引中間印給泛料不侵。故引法日壞。況用張浚開引法宣府。趙開爲總餉。以供軍糧本。以給軍需。增引日多。莫能禁止。

Under the reign of the Emperor *Kao-tsung*, in the sixt month of the 3rd year of the period *Šao-hing* (1133) a proclamation was issued (in which was said) that in the province of *Sse-tš'uen*, since the reign of the first two emperors of the present dynasty, the reserve-capital was always beforehand calculated for the number of credit-bills which were emitted to meet the expenditure of the border-fortifications, and the reason why this law did not operate badly was this that the heavier metal was always deposited in order to balance the lighter bills.

But when in the time that these bills were printed, the quantity of the different materials which must be procured, ever increased, the metallic deposit was seized upon, and gradually spent in consumption. This was the reason that the fixed rules of the circulation of credit-bills was violated daily. Moreover, since the minister *T'šang-siün* opened *Siuen-fu* [2]), and *T'šao-k'ai* was made head of the purveyance (department), in order to supply the capital for the government purchases and the pay and rations of the soldiers, the increase of the credit-bills got greater every day, and nothing was able to check it.

1) 祖宗 are the two first emperors of the *Sung*-dynasty 太祖 and 太宗。

2) This will have been about 1163—64, when *T'šang-siün* defeated the Tartars. Further information explaining the historical details of this allusion is not within my reach, but the meaning is clear that the cost of the support of the army tempted the government to expand paper money.

方　用　價　絀。有　謂　稱　最　四　高
得　錢　減。如　錢　官　提　善　川　宗
無　自　即　交　百　中　之　沈　交　因
弊。買。官　子　萬　嘗　說。該　子。論

When the emperor *Kao-tsung* once spoke of the bills of exchange of the province of *Sse-tš'uen*, he stated as his opinion, — in consequence of a saying that it were best to suppress all talk of the character of the paper money as an equivalent for the real holding of a property; — that when there were among the state functionaries who had 1.000.000 string of money in cash, they ought to use that money to buy them up themselves, in case the prices of the bills of exchange began to fall. (In this way) everywhere the result would be that they did not depreciate.

The two passages are taken from that fragment in which Ma-twan-lin treats of the credit-bills of the province of *Sse-tš'uen*. These bills were a continuance of the credit-paper issued there on the part of the government some time after the abolition of the private bank at *I-tšeu* in 970. Before proceeding to a new invention of the Emperor *Kao-tsung*, the issue of frontier-bills in behalf of the army, we shall first treat of this sort of bills of which many particulars are communicated as to the quantity issued, convertibility, depreciation, etc.

CREDIT-BILLS OF THE PROVINCE OF SSE-TŠ'UEN.

數　言　書　月。池。於　銀　請　吳　副　川　二　七
巳　引　省　中　五.　河　會　置　玠。師　陝　月。年。

In the 2nd month of the 7th year, *Wu-kiai*, second commander in *Sse-(tš'uen)* and *Šen-(si)* [1] proposed to institute silver-bonds in *Ho-tši* [2]. In the 5th month the *Tšung-šu-šang* said that the number of issued credit bills was already very great, and that the losses should be considered which would be the consequences of this law (of ex-

1) *Wu-kiai* was second in rank to the commander-in-chief *Tšang-siün*. MAYERS I. 865. He was the terror of the *Kin-Tartars*.

2) *Ho-tši* is situated on the frontiers of *Sse-tš'uen* and *Šen-si*.

即印爲添稱七十紹三百時多
止三朝印提十七與千二蜀慮
後百廷錢十七末七十交害
之萬久引萬萬年百餘書成
望委遠以貫餘積入萬放法
只之之以又貫至十令兩詔
添望處救臣以四餘三界止
印約當目之所千萬界每之
一度時望鹽有一界界蓋
百給詔不酒鐵百以通止祖
萬用添得等錢一至行爲宗
　　印請陰百四于一

pansion). Accordingly, there came an imperial decree to stop it (the issue). When in the days of the first two emperors of this dynasty bills of exchange of two (different) terms were issued in the country of *So*, every term amounted only to 1.200.000 string; when it was ordered to bring in circulation those of the third terms of redemption there were above 37.800.000 string; come to the last year of the period *Šao-hing* (1162) it was increased to an amount of more than 41.470.000 string. On the other hand the total amount of the circulating iron money was 700.000 string. As salt, wine, and other government productions were secretly (employed) to give assignats [1]) on, *Wang-tši-wang*, the official charged with the victualing of the army, suggested to expand the coining of credit notes in order to meet the perplexed state which was before the eyes. He was not able, by this measure, to prevent the far-reaching thoughts (harbored by the people) against the imperial government. The order was then given to fix the amount of the notes still to be printed, at 3.000.000 string. But (*Wang*)-*tši-wang* who was charged with the execution of this (decree), limited the quantity and coined as many as he thought would be necessary to supply the want. (The consequence was that) afterwards (*Wang*)-*tši-wang* had coined only an amount of 1.000.000 (string) more.

Soon afterwards, however, a successor of that modest official makes use of the permission once given, to issue the remaining 2.000.000 string of paper money. In the year 1178 the officials

1) 爲稱提 to make assignats.

2) The full stop ought to be put after the character 萬.

report that the total number of bills in that part of the country amounted to 45.000.000 string, and that if the issues were not discontinued, the time would soon come that they were not current any more. They insisted on placing a fixed limit upon the amount of bills which might be issued, and beyond which it should be prohibited to issue more.

從之 "that advice was followed," says the chronicle but contrary to this the next fragment tells us that 13 years later the credit-bills of the province of *Sse-tš'uen* were increased again with bills of a new term.

百 止 嘉 行。小 用 臣 開 書 萬 五 兩 寧
以 直 定　　會。不 陳 禧 放 緡。千 界 宗
下 鐵 初。　　卒 足。咸 末 益 通 三 書 嘉
咸 錢 每　　不 嘗 以 年。多 三 百 放。泰
乃 四 緡　　能 爲 歲 餉 矣。界 餘 凡 末。

At the end of the period *Kia-t'ai* (1204) in the reign of the emperor *Ning-tsung* the number of bills of two terms which were issued was above 53.000.000 string, and that of the bills of the third issue was also increased [1]).

In the last year of the period *K'ai-hi* (1207) the head official who was charged with the purveyance of the army, stated that the total amount was not sufficient for the wants of that year. They then attempted to issue small *Hoei-tsze*, but they could not bring them in circulation.

In the beginning of the period *Kia-ting* (1208), when every string had only a worth of 400 pieces iron money, and even less, 13.000.000

1) For bills of two terms, see page 173. Bills of the third term may be those who were first issued A. D. 1107. Cf. page 175. These seem to have been convertible every year. Though no express mention is made of this fact, I have arrived at this conclusion as in a subsequent fragment (page 185) is spoken of bills of which the 93rd and the 94th terms were issued. In the year 1210 there could be impossibly a 94th term of the first issue, convertible every three years and emitted in the years 1011 and 1072 the first being only of 23 terms. When we however consider that the payment was deferred every now and then, which we find expressly mentioned with regard to the *Hoei-tsze* or bonds, 1210 can be the year of the 93rd term of the bills which were first issued in 1107. In other authorities treating of the subject more systematically and minutely, we can perhaps find the confirmation of this suggestion.

出金銀度牒一千三百萬。收回半界，期以歲終，不用。然四川諸州去總所遠者千數百里，期限已逼。受給之際，吏復爲姦¹，於是商買不行，民皆嗟怨。一引之直僅售百錢。制司乃揭榜除收兌一千三百萬。引外三界依舊通行。又撤總所取金銀，就成都置場收兌。民心稱定。自後引直五百鐵錢有奇。若關外用銅錢，引直百七十錢而已。

bills calculated in gold and silver had been issued at a time. When half a term was withdrawn and had returned (to the government), they were not used any longer already at the end of the same year. For from all the districts of *Sse-ts'uen*, thousands of persons had gone away hundreds of miles to repair to the distant (from their home-steads) exchange-office (lit. the place where [the silver-bills] were collected), and the time of redeeming had already approached; but at the time when payment was to be made, (it appeared that) the functionaries had again deceived ¹) the people. Thereupon trade was brought to a stand-still and the people grumbled and were dissatisfied. The worth of a credit-note (nominal 1 string) was so (reduced) that it was disposed of for 100 cash. The functionaries who were charged by the government with this, made a proclamation that 13.000.000 credit-notes should be withdrawn and exchanged by the government, and that after this the notes of the third issue should continue to circulate in the same way as before. Moreover, at the places where the payment was to take place, a proclamation was made that, in order to receive gold or silver people must go to *Tšing-tu-fu* where a government-office (lit. enclosure) was established to withdraw and redeem them. (The result of these measures was that) the minds of the people gradually became at ease, and that then the value of the credit-notes (of a string) was a little more than 500 iron pieces. Where across the boundaries (of *Sse-ts'uen*) copper money was employed the worth of a credit-note was 170 pieces (of copper money) and no more ²).

---

1) 爲姦 to play, to make the wicked.

2) As we saw in the foregoing chapter, iron money was exclusively used in those western parts of the empire.

嘉定三年。春。制總司收兌九十一界。二千九緺。餘萬緺。其餘二百萬制以茶馬緺羨千錢及椿管司空²⁾名官告。總餘所以金銀度牒官¹⁾對鑒。餘九十三界錢引收兌。又造九十四界錢引引五百餘萬緺。以收前宣撫³⁾程松所增之數。應民間輸納者。每引百帖八千。其金銀品搭。率用新引七分。金銀三分。其金銀品色。

In the spring of the 3rd year of the period *Kia-ting* (1210) the functionaries who were charged with this, had redeemed 91 terms, to a total amount of more than 29.000.000 string. Of these they had redeemed 12.000.000 string with the balance of the account of the tea and horse officials ¹); and it was announced to the illustrious functionaries of the Board of works ²) to exchange for the notes still in the store-vaults, the value of which was calculated in the gold and silver that was in the cash of the functionaries who superintended the border-fortification, the damaged (lit. bored) *Hoei-tsze*. What then remained should be exchanged for credit notes of the 93rd term. There was also made a 94th term of the credit-notes to an amount of more than 500.000 string to redeem with these what at one time had been issued by the officer *Tsing-sung* who had been sent out to relieve the people ³). When those credit-notes were employed by the people to pay the taxes, they had a value of 8000 a 100 pieces. The sort which had been calculated in gold and silver was added to it (i. e. were accepted at the same value). As a rule (the taxes were paid) in 7 parts of the new credit bills and 3 parts of gold or silver (bills).

The quality and sort of that gold and silver was appreciated on the part of the government in such a way that there was not a single piece that was not defective and too short (all of them were of a bad

1) 茶馬司 name of officials who bartered the government-tea for horses among the *Hoei-hi-*(回紇)Tartars. They were first appointed under the *Sung*-dynasty. For particulars. See MORR. 官 n°. 115 (p. 824).

2) 司空, the superintendent of the Board of Works, who arranged the works whereon the people should be engaged.

3) 宣撫使 is the name of an officer, who was sent to relieve the people, when they were suffering from some calamity produced by natural causes. MORR. 官 n°. 111 (p. 823).

如 直 引。兩 年。蓋 二 百 每 無 官
故。遂 而 收 三 自 十 帖。舊 少 稱
昔¹⁾復 引 舊 年。元 引。納 引 腐。不

quality). For 100 old bills (*Hoei-tsze*) 20 new credit-notes were received.
(The consequence of all this was that) when in the 1st year (1208) and
in the 3rd year (1210) thus twice the old *Hoei-tsze* had been withdrawn
from circulation, the value of the new (notes) was in the end again
equal to the old ¹) ones.

We now return to the beginning of the reign of the emperor
*Kao-tsung*, when in behalf of the army a new sort of bills was
issued. [Matw. IX 24a—30a].

### THE HOEI-TSZE OR BONDS.

州 關 部 致。通。而 辨 有 州²⁾元 高
召 子。造 乃 錢 舟 合 司 之 年。宗 會
客 付 見 詔 重 楫 用 請 屯 因 紹 子。
人 婪 錢 戶 難 不 錢。椿 駐。婪 與

Under the reign of the emperor *Kao-tsung* in the first year of the
period *Šao-hing* (1131) the officials requested in behalf of the camp and
halting-stations in the province of *Wu-tšeu* ²) for the necessary money,
in order to make the palisades (fortifications). As these parts could not
be reached by water, and the weight of the money made the transport
(in another way) troublesome, it was ordered to the ministry of finances
to make frontier-bills for ready money and to send them to the province of *Wu-tšeu*, where every stranger who entered this province, was
summoned at the custom-house. As soon as those frontier (bills) had
arrived, they were forwarded to the custom-house for goods to be exchanged there for money.

If there were some (of the merchants) who wished to receive in
return receipts for tea, salt, aromatics, or other articles of commerce, this was left free to the functionaries of the districts. With
frontier-bills the government purchases of grains were paid. In the
beginning it could not be prevented that they (ready money and notes)

1) 故。昔 means obviously 故昔。 | 2) *Wu-tšen* is situated in the province of *Sse-tš'uen*.

務。椿堁見錢印造關子。
於是罷交子務。令権貨。
民何以信。
意。改爲交子。
見錢務。交子。
子臣僚有司朝廷行措置本
六年二月。詔置人皆在交
分之一。又止之以日償
権充糧本。未免抑納配²。以貨
子引者。聽於是州縣。香
錢。有願於得茶鹽貨鈔
入中。執關¹⁾赴榷貨務請

were settled on a par ¹). The custom-house for goods paid only one part on the three on the day that they were redeemed. The people complained of this, and were dissatisfied ²).

In the second month of the 6th year (1136) there came an order to establish a bank for the issue of the bills of exchange (*Kiao-tsze*) which were already circulating. The ministers then said that when his Majesty had instituted the frontier-receipts for ready money, the functionaries, charged with the execution, had entirely lost sight of the original intention. When now a change was attempted, and bills of exchange again were made, while the government was without metallic deposit, how would the people have faith in them. They concluded that it might not happen. Then the bank for the issue of bills of exchange was abolished again, and the custom-house for goods was ordered to have frontier-notes coined to (supply) the ready money wanted for the construction and repair of palisades and parapets.

1) A sinologue will observe that there are a great many difficulties in this fragment. In 執關 the monogram 關 stands for 關子, the frontier notes — and the literal translation is: the notes in hand or in possession, i. e. as soon as the notes had arrived. The position does not admit to take 關 in a locative case with the meaning of "at the frontier." For the same use of that word Cf. page 218. note 2.— 請 has here the meaning of 清 to clear, to exchange. In the following parts it occurs three times more in that same signification, Cf. p. 187, 205 and 212. A similar expression is found in WILLIAMS' Dictionary *in voce* 領 p. 540a — 抑配 is still more difficult to explain. I believe the meaning is this: In the beginning, when those bills were first issued the government settled the worth of paper and metallic-money at the same ratio, notwithstanding, at the very first redemption, the restitution was only a third part of the sum for which they had been given in payment. The same expression occurs again Matw. IX 29a Cf. page 201.

2) The single place where DE MAILLA in his Hist Gén. d. l. Chine alludes to paper money is when treating of the institution of the frontier-notes of the province of *Wu-tsen* Vol. VIII p. 502. He has only one addition to the information which Ma-twau-lin gives, viz. that those notes were stamped at ten corners (*marqués a dix coins*).

二十九年，印給公據關子，赴三路總領所。淮西、湖廣各關子八十萬緍，淮東至公據四十萬緍，凡五等，自十千至百千。內公據關子作三年行使。第二年許見錢銀中半入納。三十年，戶部侍郎錢端禮被旨造會子，椿見錢於城內外流轉，其合發官錢並許兌會子，赴左藏庫送納。明年二月詔會子赴茶場，筭請茶鹽香礬等歲以一客旅。

In the 29th year (1159) the government coined frontier-bills in order to provide for the whole garrison [1]). To receive them people) went to the central-office of three districts. *Hoai-si* and *Hu-kwang* were each to receive frontier-bills for 800.000 string, and *Hoai-tung* bills in behalf of the general garrison for 400.000 string. Those bills were of 5 different sorts of from 10.000—100.000 pence (10—100 string [2])). These bills for the general garrison were made for a circulation and use of three years. In the second year it would be allowed when payments (of taxes) were made in copper money or silver at the government offices, to pay in these bills half of the sum due.

In the 30th year (1160) *Tsien-twan-li*, vice-president of the ministry of finances possessed of an imperial authority issued again *Hoei-tsze* (to meet the necessities) of the palisades (fortifications). Of the ready money circulating within and without the fortified places, that which agreed with the pieces issued by the government, might be entirely exchanged for *Hoei-tsze*. People went to the left government-treasury to deliver it. In the second month of next year an order was dispatched to the *Hoei-tsze* bank and to the officials attached to the government stores [4]) of tea, in which was said that it would be expedient to settle [5]) the accounts of

---

1) 公據 lit. the whole occupation. We see here a considerable expansion of the first issue, which was only for the fortification of the encampments. The fact reminds us of the time of Louis XIV of France, when similar billets were issued, called, *"Billets de l'extraordinaire des guerres, de l'artillerie, de la marine"* Cf. Les Economistes du dix-huitieme siècle. Paris, Guillaumin. 1843. page 444.

2) They were probably for such a large amount as they ought not to circulate as money, but only served to pay the merchants who purveyed the army.

3) The sentence 見錢....會子 is an example of a rhetorical inversion or ante-position.

4) 茶場 government-stores of tea. 場 is an enclosure, set apart for the gathering of grain.

5) 請, this is the second passage in which this word is used in the meaning of 清 Cf. p. 187.

押。每一萬道。解赴戶部

者聽⁴日造會子。監官分

件²）賞錢或願補前名目³）

告首¹）特與免罪亦支上

徒中及窩藏之家¹）能自

支賞與補進義校尉。不若願

斬。賞錢一千貫。

僞造會子之罰。犯人處

三十二年。十二月。詔定

也。

非全仰會子以佐國用

不獨恃見錢以為本。又

千萬貫。可以陰助 稱提。

the travelling merchants (with the government) by means of receipts for tea, salt, aromatics, alum, and other government productions, which (estimated in money) annually represented a sum of 10.000.000 string. In secret it might serve to support (the State-finances, as these receipts) balanced an actual possession of merchandise, (and the government had moreover the advantage) that it had not to rely on metallic money alone as basis (in exchange), while on the other hand it had not entirely to look up to the *Hoei-tsze* to meet the wants of the empire.

In the 12th month of the 32nd year (1162) an order was issued to institute punishments for forgery of *Hoei-tsze*. The offender was put to death, and the reward (given to the informer) was 1000 string. If he did not claim that reward, it was given as an perquisity to the master-controller. If there were among the villains and their accomplices¹) some (who denounced themselves) by confessing and avowing their crime, they could by special permission be exempted from punishment. They were also allowed to receive a reward in money, or if they wished it they were free to be rehabilitated in their former reputation and honor³).

Now *Hoei-tsze* were made daily. The functionaries of the mint partly impressed their seals on them, and every 10.000 bills were forwarded to the ministry of finances to be sealed there again.

The paper for the *Hoei-tsze* was at that time taken from the provinces of *Hoei-tšeu-fu*⁵) and *Tši-tšeu*⁶) and afterwards they were made in *Tšing-tu-fu*⁵) and also in *Lin-ngan-fu*⁶). In the beginning the *Hoei-*

1) 窩藏之家 are accomplishes.

首 has here the 3d tone and the meaning of to confess guilt.

2) 件 a numerative.

3) 名目 reputation and honor 補

前 | | to rehabilitate.

4) 聽 it is allowed, it is at liberty.

5) *Hoei-tšeu* en *Tšing-tu-fu* were situated in *Sše-tš'uen* and thus supplied the frontier-bills for the encampments.

6) *Tši-tšeu* and *Lin-ngan-fu* are situated in the province of *Tše-kiang* in the east of the empire; they supplied the capital and the regions of *Hoai*.

覆印。當時會紙取於徽池州。續
造於成都府。又造於臨安府。本行會
子初止行於兩浙。除後又詔通行會
於淮止湖北京西。
並用浙錢外。其
上供等錢許盡不用。會子解發²其處。
沿流州軍錢會中半。民間典賣其處。
田宅牛畜車船等如之。或全用
會子者與聽³。
孝宗降與元年。詔官印會子之印以
隆興尚書戶部官印會子
為文更造五百文會。又造二百
三百文會。五年置江州會子務。

tsze circulated only in the parts of the two *Tse* rivers, afterwards it was ordered to circulate them in *Hoai*, *Tse(kiang)*, *Hu-pek* and west of the capital. Except at the offices where the duty on salt[1]) was paid and metallic money was used exclusively, it was allowed at places which could not be reached by water or by roads, so that the government could not furnish another kind of money, entirely to make use of *Hoei-tsze* in exchange[2]). In the districts and encampments situated along the river it was a rule that people paid one half in money and the other half in *Hoei-tsze*. When a mort-gage was made, or lands and houses, cattle, food, waggons, vessels, and other similar things were sold the people were free[3]) to use only *Hoei-tsze*.

Under the reign of the Emperor *Hiao-tsung* in the first year of the period *Lung-hing* (1163) it was notified to the officials who coined the *Hoei-tsze* that the year-name of *Lung-hing* and the state-seal of the minister of finances should be the seals to be used to stamp the *Hoei-tsze*. Then *Hoei-tsze* of 500 *cash* were made, also were there made of the value of 200 and 300 *cash*[4]).

In the 5th year (1167) a *Hoei-tsze* bank was established in *Kiang-tseu*.

---

1) An income-tax levied on every one of the people. It is remarkable that the government did not accept those taxes in paper money.

2) 解 to transmit, to hand over. — 發 to pay out.

3) 聽 has here the same meaning of to be allowed as at the foregoing page 189 note 4.

4) Since the *Hoei-tsze* were generally used as medium of exchange, they were no more of those large amounts of 100 strings of *cash*.

之。萬 銀。及 出 予 祐。司 年。乾
兩 一 南 內 之 言 諫 因 道
收 百 庫 庫 做 會 陳。左 二

In the second year of the period *Kien-t'ao* (1166) in consequence of
what was said by the councilor of the left side, *Yen*[1]), viz. that the
*Hoei-tsze* had greatly diminished in value, a sum of 1.000.000 ounces
of silver was given out of the left and south treasury (to redeem the
depreciated paper money).

After these fragments we have a minute report of an official
of the ministry of finances, from which it appears that in the
last seven years (1161—66) especially, an enormous quantity of
paper money had been issued. When afterwards the government
ordered that the taxes for the full amount should be paid in ready
money, these bills were soon reduced in value. In order to avert
the dangers resulting from a depreciation, arrangements were made
to convert the old worthless *Hoei-tsze* into another sort of paper
currency; a measure which seems to have succeeded.

But when a large number of *Hoei-tsze* had been redeemed in
this way, new notes were issued again. The worn and torn bills were
accepted by the government at 10 per cent of their original value
and, it is a noteworthy instance of tyrannical government that a
heavy punishment was inflicted on such private persons as ventured
to vie with the government, and buy them at a lower discount.

Our chronicle relates the particulars in the following way:

道²。百 二 過 月。二 至 十 詔 璿。耶 月 三
止 餘 千 會 共 年。乾 一 與 言 中 庋 年。
乾 萬 八 予 印 七 道 年。三 自 唐 支 正

In the 1st month of the 3rd year (1167) *T'ang-tšuen*, the official who
was charged with the disbursements at the ministry of finances, reported
that from the 31st year of the period *Šao-hing* (1161) till the 7th month

---

1) *Yen* is the same as *Liang-yen*, a functionary who continually warns the government against the perils of an overissued popel

currency. Cf. p. 203.

2) 道 a classifier of dispatches.

往　輸　要　萬　大　餘　收　自　在　道　共　道
商　納³⁾十　緣　約　貫　換　民　除　二　支　二
買　會　分　諸　每　尚　截　間　在　年　取　年
低　子　見　路　月　有　一　者。官　十　過　十
價　是　錢　綱²⁾收　三　月。司　一　千　一
收　致　州　運　換　百　三　有　椿　月　五　月
買　在　縣　依　不　一　年　九　管　十　百　十
輻　外　不　近　過　十　正　百　循　四　六　四
湊⁴⁾會　許　指　六　萬　月　八　環¹⁾日。十　日。
行　子　民　揮　七　貫　六　十　萬　以　餘　以
在。往　戶　並　十　未　日　後。外　前。萬　前。

of the 2nd year of the period *K'ien-lao* (1167) all together more than 28.000.000 *Hoei-tsze* had been printed. Before the 14th day of the 11th month of the year 1167 there were paid and received above 15.600.000 *Hoei-tsze* (total 43.600.000). Besides those which were in deposit with the functionaries who kept the frontier-fortifications in repair in order to bring them in circulation ¹), there was a number of 9.800.000 which already circulated among the people. Since that 14th day of the 11th month the repayment had begun, up to the 6th day of the 1st month of the 3rd year there were presented for repayment above 1.189.000, so that there remained more than 8.000.000 which had not been received. Upon the whole the number which was redeemed monthly did not exceed the amount of from 600.000 to 700.000.

According to a law ²) to which all the districts were subject, and in accordance with a regulation lately prescribed, the people were not allowed to pay their taxes ³) any more in *Hoei-tsze*, but were obliged to pay every 10 parts in ready metallic money. The consequence of this was that the excluded *Hoei-tsze* by and by were accepted by the merchants at a reduced value, when something was bought. (In order to prevent a further depreciation which might be fatal to the credit of the state), and to collect together ⁴) all the *Hoei-tsze* that were in circulation,

1) 循環 to go in a circuit.

2) 綱 a law.

3) 輸納 to pay taxes.

4) 輻湊 (= 輳) lit. the spokes of a wheel together with the nave, is a methaphorical expression meaning to collect in one centre (the bank) the circulating bonds from all quarters. Cf. p. 206.

所以六務支取擁并。給降度牒及諸州助教[1]帖，詔五千道，付權貨務召人全以會子入納候出賣欲盡收[2]，節續給降務將盡收取。會子除收也。六月戶部曾懷[3]言會子還外尚有四百九十萬貫在民間，乞子存留行使者。十二月以民間會子有破損者，別造五百萬換給。他日又詔損會貫買百錢數可照者並作上供錢解發。鉅室以低價收者坐罪。

for which purpose six different banks were established to receive and collect them, it was ordered to issue bills estimated (at a certain sum), and (further) it was ordered to give a number of 5000 to the support of every *Tšeu*-district in the country, and to send them to the custom-houses (in those districts) and then to invite the people to exchange their *Hoei-tsze* there (for those new bills). After this the government should wait till (those 5000 bills in every province) would be sold out. If the demand for them continued steady, the government, if it wished entirely to withdraw the *Hoei-tsze* from circulation, for a certain time might continue to emit these bills at the banks. In the 6th month *Ts'ang-hoai*, the minister of finances [3]), reported that besides the *Hoei-tsze* withdrawn from circulation (by the government), there still circulated (*Hoei-tsze*) for an amount of 4.900.000 string among the people. He requested to keep these in circulation (and not to redeem them). In the 12th month (1167) there were separately made *Hoei-tsze* for 5.000.000 string, because there circulated among the people many that were damaged and worn. Shortly afterwards another decree was issued that the value at which worn *Hoei-tsze* of a nominal worth of 1 string could be exchanged should be 100 cash. This might frequently be repeated till the money, procured by the government for this purpose, would be wholly spent. The obstinate houses that would continue to receive them at a reduced value should be tried and punished for the offence [5]).

1) 教 to give instruction.

2) 申取 the demand increasing.

3) 戶部 is here for ｜｜尚書,

4) 收還 to draw and pay back.

5) By this the government would compel the holders of torn bills to exchange them

see the next fragment.

The next fragment is remarkable for the great many particulars it contains regarding the exchange of old bills for new ones. The way in which the conversion was effected was now much less tyrannic than the one just mentioned; and this must be mainly attributed to the cleverness of the man who managed these affairs. But the end shows again that the best measures were ineffectual when the state finances are so hopelessly deranged. Immediately afterwards we read that twice in succession the redeeming the *Hoei-tsze* was deferred, each time for a period of three years, while at the same time the issue was increased.

收稅。蔣芾奏曰。
經過務場不得
庫推賞其將帶
子庫庫印依左藏
鑄懷提領措置
曾同共措置
舊逐戶部尚書
額界一千萬貫換
以一界爲
年立爲一重界
會子毀抹截鑿
會毀抹截鑿三付
四年。以取到舊

In the 4th year (1168) the old *Hoei-tsze* which were already drawn back and which were damaged, obliterated, quite torn to pieces and full of holes, were forwarded to the *Hoei-tsze* bank (with the order) to make them heavier (in the future). In the previous (third) year a new issue of *Hoei-tsze* had been coined for an amount of exactly 10.000.000 string, and in proportion as (the bills) of that issue were coined, new bills were exchanged for the old ones. *Ts'ang-hoai* who was the head of the ministry of finances had, at the same time that he carried into effect the command (to make bills) ordered that money should be cast. The *Hoei-tsze* already printed and put up, were transferred to the left treasury. Those of them which would be smuggled and get outside the issue-department should not be accepted in payment of taxes.

*Tsiang-fei* said in a report: During the last month the *Hoei-tsze* which were in use have been withdrawn and redeemed with gold and silver (now the same course must be pursued), and if the number of

at 10°/₀ of their original worth, and every private person who continued to ac- | cept them at a higher rate should be punished.

此月用會子收回金銀。若會
子稍多又出錢銀收之。陳俊
卿奏曰歛散抑揚權之在上。與
可以無斂。其年四月一日
工印造至歲終可造一千萬
貲措置收換舊會。每道收舊
貫錢二十足零百半之應舊糜
會破損。但貫百百存印。文將可
驗者。即與兌換。內有假偽
辯驗人吏送所司。其監官取
朝廷指揮每驗出一貫偽會。
追究元收兌會子人錢三貫
與辯驗人。如官吏用心訐事

issued *Hoei-tsze* gradually increases, gold and silver must continually
be given to withdraw them.

Developing (this principle), the report of this excellent minister says
further: The means to make that they do not depreciate, is now to
collect them together, and then again to expand them, at one time to
withdraw them and at another time to bring them in large quantities
in circulation, and in this way always to balance them that they may
remain at full value. Now if on the 1st day of the 4th month of this
year workpeople are appointed to print and coin them, an amount of
10.000.000 string may be ready at the end of this year. When at that
time the exchange of the old *Hoei-tsze* begins, on every bill which is
exchanged a premium of 20 *cash* shall be demanded. It will be sufficient that the piece which is left of the bill presented, is a little more
than half (the original paper); and when of the old bill which is torn
or damaged only the character 貫 (*Kwan*-string) or the character in-
dicating the number of hundreds of *cash*, is left, and the seals can
still test the genuineness, it may be presented to be exchanged. Now
when among those bills are forged ones, the functionaries who examine
them must dispatch them to the department (where they are made).
Those functionaries who examine them will receive further instruction [1])
from the government. Every time when the examination brings to light
a forged bill of a string, the person who after having been traced out,
is proved to have exchanged this bill first, shall have to pay a sum of

1) Probably further information, f. i. | uineness could be recognized.
about secret marks by which the gen-

於外者。綫二百萬耳。行
銀換收者四百百萬。流金
半爲會子。而南庫以其
部歲入一千二百萬。萬戶
萬。赴南庫一千二百萬。其
板接續印庫椿管。當時百銅
易會子庫。造會子二界茶四
界各展限將第四令都界
淳熙三年。詔第三年。第三界
盡絕更不年。不行用三
換絕更明年。三月十日終。
十二月。一日始。置局。收
無假僞。具姓名推賞。自

3000 copper pieces in money to the functionaries who have verified and proved it. When those functionaries use their common sense they will terminate the whole affair without having forged bills. Both the name and surname of the. offenders shall be published as a punishment for their offence. From the 1st day of the 12th month the office for the exchange of *Hoei-tsze* was opened, this lasted till the end of the 10th day of the 3rd month of the next year (during 3 months and 10 days). After that time it was all over, nor was it practiced again.

In the 3rd year of the period *Sun-hi* (1176) it was proclaimed that the 3rd and 4th term of payment [1]) should be delayed three years each. Furthermore it was ordered that the depot where the government stores of tea were kept and the *Hoei-tszè* were issued, should take the copper plates of the 4th issue, and continue to coin and print *Hoei-tsze* for an amount of 2.000.000 (string) and to send them to the Southern treasury, charged with the administration of the border fortifications.

At that time the amount of the revenues at the Department of finances was 12.000.000 string in the whole year, half of which consisted of *Hoei-tsze*. Of these the Southern treasury took 4.000.000, exchanging them for gold and silver, and what was then again brought in circulation did hardly amount to 2.000.000 string.

1) This is the first time that we read of periodical terms of the *Hoei-tsze*. The first issues of the year 1131 seem not to have had those regular terms of redemption as the bills of exchange of *Sse-ts'uen* (p. 171). The *Hoei-tsze* were originally a sort of currency used in the army, very much the same as that issued in times of war in Europe for instance by Frederic the Great and in the late French-German war, convertible either after a fixed term or immediately after the expedition. In China this sort of bills was issued to be redeemed after 3 years; other issues followed probably for the same interval of time till at last they were also made with periodical times of redemption; but we do not know how long the whole time of circulation was then regulated. Now we find it instanced that when a term to repay the notes had come, the necessary money was wanting and the payment was delayed for another period of three years. We shall soon see that the imperial government was not ill-pleased with the measure, as afterwards the redeeming of new issues was likewise postponed.

The two following fragments contain some information on the money among the Tartars who had established themselves in the northern parts of the empire and in *Kai-fung-fu* the Chinese capital. In many respects this part is important. It corroborates the fact mentioned before that the Tartars had learned the use of money from the Chinese, and how they managed to transport Chinese money from the neighboring southern parts over the *Hoang-ho* and to bring it in circulation in their own territory. Furthermore we are told how the notes were signed and sealed, and herein do we find the key to decipher some difficulties presented by the almost invisible seal-marks on the note of the *Tai-ming*-dynasty, a photograph of which has been subjoined to the Addenda. As the whole system of paper money among the Tartars was borrowed from the Chinese we may safely conclude, that the Chinese notes were signed and marked in the same way as related in this fragment.

局 於 中 於 不 國 餘。錢 一 場 本 轡 范
造 汴 國 河 欲 舊 悉 絕 鑄。王 無 錄¹。成
官 京³)楷 南。留 錢。用 不 正 亮 錢。載 大
會。置 幣。效 錢 又 中 多 隆²)嘗 惟 虜 攬

*Fan-tsing-ta*'s "History of the grasp of the reins ¹)," contains the information that originally the captives of war had no money about them. Only *Yang-wang-ling* has once tried to cast it. When the money of the period *Tsing-lung* ²) (1156—61) was not supplied any more, (lit. was cut off) and circulated only in a small quantity (the *Kin*-Tartars) employed the old money of the Middle Empire exclusively, and not liking to leave money behind them in *Ho-nan*, they also imitated the paper money of the Chinese, and established in *Pien-king* ³), (their ca-

1) *Fan-tsing-ta* is a distinguished Chinese author however, I have not found that mention was made of the 攬轡錄 which I literally translate by "The history of the grasp of the reins."

2) A yearname of the *Kin* or *Niu-tši-* Tartars.

3) 汴京 the court of *Pien* was the name of the town 開封府 *Kai-fung-fu*, in the province of *Ho-nan*, at the time of its capture by the *Kin*-Tartars.

後　偽　年　輸　赴　南　例　京　尚　日　即　陰　謂
有　造　納　工　庫　路　交　置　書　南　用　收　之
戶　者　換　墨　支　官　鈔　鈔　省　京　錢　銅　交
部　斬　別　錢　取　私　許　局。印　批　不　錢。鈔。
管　賞　給　一　即　作　人　造　降　用　悉　擬
當　錢　以　十　時　見　納　一　檢　鈔。運　見
令　三　七　五　給　錢　錢　貫　會　準　而　錢
史　百　十　文　付。流　給　至　鈔　北。行
官。千。為　候　每　轉。鈔。昨　文　過　使。
交　前　陌。七　貫　若　河　貫。南　奏　大　河　而

·pital) a bank for the coining of *Hoei(tsze)*, and called this paper money *Kiao-tšao* (i. e. bills of exchange). Like the ready metallic these notes circulated, but unobservedly they drove the copper money out of circulation there, and entirely transferred it to the North. And no sooner had they crossed the (*Hoang-)ho* than they used money and no notes. The design of those notes was mostly "Bills of exchange of the Southern Capital')," and it was the wooden seal of their department of finances which determined their value. From a report lately published, of an assistant-official of the *Šang-šu-šang* 2), who was charged with the issue and management of the *Hoei(tsze)*, appears that in the "Southern Capital" was the issue bank for the notes, and that they were made of a value of from 1 to 3 string. As soon as those bills of exchange were regulated, the people were allowed to bring their money and receive notes in return. The state money and the money coined by private persons, circulating in the districts south of the river, was sent (to the north) as soon as it was received in payment at the treasury. The cost of the bringing (them) in circulation, labor and ink amounted to 15 *cash* a string. After a term of 7 years they were redeemed. When redeemed before the proper time only 70°/₀ of the value was received. He who forged them was beheaded and the reward of the denunciator was 300.000 *cash*. On the front and back of the paper they were warranted by the seals impressed on them by the officials charged with the control at the department of finances, and by the officials appointed

1) The Southern capital of the Tartars in the Chinese dominions.

2) 尚書省批 an assistant officer of one of the ministers is here a Chinese, not a Tartar official, nothwithstanding the

尚書省 is the name of a prime minister of the *Kin*-Tartars and the *Yuen* or Mongol dynasty. Matw. speaks of his own time when the *Yuen*-dynasty, sat on the throne.

鈔庫使副書押。四圍畫龍鶴有飾。乾道間。充泛○右石湖國汴京。有交使入金國以見如此。其鈔所載其有幣權錢。然時中國。亦湖會子。又有東南之地。不會。而鼓鑄川引淮交而一。所以常之所。亦復惟賤秤提無困錢幣多中以交鈔行策。而彼則反國舊錢行之。河南以簡易也。之河北。似

at the bank of issue. At the four corners of the notes dragons and cranes are engraved as ornaments.

When in the period *K'ien-tao* (1165—74) on the part of the districts of *Yeu-Si-* and *Hu*, *Tsung-fan* was sent to *Pien-king*, the capital of the empire of the *Kin*-Tartars, there circulated bills of exchange which contained all that we have just seen. At that time shreds of paper weighing against money, were employed in China. In this way *Hoei-tsze* were found in the eastern and southern provinces; moreover there were credit notes for the province of *Sse-ts'uen*, bills of exchange for the *Hoai* regions, and *Hoei-tsze* for the *Hu* country; and when at the places where metallic money was cast, they worked no longer after one and the same model, and because of the continuous want of metallic money, (the number of notes) had ever increased while they had fallen in value, (this resulted) that they were no longer a medium of exchange weighing against a real property¹); and this was the reason that they (the *Kin*-Tartars) employed only the bills of exchange in circulation, and (that they collected) in *Ho-nan* the old Chinese money and carried it over to the north of the river. It seemed that the exchange for bills was very easy.

光宗紹熙元年。詔第七、八界會子各展三年。臣僚言會子界三年爲限。今展至再則爲九年矣。何以示

In the 1st year of the period *Sao-hing* (1190) under the reign of the emperor *Kwang-tsung* it was ordered to prolong the 7th and the 8th term with three years each. The ministers observed that the fixed term for *Hoei-tsze* was three years, but that now in consequence of the double

¹) In the expression 稱提 the character 稱 is here superseded by 秤。

行．執　更　額．千　界．詔　元　寧　限．立　第　信。
奏　增．額　萬　以　會　元　宗　　定　十　詔
不　許　外　爲　三　子　年．慶　　年　界．造

expansion, (that term) had already come to 9 years. By what means
was the confidence of the people to be preserved. (For answer) there
came an imperial order that with the 10th term the regular intervals
should be restored.

In the 1st year of the period of *King-yuen* (1193) under the reign
of the emperor *Ning-tsung* an order was issued that the limits of the
*Hoei-tsze* should be a fixed amount of 30.000.000 string. And when
they (the *Hoei-tsze*) were increased beyond that amount, it was allowed
to stop them, and bring them forward that they might not circulate.

The phrases and expressions especially of the latter part of
the fragment which now follows, are so vague and obscure that
I have long hesitated whether I should insert it. However, as I
have till now never shunned the difficulties in Ma-twau-lin's text,
I will try also to explain these to the best of my ability, the
more because the fragment gives a lively picture of the always
increasing misery caused by an imprudent issue of paper money.

免　提　新　以　舊　安　二　綾　金　策．目　言　嘉
告　新　會　舊　會．府　十　紙　銀　詔　滋　三　定
許　會　之　會　品　官　萬　乳　度　封　多．界　二
肆　最　一．之　搭　局．添　香．牒　椿　稱　會　年。
起．嚴　而　二．入　收　貼　湊　官　庫　提　子．臣
根　未　稱　換　納．換　臨　成　詰　撥　無　數　僚

In the 2nd year of the period *Kia-ting* (1209) the ministers reported that the
*Hoei-tsze* of three terms (of redemption) were so increased in number that
they were no more a means weighing against an actual possession of money.
Then an order was given to the treasury which supplied the wants of the
border fortifications to issue notes estimated in gold and silver, (and which
should be printed) on the part of the government on paper mixed with
satin, and (saturated with) olibanum. Of these should be collected to a
number of 200.000, to supply therewith the state bank at *Lin-ngan-fu.*
When this sort which had been added to (the already circulating bills)

志。酷 敷 提¹。用 而 并 徒 出。而 連
吏 抑 而 假 重 相 流。佸 苟 株
得 配²。科 稱 刑 望。鄕 籍 政 逮

was received (at the Bank), in the withdrawing and redeeming of the old *Hoei-tsze*, a new note was exchanged for 2 old ones, and it was looked sharply to that those new *Hoei-tsze* should balance an actual possession (of money). It could not be prevented that accusations and denunciations arose everywhere, for the root was torn up, trunk and all, (i. e. they sought to get out of it as much as possible) and consequently there arose an inquisitive government. In vain there circulated lists of prices (i. e. nothing was either bought or sold); the different villages and places looked out for each other, and the punishments for the use of forged assignats were made severer [1], and moreover it was dictated that (the notes) should be put on a par [2] (with money); the tyrannic officials carried their point [3].

In the last part of his "Examination" [IX 32*a*—33*b*] Ma-twan-lin treats of the paper money of the Eastern provinces of *Hoai* and *Hu*, instituted there at the time that the government had already enjoyed in the North and West the large profits accruing from an unlimited issue of a currency which could be made at so little cost. The following passages taken from these chapters are interesting as they reveal the causes which ultimatily led to the total depreciation of the paper currency in consequence of its being circulated over the whole of the immense realm.

1) 用 假 稱 提 Cf. page 164.

2) 抑 配 is the same expression which in the beginning of the history of the *Hoei-tsze* caused difficulties. Cf. page 187.

3) Cf. with this passage and that of p. 207—209 the next fragment painting the misery causedly an overissue of paper money in Austria, quoted from Prof. SUMNER, "History of American Currency" p. 313. In 1810, the next stage was reached, a stage which the student of paper money meets so regularly in its history, that he anticipates it sooner or later, in one form or another, in every new instance. A new class of notes was issued called "redemption-notes," to represent coin, and to exchange for paper at the rate of one for three. By using these, the government prevented its expenditures from running up such enormous figures. This plan, and others intended to support it, failed to attract even the popular attention; all confidence in the promises of the government was lost. The misery was wide and deep, reaching even the well-to-do classes. Persons on salaries found themselves in the pecuniary position of day laborers; the peasants and country people who tilled the soil had its products for food, but trade was brought to a stand-still."

## THE BILLS OF EXCHANGE OF THE REGIONS WATERED BY THE HOAI-RIVER.

紹興末年、會子行、未有兩淮
湖廣之分。乾道元年、戶部侍郎
林安宅、言督府妄費、印給會子、
而本錢不足、遂致有弊。乞別
給會子二十萬。背印付他路、
州軍行使、不得越過印
二年六月。詔別印三百萬、止於
五百一貫、交子三百萬止
兩淮州縣行使。其日前舊會、
聽對換、應入納、買賣、並以交會
子見錢中半。如往來不便詔。

In the last year of the period *Šao-hing* (1162) regarding the circulation of *Hoei-tsze* there was no distinction made as yet between the two *Hoai*-districts and *Hu-kwang*.

In the 1st year of the period *K'ien-tao* (1163) *Lin-ngan-tséu*, vice-president of the department of finances, reported that in consequence of an inquiry (made) at the department, (it appeared that) the reckless cost of printing and the supply of the *Hoei-tsze* were very great, and as the deposited capital was not sufficient, the result would be that the paper should fall in value. He therefore insisted upon procuring a separate number of 200.000 *Hoei-tsze* on which should be printed on the reverse that sent to *Hoai-nan*, they should circulate in these districts of the country and in the encampments, while they might not pass the boundaries to other districts.

In the 6th month of the 2nd year (1166) it was ordered to coin separately bills of exchange (*Kiao-tsze*) for an amount of 300.000 string, of a value of 200, 300, 500, cash and of one string, which were to circulate only in the subdivisions of the *Hoai*-regions. To further the withdrawal of the *Hoei-tsze* circulating before that time, they must be received as payment in exchange at a general rate of one half in bills

---

1) *Hoai* is in the North-East, *Hu* in the South-East of China. The bills of the *Hoai* regions were afterwards allowed to circulate in the *Hu*-regions.

給交子會子各二十會。付
鎮江建康府榷貨務。使准
人之過江江南人之渡准
者。皆得對換循環使用。然
自紹與末年以前。銅錢禁
用於准而易以鐵錢。會子
既用於准而易以交子於
是商買不行。淮民以困。右
司諫陳良祐。言莫若如舊
從民便令鐵錢已散銅錢已
收。且兼行以鐵錢二當
銅錢一。交子可以盡罷。無
疑也。上曰。朕亦知其不可

of exchange (*Kiao-tsze*) and the other in metallic money. This not being convenient to the coming and going[1] (the merchants), it was ordered to provide for a quantity of 200.000 *Kiao-tsze*, and for as many *Hoei-tsze*, and to send them to the custom-house for commodities of *Kien-kang* and *Tsin-kiang-fu*, in order to make that the people coming from *Hoai* (i. e. the North) and crossing the *Kiang*, and those who coming from the South of the *Kiang* crossed the river *Hoai*, could all exchange their money (at that office) for the money which was current (within the boundary-line) where they made use of it. Before the last year of the period *Šao-hing* (1162) the use of copper money was prohibited in the district of *Hoai*, and iron money had been substituted for it[2], and the *Hoei-tsze* which had been employed till now, were also superseded by *Kiao-tsze*; and when this paralyzed trade and the people of the district of *Hoai* were in want, *Liang-yen*, an councilor of the right side said that there was nothing so good as the old regulation and (that nothing was) so convenient to the people, as when the iron money was spread and the copper money was (generally) received, and that, if it was ordered that the two sorts should circulate together, so that 2 pieces of iron money were equal to 1 piece of copper, this would undoubtedly result in the abolishment of the bills of exchange. The emperor said, we too know that this will not do any longer, were it alone because in those parts a legion (*Kiün* = 12.500 soldiers) of lancers is encamped; and when *Liang-yen* too reported that the *Kiao-tsze* were inconvenient, all the

1) For in that case they were still obliged to carry with them the heavy copper money.
2) Compare what is said on this measure in the passage quoted page 147. When confronting these two passages it appears pears that the whole circulating medium in the Eastern regions coin as well as the paper money has undergone a change in that period.

行。只爲武鋒一軍在彼。艮祐又
奏交子不便詔兩准郡守漕臣。
各條其利害乃謂所降交子數
多。而銅錢并會子又并不過江。子是數
致民旅未便。詔銅錢并會子。
舊過江行使其民間交子。
見錢納官。應在官交子。日下盡
數赴行在左藏庫交納。
○後又詔銅錢并會子。民間依舊過
江行使又詔江南州郡。民間行
使准交者從便。至嘉定十五年。
增印及三百萬。其數日增價亦
日損。稱提無其術也。

magistrates and officials for the transport of grain in the two *Hoai*-
regions were directed that each of them should send in a report on the
advantages, disadvantages (in use), and the number of the bills that
was issued.

But the copper money and the *Hoei-tsze* not being allowed yet to
come across the *Kiang*, this made that the people living there as well
as the travellers still experienced the inconvenience. On this the order
was issued that the copper money and *Hoei-tsze* on the same footing
as before might circulate and be employed across the *Kiang*. The *Kiao-
tsze* which at that time still circulated among the people might be received at the government offices in exchange for a metallic currency
made for this purpose. The *Kiao-tsze* in store at the government (offices) which were still extant, were from that time to be sent up to the
left government treasury in order to be converted there.

After the order was issued that the copper money together with the
the *Hoei-tsze* as in olden times might circulate over the *Kiang* (in the
districts of the *Hoai*), it was also ordered that in the divisions and subdivisions south of the *Kiang*, where the *Hoai-kiao-tsze*, circulating there,
were considered by the people to be very convenient, up to the 15th year
of the period *Kia-ting* (1222) should be printed in addition for an amount
of 3.000.000 (string). However, since that time this number was increased daily, and the value of this paper consequently diminished daily
and the character of the paper money, i. e. the balancing an actual possession of the merchandise, lost its effect also here.

湖廣會。孝宗隆興元年。
餉臣王珏言。襄陽郢
復等處。大軍支請以
錢銀品搭。見錢印
大軍庫堆垜措置。於
造五百并軍見當便
會子發赴軍前買直見
錢流轉於京西湖北
路行使乞鑄勘⁴⁾會子
覆印會子印及下江
西湖南漕司根刷舉
人落卷及巳毀抹茶

Under the reign of the Emperor *Hiao-tsung* in the 1st year of the period *Lung-hing* (1163), *Wang-kiö*, superintendent of the purveyance for the troops in *Hu-kwang*, said that at *Siang-yang(fu)* (in the north of *Hu-pĕk*) and *Ying* (the then capital of *Hu-kwang*), and at other places the heavy payments for the army were settled[1]) both in copper money and in those (notes) for silver[2]). Therefore at the great army-cash where the money for the border fortifications was deposited, "convenient" *Hoei-tsze* of a value of 500 and 1000 *cash* had been printed. Emitted in behalf of the camps they circulated as ready money west of the capital and in the districts of the province of *Hu-pĕk*, where they were in general circulation and use[3]).

(As the want of paper money was thus obvious) he requested, in case the *Hoei-tsze* were coined again, to have printed on the *Hoei-tsze* which should be emitted, that they should reach (lit. below i. e. to the south) as far as the territory of the transport-officers of *Kiang-si* and *Hu-nan*[5]). Furthermore the bills presented (at the offices), and circulating among the people ought to be closely examined, and the torn and illegible (effaced) old tea-receipts should be confiscated by the officials in order to make again *Hoei-tsze* of them. That advice was followed. After the

1) 請 occurs here once more in the signification of to settle, to pay.

2) 銀品搭 lit. those notes for silver which were added to the already circulating credit notes; it is the notes which were estimated in silver. Cf. p. 185 and 200, where the same expression is found.

3) Originally issued in behalf of the army they soon got a more extensive circulation in *Hu-pe*, and in the neighborhood of the capital of *Hu-kwang* (*Ying*).

4) 鑄 勘 is here borrowed from the making of money. 勘 is to be taken in the meaning of "to collate,"

5) The meaning is that they were to be current also in these southern parts, and for that reason should be given in payment by the functionaries who bought there grain for the government.

鎮　將　貨　動　旅　毀　撥　以　由　路　數　及　引
江　會　又　以　輻　而　茶　印　之　而　日　印　故
等　子　湖　數　湊　總　引　造　地　京　印　造　紙。
處　就　北　百　之　領　及　銅　流　南　增　之　應
與　買　會　萬　地²　所　行　板　通　水¹　且　權　副
販。　茶　子　緡　每　謂　在　緻　不　陸　總　既　抄
今　引　不　自　年　江　會　申　便　要　所　專　造
既　回　許　來　客　陵　子　尚　乃　衝　所　則　會
有　往　出　難　販　鄂　收　書　詔　商　給　印　子。
行　建　界　得　官　州　換　省　商　總　止　造　從
在　康　多　回　鹽　商　焚　又　必　本　行　之　之。

license to make and issue them had been granted (to the army-cash),
the number of the bills which were coined, also increased daily. But
now the bills issued by this office circulated in the above-mentioned
districts and in *Kiang-ling*[1]), situated south of the capital, a place where
trade was very brisk, and to the merchants of those parts (such a limited circulation line) not being convenient, the office for the issue
was ordered to transfer the copper plates from which the bills were
printed to the *Šang-šu-šang*. Further (it was ordered) to redeem the burnt
and torn notes of the issued tea-receipts and the circulating *Hoei-tsze*,
and that the central office for issue should be called "the meeting-place
of the merchants of the districts of *Kiang-ling* and *Ngo-tšeu*"[3]). The
government salt annually bought and sold by the merchants produced
returns to an amount of several millions of strings of money.

As (on account of the cost of transport) it was difficult to get in
return a remittance in goods, and as the *Hoei-tsze* of the province of
*Hu-pĕk* might not cross the boundaries of that province, *Hoei-tsze*
were generally taken with which tea-receipts were bought, and these
were sent to the districts of *Kien-kang* and *Tsin-kiang-fu*, and other
places where they were in demand in trade. But who shall of his own
accord go and buy tea-receipts now that the circulating *Hoei-tsze* are

1) 水 陸 I take for *Kiang* (江) *ling*,
situated in the south of *Hu-pĕk*; three lines
lower mention is made of 江 陸 and the
substitution of 水 water for 江 river is
very possible.

2) As to the signification of 輻 湊
(= 輳) Cf. p. 192.

3) *Ngo-tšeu* is an ancient name of *Wu-
tšang-fu*, 武 昌 府 in de prov. *Hu-pĕk*,
situated east of *Kiang-ling*.

舊 萬 會 印 其 朝 軍 若 降 緣 就 通 會
會 貫 子 給 義 廷 食 賣 引 每 買 行 子
換 二 湖 乃 遂 必 不 數 年 茶 誰 可
收 百 北 再 寢 關 行 多 帖 引 肯 以

current everywhere. Because the number of credit bills was increased
every year, and because they were not current any longer in trade,
the army should positively be in want of food. But notwithstanding
this the government lost sight of the warning embodied in the course
of things, and caused again *Hoci-tsze* for the province of *Hu-pĕk* to be
made for an amount of 2.000.000 string to redeem with them the old
*Hoei-tzse.*

The fragment which follows now is found in Ma-twan-lin IX
29*a—b* succeeding that of page 201; we have purposely given
it here at the end of the historical part, as it is a real cry of
distress which broke from the hearts of a people bending under
the insupportable burden of a totally depreciated paper currency,
a condition at last resulting from the thoughtless extension of
the representative medium of exchange as we have seen from our
chronicle.

而 支 以 軍 倅 楮 楮 然 特 民 歲 失 皆
非 吾 楮 士 給 百 鹽 糧 以 不 月 職 以
楮 無 州 支 以 官 本 本 畏 以 扶 自 稱
銅 一 縣 犒 楮 之 以 以 耳 信 持 是 提

(*Some provincial magistrates of which I omit the names* [1])) lost
their offices because of the assignats [2]). After having tried for years
and months to support and maintain (these notes), the people had no
longer any confidence in them, but were positively afraid of them.
For the payment for government purchases was made in paper, the
fund of the salt manufactories consisted of paper, the salaries of all the
officials were paid in paper, the soldiers received their pay in paper.
Of the provinces and districts, already in arrear, there was not one
that did not discharge its debts in paper. Copper money which
was seldom seen was considered a treasure. The capital collected together

1) The translation is a little freer | 2) Cf. p. 164.
than of other passages.

楮之弊也楮以製楮錢爲

國家建隆之初賦入尚少

東征西伐兵饟不絕于道

欲楮之不弊不可得也且

楮實爲病不可得也。且

楮實爲便。今況僞造日滋。製

亦皆昔也今也錢重而製楮

嘆皆楮之弊也楮以製楮錢

憂州縣悴戰士無以養廉¹⁾飽之

生物價皆翔騰楮價不損折爲民

宜物價皆絕口而不言矣是

之本皆絕口而不言矣。是

錢以罕見爲寶。前日椿積

in former days to supply the border fortifications was quite exhausted and was a thing not even spoken of any more. So it was natural that the prices of commodities, rose while the value of the paper money fell more and more. Among the people this caused them, already disheartened, to lose all energy, the soldiers were continually anxious that they should not get enough to eat, and the inferior officials in all parts of the empire raised complaints that they had not even enough to procure the common necessaries. All this was a result of the depreciation of the paper money. And is the paper money depreciated, the metallic money is consequently depreciated likewise [2]).

When in ancient days, as the money had its full value, paper money was issued, the effect was convenience and profit, but when at present, while there is a total want of metallic money, paper money is made, the effect of that paper money is corruption and disease, and moreover forgery increases daily.

Even when it was earnestly desired that the paper money should not depreciate, it is not possible to attain that end now.

And yet in the beginning of the period *Kien-lung* (960) under the reign of this family, the proceeds of the taxes were little as yet. In the east the rebellious tribes were subdued and, in the west the enemy was defeated, but arms and food [4]) were not cut off on the roads, and they (the rulers of that time) did not try to have recourse to paper money

1) 養廉 a legal addition to the salary of officials.
2) This means perhaps that copper coin was then issued so base as to be on a level with the depreciated paper as it was in Austria in the year 1810.

3) 實 the effect, the result, the fruit.
4) 藉 to lean on for aid, to have recourse to.

嘗藉楮以開¹⁾國也。靖康以來。外壞夷狄。內立朝廷。左支右吾。日不遑。末嘗藉楮以濟中興²⁾也。至于詔諭及此。未嘗不曲盡其心。孝宗謀慮。內有三宮之奉。外有歲幣之賚。而造楮惟恐其多。以示民信。或無以收。換愈多而弊愈甚。其所幸者。恭儉節用。無錫賚子之泛。所以楮雖弊而有以養其原也。

to make the state firm, strong and united [1]). Since the period *Tsing-k'ang* (1126—27) abroad, the Barbarians were driven out of their country, and at home, a new dynasty was established [2]). (Then there was really a great want of money) but at the left advances were made, and at the right the payment was delayed, and there was no day when this did not occur, and yet they have not tried to take recourse to the paper money to mend that condition [3]). When come to the last year of the period *Sao-hing* (1163) projects were made to meet the general want of a medium of exchange, and, come to the emperor *Hiao-tsung* (who ascended the throne in 1163), ever making projects and inventing means, this (paper money) was devised, but it was not yet attempted to do to the utmost what was not wrong [4]). In that time at home there were three imperial palaces built, and abroad there were the usual yearly expenses, but in making paper money the only fear was the over-issue (that too much would be made) and in redeeming them it was feared that it would be impossible to pay them up to the last, or that there would be something by which the confidence with the people might be shaken. But since the reigns of the emperors *Kwang-(tsung)* and *Ning-*

---

1) 開國 is literally to found a state. With the consolidation of China into 960 after the division under the "five families" in view, the rendering, though free, is justified.

2) In 1127 the southern *Sung* ascend the throne. The driving out of the Barbarians is little more than boasting. Cf. p. 178.

3) 中興 to repair, to fit up, to renew.

4) i. e. the issue of paper money was not yet so far extended as might have been without risking the credit of the state; 不曲 is by ante-position put at the beginning of the phrase.

*(Tsung)* the number that was made exceeded all limits and the depreciation was worst. And yet (however wretched the condition may be) there is a luminous point. When a proper and moderate use is made of them without awaiting help from boggies in caves and woods, and it is attempted to observe a due proportion in motion and rest, so that there is not at once a flood of issue, such a proceeding, notwithstanding the present depreciated condition may be the means by which it is possible to rear the paper money up to its original state.

Now that the historical parts are treated of as far as Ma-twan-lin's book gives them, I will proceed to give the criticism of the authors who witnessed the social ruin of those times. First of all the opinion of Ma-twan-lin himself, a piece so excellent as to the economical principles which are promulgated in it, that for this little fragment alone the author has already a high reputation[1]) in the eyes of our modern writers on money. And indeed, albeit that his theories have been somewhat altered and modernized by authors who copied from each other the passage of M. E. BIOT's essay[2]), which is already translated rather freely, Ma-twan-lin nevertheless fully deserves the praise which has been lavished on him. Our author's opinions on paper money are so true and correct, his criticism of the history of his time so sound and judicious, that this passage, which moreover excels in elegance of style and language, is unquestionably the best in the whole book. [IX. 33*a*—35*b*].

---

1) Cf. Dictionnaire de l'Economie politique article Papier-monnaie, par COURCELLE SENEUIL. A. N. BERNADAKIS, Le papier monnaie dans l'antiquité.

Journal des Economistes, tome 33 (1874) pag. 366—367.

2) Journal Asiátique (1837) *in locu* page 248.

## MA-TWAN-LIN'S CRITICISM.

○按錢幣之權。當出於上。
則造錢幣之司。當歸于一。
漢時常令民自鑄錢。及于武
帝則專令上林三官鑄之。
而天下非三官錢不得行。
郡國前所鑄錢皆廢。銷輸
其錢以銅鐵鉛
錫。搬運
重難。是以歷代多即坑冶
附近之所置監鑄錢。亦以
錢之直日輕。其用日廣。不
容不多置監冶。鑄以供用。
中興以來始轉而為楮幣。

If we observe the great power and significance of money, (and) that it must be issued by the supreme government, it is also necessary that the function of the state officials who make the money returns to one (person or institution).

During the *Han*-dynasty the people had been allowed for a time to cast money for their own use, till the emperor *Wu-ti* carefully charged a college of three officials from the *Sang-lin* with the coining of money, and in the whole empire there might not circulate any other money than what was made under the supervision of that college. All the money formerly cast in different districts and provinces was abolished, melted, and the copper (bullion) carried to the (new) mint-college. Thus was the money made of a composition of copper, iron, lead and tin. But as the transport of it by water as well as over land was difficult and troublesome, the later dynasties in the immediate neighborhood of the money mines and foundaries, then existing, have established government work shops for the casting of money. But because the relative value of the money continually decreased while the use made of it increased daily, and the number of foundaries and government work shops could not be made larger in order that, by casting constantly more, the want (of money) might be supplied, (therefore) since the empire (under the *Sung*-dynasty) was re-united under òne scepter, the government has

---

1) 中興 to renew, to repair, refers to the consolidation of China under the *Sung*-dynasty (960)

則　一　平　耳　引　即　哉　也　引　有　則　以　夫
止　鈔　時　然　之　以　盍　收　湖　行　就　鑄　錢
於　請²⁾　解　鈔　屬　會　置　換　會　在　行　之　重
一　鹽　鹽　引　視　為　會　不　各　都　會　可　而
貫　二　場　則　之　錢　子　行　自　印　子　也　直
下　百　四　所　而　盍　之　稱　印　又　印　楮　少
至　斤　貫　直　以　初　提　造　有　足　造　輕　。
三　而　八　者　重　意　無　而　川　矣¹⁾　輕　則
百　會　百　承　錢　鹽　策　其　引　而　直　多
二　子　售　鈔　權　鈔　何　末　准　既　多　置　監

begun to make and circulate bits of paper made of the bark of the
mulberry-tree. That at the time when the money was heavy and of
slight value, several government work shops were established for the
casting of it, stands to reason, but with respect to the paper money
which is light of weight while it has a great value, it had, in my opinion,
been sufficient, when only the capital (of the empire) had been resorted
to to have it printed and made.

At present there are, besides the already circulating *Hoei-tsze*, the
credit notes of (*Sse*) *ts'uen*, those of the *Hoai* provinces and the *Hoei-tsze* of the *Hu* regions, and each of those provinces prints and makes
them for itself, and the end of it is that the re-payment does not take
place, and that they are no more a means balancing the actual possession (of money). How is this? With the very first intention to institute
*Hoei-tsze*, it was not originally so that the *Hoei(tsze)* were looked upon
as money, but they were then considered to be of the nature of the
receipts for tea, salt, and other government productions, balancing
money only temporarily. (Only these points of difference there were
between these three sorts of credit notes) that the receipts for commodities were upon the whole of a greater value. When one took a sum
of 4 string 800 *cash* (4800) to the government salt stores, one received
in return a bill which could be exchanged for 200 pounds of salt. The
*Hoei-tsze* however were only of one string and lower down to 300 and
200 *cash*. Furthermore there was only printed on the receipts that
the merchants must present them in order to receive for them tea,

1) 矣 is here an exellent instance of
expressing the subjective meaning of the
author in contradistinction to the foregoing
也. I have, therefore, rendered it by
in my opinion. See the preface.

2) 請 = 清 Cf. p. 187.

百。鈔引只令商人憑以取茶鹽香貨故必須分路如顆鹽鈔只可行於陝西末鹽則鈔只可行於江淮之類而楮子用。則公私可買賣給無往而不用。之自一買賣支至二百。則是明而以代見造錢矣。又況以尺會里代數斤之銅資輕用之重。千尅之遠。數數萬之絹一夫之力自日可到則。而何必川自川淮自淮湖自湖而使後來或廢或用。號令反覆。民聽疑惑乎。蓋兩淮荊湖所造朝廷初意。欲

salt, aromatics (or other) articles, and therefore for these notes a sepa-ration and division into several districts was necessary, as, for instance. receipts for lump salt could only circulate in Šen-si, while receipts for crushed salt are current only in the *Kiang* and *Hoai* regions.

The *Hoai-tsze*, on the contrary, served to be given and taken in pay-ment, when private as well as public persons bought or sold something, without the occurrence (of the fact) that they disappeared, not to be used any more (like the receipts). Moreover, another evidence that they served as a substitute for the ready metallic money, is that they were made of the value of from one string to 200 copper pieces. And so much the more, now by means of a shred of paper of the size of one foot a quantity of many pounds of copper could be substituted, now by circulating the lighter, the heavier was actually employed, and the strength of one man was sufficient to make that a quantity of tens of thousands of strings at a fixed time arrived at places some thousands of miles distant, what necessity was there then that *Sse-tš'uen* should have *Sse-tš'uen* receipts of its own, and *Hoai*, its own *Hoai* notes, and *Hu* its own *Hu* bonds; and this must needs be the reason that afterwards some were abolished and some remained in use, that the names (of the notes) were continually altered, and that in this way the people not knowing any more what to trust, grew suspicious? When the various notes were made for the two *Hoai* districts, for *King-(tšeu-fu)* and other districts of *Hu-kwang* and *Hu-pĕk*, the original intention of the government and its desire was that they should be used only for a short time, and then to abolish them. But it did not know that, once fal-

1) lit. pearl or bullet salt and salt powder.

暫用而即廢。而不知流落民間。便同見鏙。所以後來收換生受。只得而造。遂愈多而愈賤。亦是立法之初講之不詳故也。

len and streaming among the people, they would be considered as advantageous as the ready money strung together. The reason why later withdrawals and re-payments only produced new issues, and that after having been repeatedly increased (in number), they at last fell in value in proportion as the number issued became greater, is because in the beginning when the law (of the issue of paper money) was made and the plan was discussed (the government) had not penetrated all the particulars of that institution.

The two following accounts of paper money have not the high economical interest of Ma-twan-lin's own criticism, but nevertheless they are worth being communicated, bearing witness of the impression, the utterly failure and ruin of paper money made on the intelligent and thinking part of the contemporaries.

*Tung-lai* of the family-name *Liu*, [Matw. IX 39a—b] without being aware of it himself, advocates the free-banking system; the system as it had developed itself in the province of *So* where paper money had been introduced as a substitute for iron. "For that reason," he says, "the bills of exchange, though they were properly no money, could for a long time continue regularly to circulate as money, but as to the other parts of the empire the advantages and disadvantages of the use of paper money by no means were the same." "Its power lies herein," he proceeds, that it was made by the people themselves and was put confidence in by the government."

"But," he continues, — and here his opinion is entirely influenced by his prejudice, because of the paper money having had such a bad effect — "but in the other parts of the empire where copper money was the common medium of exchange, paper money was not wanted; and a favorable result of the use of paper money can be imagined only when there is no other medium of exchange than the inconvenient iron, and even then it should be allowed to regulate the circulation only for a short time. In the present time, however, copper money is much better adapted to the purpose than paper."

To avoid the repetitions of our Chinese economist only the substance of his long discourse has been communicated. The following criticism on currency by *Šui-sin* of the family-name of *Ye* is, however, remarkable enough to be given again in full. [Matw. 42*b*—43*b*].

### CRITICISM OF ŠUI-SIN OF THE FAMILY YE.

道。惟通融流轉。
無留藏積蓄之物。
錢貨至神之物。
來不可逆知。然送
賤其輕重送往送貴
之變世輕重。數貨之易。物之
錢耳。行夫之古今物之惟
通行隱沒於世不見。而
物隱沒不見天下之非
錢不行度。亦之非雖
私家用度。征。則雖
上下相征。

Of all that is transacted there is nothing which does not circulate by means of money, even though the regulation of the money is left to private persons, and it is the money alone which, unobservedly and without (its influence) being seen, causes all productions of the earth to circulate among the generations. All the changes that we have observed in ancient and modern times, during the succession of a many generations, those constant changes in the prices of commodities and in the value of the money, and its continual fluctuations even in those different periods, all these are phenomena which we cannot know beforehand. The currency comes near to a supernatural object, no fixed rule can be given to keep it and gather it; it ever goes on and, like the steam issuing forth from the kettle, it diffuses itself and whirls, and everywhere we see its effect and its use.

方見其功用。今世富人。既務藏錢而已。朝廷亦盡征天下錢入於府。以待¹⁾之者不使之出。乃立楮於天下為利。錢雖積之甚多。以與他物何異。人用不究其本原。但以錢益少。故只當用楮。楮行而錢亦少。將物不可得而見。然自古今之物變則相續至于今日。事極則變。物變則反必須更有作新之道。但未知其法當如何變。得其決不可易者。廢交于然後可使所藏之錢

The rich people of the present time have made it their business to hoard up the money in their depositories, and likewise, after having exhausted the taxes, the government has put the money of the empire in the royal treasury. And what is once put in it cannot be got out again; and then the paper money has been instituted and brought out to supersede ¹) (the copper money). But that (paper money) is not so advantageous as the copper money to circulate through the empire. Though ever so much copper money has been hoarded up, what then is the difference between this and other goods? But people do not search into the basis and origin of things, and they think that paper money should be used only because there is a want of copper money. But now the paper money circulates, and the quantity of money is little, the result of this will be, not only that no commodities are to be had or to be seen, but also will it be cause that even no money will be had or seen any more. But since the corruption and misery of ancient and modern times have succeeded each other till this very day, it has always been seen that when matters had reached a climax, a change was nigh, and as once that change comes a whole revolution is the result, and so it must be positively now that a new way will be opened, but we do not know what that way shall be. If once that revolution has been brought about, it cannot be changed any more. When the paper money is now abolished it may result in the re-appearance of the stored up metallic money. Now as the way of wealth and power is situated

---

1) 待 *tai* is here again very probably used instead of 代 *tai* to supersede. Cf. page 45, note 2.

復出．若夫富強之道在於物多．物多則賤．賤則錢貴．錢貴然後輕重可權．交易可通．今世錢至賤．錢賤由乎物少．其變通之道．非聖人不能也。

there where is abundance of commodities, and in consequence of those commodities being in abundance they are cheap, and for that reason the money is dear, (i. e. gets back its original value [1]), and if the money has again its value it may be weighed in light and heavy, and barter and exchange can go on again, so at present, now the money is of very little value, and this again results from the scarcity of commodities, not even a saint would be able to point out the means to bring about a radical change in this condition [2]).

But no saint did descend from Heaven and the Chinese, earthly beings as they were, continued to involve themselves in still greater difficulties, and the revolution which the prophetic look of our last quoted author had foreseen actually came but too soon.

Ma-twan-lin has brought his "Examination" down only to this time, but from *Wang-k'i's* Continuation of Ma-twan-lins work [3]) we learn how one issue succeeded the other, how every time new names where invented to delude ·the people, solemn promises were made that henceforth the government should fulfil what it had charged itself with, and how the result was that again and again old debts were paid by incurring new in order to defer the impending bankruptcy of the state.

I will not weary my readers with the details of the sad his-

---

1) In contradistinction to the condition of the present time when money is cheap or has no value whatever ·when people wants to buy something with it.

2) The construction of this phrase is: "to point out a means by which a radical change might be brought about, he who is not a saint would not be able to do.

3) 續文獻通考． Continuation of the General Examination of History and Scholars by 王圻 *Wang-k'i,*

tory, but only quote the last few lines of *Wang-ki's* monetary history of the *Sung*-dynasty which run as follows: [*Wang-k'i* XVII, p. 15*b*.]

價 銀 見 改 稱 是 如 苦 民 物 會 寧 ○
頓 關²⁾ 錢 造 提 似 之 朝 不 價 子 宗 按
踢 行 關 金 楮 道¹⁾ 何。 廷 勝 踢 壅 之 宋
矣。 物 子。 銀 幣 請 至 無 其 甚。 滯 世 史

It we examine the historiographers of the *Sung*-dynasty, we see that already in the time of the emperor *Ning-tsung* (1195—1225) the *Hoei-tsze* did not circulate any longer (lit were stopped in their course). The prices of all commodities rose enormously. The people could not endure their misery any more, and the government did not more know what to do. As it had come so far (*Kia-*)*sse-t'ao*²⁾ suggested to alter the paper parcels which balanced the actual possession, and to exchange them for frontier-bills for ready money, estimated in gold and silver. But when those silver-bills circulated the prices of commodities suddenly rose still higher.

The incessant attacks of the Mongols who already under Ghengis Khan had conquered a great part of Asia, at last overthrew the feeble structure, and made an end of the *Sung*-dynasty. An alien mounted the throne, and since that time the nomadic princes have ruled over the Middle-Empire for about a century.

The assertion that paper money has been one of the leading causes of the fall of the *Sung*-dynasty is a thesis which will hardly be gainsaid by those who have read the history of this institution from its glorious beginning to its wretched end.

It is indeed not to be wondered at that after those fatal results which China was to experience twice more in after times, the government superseded the paper money by a metallic currency, and for ever abolished paper money issued by the State.

---

1) *Kia-sse-t'ao*, was the perfidious premier of the emperor *Tu-tsung* (1265—75) under whose government the Mongols conquered the whole of China. MAYERS 1. 252.

2) 關 = 關 子 Cf. p. 187 note 1.

Had that history been known earlier, it might have taught a great lesson to Europe and America, and preserved them from those evils which were to work incalculable misery and irreparable loss; evils which in many countries of the world reveal themselves, alas, too strongly in the social condition of the present time, and which are so well expressed by WEBSTER who, speaking of paper money, says: "We have suffered more from this cause than from every other cause or calamity. It has killed more men, pervaded and corrupted the choicest interests of our country more, and done more injustice than even the arrows and artifices of our enemy."

# ADDENDA AND ERRATA.

Page 14 Chin. text Column 3 n⁰ 6 for 縉 read 縉.

» 31 line 1, for remonstancing read remonstrating.

» 34 note 2, Cf. page 110 note 1.

» 42 note 1 at the end for 外象天圓, read 外圓象天.

» 94 Chin. text. Columu 3 and 12 and line 6 from the bottom for 郎 read 即.

» 95 note 1. When the proofheet was ready to be printed, I found in another Mint-book, 欽定錢錄, kindly lend to me by Prof. SCHLEGEL, the information that the country *Wu-yĭk-san-li* was situated east of Cophine on a distance of 12.200 *li* from Peking. 烏弋山離國 去長安萬二千二百里東與罽賓國 etc.

» 166 note 1 for Capus read Caput.

220a

大明通行寶鈔

dragon

balustrade of flowers

balustrade of flowers

壹貫

design
ten strings
of 100 *cash*
each.

天下通行

大明寶鈔

戶部

奏准印造

大明寶鈔與銅錢通行

使用僞造者斬告捕

者賞銀貳伯伍拾兩

仍給犯人財產

洪武年月日

spend it be economical." In every octogon of the border one of the eight diagrams of the emperor *Fu-hi* is put as ornament.

The inscription outside the border reads again, "Bill corresponding with copper coin *littera Kien* n° 170". That column which on this note is accidentally preserved in its whole, is generally cut through, for when the bill is issued, the one half remains in the book of the banker as a means of controlling.

Another bill, belonging to the "*Ecole des langues orientales vivantes*" is issued by a joint-stock bank (lit. money-shop erected in association) 合興錢舖 at *Shang-hai*. Besides, almost the same inscriptions as the government note above treated of, it contains the remarkable addition by which its character as a bill to the bearer is expressed, 認票不認人 i. e. "The bill not the man is recognized".

# II.

---

The four characters at the top of the bill contain the name of the Bank. "Everlasting flourishing State-bank". The seal mark at the bottom on the original printed in red and seal characters, likewise contains that name.

. The vertical column of characters at the right side reads as follows "Valid bill equalizing 60 *cash* of copper money, certified". The column of the left side, "20$^{th}$ day of the 10$^{th}$ month of the 18$^{th}$ year of the period *Hien-fung* (1858) mark; (*littera*) *Kien*, n° 170".

The square seal mark between the two columns is also printed in red, and contains 16 characters. It reads:

"It is given in payment of taxes. "Among merchants and "people, current together with coined copper cash, it is successively "given in payment and circulates".

At the bottom another seal of an octangular form contains the two following fragments of a sentence taken from "*the Great Learning*" Ch. X, 19. and having reference to wealth. The meaning is:

"Let those who produce it (wealth) be many, and those who

# I.

## DESCRIPTION OF THE FAC-SIMILE OF THE CHINESE BANKNOTE
## OF THE TAI-MING DYNASTY.

belonging to the Collection of the Asiatic Museum of the Imperial Academy.
of Science at St. Petersburg.

#### ACCORDING TO SU-WEN HIEN-T'UNG K'AO.

*Size of the original 32—21 cent<sup>m</sup>.*          Vol. XVIII p. 10*b*.

---

下 十 通 日 旁 通 橫 質 六 其 鈔 中 太
日 串 行 大 復 行 題 外 寸 制 取 書 祖
則 中 明 爲 其 爲 許 方 桑 省 洪
爲 圖 寶 篆 鈔 額 龍 以 高 穰¹⁾ 造 武
一 貫 鈔 文 內 曰 文 靑 一 爲 大 八
貫 貫 天 八 上 大 花 色 尺 鈔 明 年
其 狀 下 字 兩 明 欄 爲 闊 料 寶 令

In the 8th year of the period *Hung-wu* (1375) the emperor *Tai-tsu* issued an order to his minister of finances to make the *Pao-tsao* (precious bills) of the *Ta-ming* dynasty, and to employ as raw material for the composition of those bills the fibres of the mulberry tree ¹). They should be made of a square form, one foot in length and six *tsün* (⁶/₁₀ foot) in width; the substance (the paper to print the bill on) should be of a green-blue color. Outside (in the upper border) was the figure of a dragon, and the crossbars which were at right angles with the front, were ornamented as balustrades of flowers. Of the inscription the front part runs "General current precious bill of the *Tai-ming* dynasty". At both in and outside there are eight characters in seal writing running "Precious bill of the *Tai-ming* dynasty current, in the whole empire". In the centre a drawing is made on the bill, representing a string of 1000 *cash* in the form of ten strings of 100, which thus makes one *Kwan* (string of 1000). Below this the inscription runs: (*Chinese text on the bill*).

1) 桑穰. The translation by the fibres of the mulberry tree is a little free, 穰 properly signifies the culm or stalk of grain. But we know from elsewhere that paper is made of the 桑 *Morus* or more generally of the 楮, the *Broussone-tia papyrifera*, and not of the straw of cereales, I have closely examined the stuff of the original bill and found no traces of straw whatever; I have therefore 桑 taken in the possessive case and 穰 in the signification of the fibres.

"According to a memorial presented by (our) minister of fi-
"nances it is assented: to print and coin the precious bills of the
"*Tai-ming* dynasty, which together with copper coin are every-
"where current. He who makes and uses forged bills shall be be-
"headed, and he who denunciates or arrests (the forger) shall receive
"a reward of 250 taels of silver; besides he shall receive the
"moveable property and real estate of the criminal.

"The -- day of the -- month of the -- year of the period
"*Hung-wu* (1368—1399) [1])."

Of the two red seals there is quite as much discernible on the
photography as on the original. With the aid of the magnifying
glass and by consulting *Wang-k'i*'s history I have tried to make
them out and believe them to be as follows.

1                                    2

1. Seal of the officials under the *Tai-ming* dynasty
who bring the bills in circulation [2]).

2. Seal of the bank were the precious bills are printed
and coined.

---

1) The just date is not readable on the original. Perhaps it was written in pencil and has disappeared in the course of time. The fold in the midle of the bill and its contrited state in that part are evidences that it has been in circulation and carried folded in the breast pocket or money belt. The fold is easily to be distinguished on the photography.

2) 舉提司 Cf. MORR. in voce 官 n° 114. Those officials occur in *Wang-k'i*'s Chronicles as issuers of the credit bills. Cf. further p. 189, 190 and p. 198, where likewise is spoken of the red seal marks of banknotes.

堅字第百七拾號合同錢票

永豐官局

憑條準銅錢陸拾文照

納投完課
商民通行
鼓鑄銅錢
陸續支通

咸豐捌年拾月廿日堅字百七拾號

永豐官局

泉舒
者者
之之
生用

# STELLINGEN.

# STELLINGEN.

---

## I.

Het gezegde van BEKKER (Processualische Consumtion p. 14) „Ein Wissen das nie ausgesprochen wird, ist bei Niemand zu vermuthen, und die Behauptung dass wir das Wesen der Exceptio tiefer ergründet als die Römischen Juristen scheint überkühn"·is onjuist, zoowel in het algemeen als in het bizondere geval betrekkelijk KELLERS ontdekking van de dubbele functie van de werking der exceptio rei judicatae in het Rom. recht.

## II.

De bewering van Dr. RÜMELIN (“Zur Lehre der Exceptio rei judicatae Tübingen, 1875)" dat de negatieve functie der Exceptio rei judicatae in KELLERS brein maar niet in het Romeinsche recht is ontstaan, is onjuist.

## III.

Art. 226 B. W. is overbodig en onnadenkend vertaald uit de C. N., alwaar de 2de zinsnede van art. 1292 B. W. niet was opgenomen.

## IV.

De toepassing van art. 538 B. W. in art. 541 en 548 is in strijd met gezonde rechtsbeginselen.

## V.

Wanneer effecten zijn gelegateerd, die geen rente betalen gedurende den tijd tusschen het openvallen der nalatenschap en de uitkeering van het legaat aan de legataris, is de erfgenaam geen intressen verschuldigd.

## VI.

Terecht beweert Pothier (Traité du prêt à usage N° 73).

"Si celui à qui j'avais prêté une chose afin qu'il s'en servit pour son usage l'a loué à un autre et en a rétiré un loyer, le loyer est un fruit civil de ma chose qui doit m'appartenir et qu'il doit me rendre, ne la lui ayant prêté pour qu'il en retirât des loyers."

## VII.

In geval van verkoop krachtens onherroepelijke volmacht (a 1223 B. W.) heeft geene zuivering plaats tenzij de voorschriften van art. 1255 zijn in acht genomen.

## VIII.

Hoewel eene overeenkomst niet tot stand komt voor en aleer de aanneming tot de kennis van den voorsteller is gekomen, zoo kan de voorsteller toch tot schadevergoeding gehouden zijn.

## IX.

Verkeerd is de bepaling van het Duitsche Handelswetboek dat de overeenkomst tusschen afwezigen bestaat op het oogenblik dat de verklaring der aanneming ter afzending is afgegeven (art. 321 D H. G. B.).

## X.

In jure constituendo behoort ook de Nederlandsche handelswet aan het aanbod aan een afwezige gedaan rechtsgevolg te verbinden.

## XI.

De verbintenis van den acceptant voortspruitende uit eene voorwaardelijke acceptatie behoort ook in ons recht te zijn opgenomen.

## XII.

De acceptatie eener assignatie heeft hetzelfde karakter als de acceptatie eens wissels en doet voor den acceptant eene dubbele verbintenis zoowel tegenover den aanwijzer als den houder ontstaan.

## XIII.

Onbillijk is de bepaling van het W. v. K. art. 838ᵇ dat geprivilegeerde schuldeischers geen stem hebben bij de beslissing van het accoord, tenzij zij van hunne voorregten afstand doen.

## XIV.

Indien de schipper in het geval voorzien in art. 372 W. v. K. een wissel trekt op de reederij of den boekhouder, en deze laatsten abandoneeren het schip, dan is de schipper tot betaling verplicht.

## XV.

De bepaling (art. 729 W. v. K.) dat de vracht van den marktprijs moet worden afgetrokken bij de waardeering van geworpen goederen, is in strijd met art. 481 W. v. K.

## XVI.

Terecht brengt de dagvaarding voor den onbevoegden rechter stuiting van verjaring te weeg.

## XVII.

Terecht wordt door de aanmaning van den rechthebbende de verjaring gestuit.

## XVIII.

Vorderingen van een faillieten boedel tegen zijne debiteuren behooren niet gebracht te worden voor den rechter die het faillissement heeft uitgesproken, maar blijven ter competentie van hun natuurlijken rechter.

## XIX.

Het denunciatiestelsel in het Chineesche strafrecht heeft steeds nadeelig gewerkt.

## XX.

In het Ontwerp Wetboek van Strafrecht is het minimum van 6 dagen te hoog voor misdrijven waartegen alleen een geringe gevangenisstraf is bedreigd (art. 337).

## XXI.

In beginsel is elke uitgifte van papiergeld door den Staat af te keuren.

## XXII.

Hoewel het stelsel van vrije banken tegenwoordig in China gunstig blijkt te werken, is dit stelsel onvoorwaardelijk af te keuren voor elke Europeesche maatschappij.

## XXIII.

Zoodra de uitgifte van niet inwisselbaar papiergeld de bij de gebruikers gevoelde behoefte aan ruilmiddel overschrijdt, herstelt zich het evenwicht daardoor, dat de waarde van elk billet daalt in gelijke verhouding als de overmatige uitgifte toeneemt.

## XXIV.

De nadeelen onvermijdelijk bij eene inwisselbaarstelling van vroeger niet inwisselbaar en gedeprecieerd papiergeld worden gewoonlijk te gewichtig voorgesteld.

Grooter toch dan die alle is het nadeel, dat alle maatschappelijke instellingen treft zoolang een niet inwisselbaar papiergeld op den wisselkoers op het buitenland en de prijzen van alle handelswaren invloed uitoefent.

## XXV.

Een eigenaardig onderscheid tusschen metaal- en papiergeld is, dat metaalgeld in waarde moet verminderen om in meerdere hoeveelheid in omloop te komen, terwijl niet inwisselbaar papiergeld door in meerdere hoeveelheid in omloop te komen in waarde vermindert.

## XXVI.

Het strijdt zoowel met economische als met juridische beginselen dat een verloren muntbillet niet door den Staat wordt vergoed onder borgtocht tegen namaning (Art. 7 Wet van 1852) Eveneens is dit het geval met de bepaling waarbij de vergoeding van een verloren bankbillet facultatief wordt gesteld. (Art. 23. Wet van 1863.)

## XXVII.

De wijze, waarop volgens de Grondwet en volgens aangenomen gebruik groote codificatiewetten zoowel aan het ministerie als door de Staten-Generaal moeten behandeld worden, is eene belemmering voor het tot stand komen van eene goede nationale wetgeving.

## XXVIII.

De instelling van een permanente commissie, wier taak zou zijn het geschreven recht in overeenstemming te houden met eene voortgaande ontwikkeling der rechtswetenschap en rechtsovertui· ging, is af te keuren.

## XXIX.

Het kiesstelsel door THOMAS HARE voorgesteld is voor ons land niet toepasselijk.

Een stelsel gegrond op HARE'S groote beginsel ten doel heb- bende om de kiesdistricten weg te nemen, gelijk door prof. FRUIN is voorgesteld, geeft meer waarborgen voor de zamenstelling van een ware Volksvertegenwoordiging dan ons tegenwoordig gel- dend stelsel.

## XXX.

De vrees voor eene gevaarlijke overmacht van de Chineezen bij eene steeds toenemende immigratie uit China naar Indië en Amerika, door MADIER DE MONJAU uitgesproken in zijne rede- voering "De l'Emigration des Chinois au point de vue des intérêts Européens" Paris, 1873. "*Les Chinois sont en marche vers l'Europe*", is volkomen ongegrond.

Integendeel ware van eene immigratie uit China naar Europa in den tegenwoordigen tijd heil te verwachten.

## XXXI.

Het onbesuisde hervormingswerk in Japan ontwikkelt een ver- keerden trek van het Japansche volkskarakter, vernietigt vele zelfstandige, oorspronkelijk goede eigenschappen en zal onver- mijdelijk eene reactie na zich slepen.

Te recht oordeelen daarom de aanhangers van de Nationale partij in Japan dat de openstelling der Japansche havens voor land en volk eene ramp is geweest.